SHOPPING CENTER TENANT COORDINATION

SHOPPING CENTER TENANT COORDINATION

International Council of Shopping Centers
New York

About the International Council of Shopping Centers

The International Council of Shopping Centers (ICSC) is the trade association of the shopping center industry. Serving the shopping center industry since 1957, ICSC is a non-for-profit organization with more than 54,000 members in 96 countries worldwide. ICSC members include shopping center

- owners
- developers
- managers
- marketing specialists
- leasing agents
- retailers
- researchers
- attorneys

- architects
- contractors
- consultants
- investors
- lenders and brokers
- academics
- public officials

ICSC holds more than 200 meetings a year and provides a wide array of services and products for shopping center professionals, including publications and research data.

For more information about ICSC, please contact:
International Council of Shopping Centers
1221 Avenue of the Americas
New York, NY 10020-1099
Telephone (646) 728-3800
Fax: (732) 694-1755
www.icsc.org

Companies, professional groups, clubs and other organizations may qualify for special terms when ordering quantities of more than 20 of this title.

Published by
International Council of Shopping Centers
Publications Department
1221 Avenue of the Americas
New York, NY 10020-1099
www.icsc.org

International Standard Book Number 1-58268-067-1

ICSC Catalog Number: 259

Contents

Acknowledgments

Special thanks go to the following people for reviewing and contributing to this book.

Nick Galloro—Director Retail Tenant Coordination Services & Technical Services, Oxford Properties Group

Greg Gunter—Vice President, 3rd Works

Bruce Harrell—Director of Tenant Coordination, Simon Property Group

Sean Johnson—Vice President, the Related Companies

Judy Murtaugh—Director Site Information Management, Store Design and Construction, Limited Brands

Bill Rowe—Vice President, Forest City Commercial Group

Kristine Sandrick—Sandrick Communications

Brad Smith—Director of Retail Tenant Coordination, Forest City Commercial Group

Martha Spatz—Senior Vice President Architectural Services, Urban Retail Properties Co.

Their time, advice and comments were very much appreciated and added immensely to the breadth of knowledge shared within this book.

In addition, I would like to thank Rudy Milian and Patricia Montagni with ICSC who said "Yes!" enthusiastically when approached about the need for an industry book on tenant coordination. . . .

To the many professional associates actively involved in Tenant Coordination who said "Yes!" when asked if they felt this project would be beneficial and provided encouragement. . . .

Finally to Skip Greeby, George Khouri, Dale Scott and David Scott, friends and mentors, who said "Yes!" when I told them I wanted to write this book. . . .

Karen M. Scott, SCMD

Introduction

The first time I heard the term "tenant coordinator" was after the grand opening of a small specialty center in Orlando, Florida, in 1995. The owners had hired me as a property manager/marketing director. However, as we rushed to get tenants ready for our grand opening, I also assumed responsibility for construction oversight. In this industry it's not unusual for the property manager to multitask, and since our goal was to open the center and begin collecting rent, I naturally assumed the responsibility.

After the opening, in casual conversation with the general contractor's marketing manager, he suggested I consider tenant coordination as a career. I picked up the phone and started calling some of my industry associates and, after listing the required responsibilities, asked if they thought me capable of making the switch from marketing and management to construction. After all, this seemed like a big leap for me. Those I talked to assured me that I had already worked in this capacity and that I should make the move. That's when my career in retail tenant coordination was born.

Today, tenant coordinators in the shopping center industry play a vital role for developers and retailers alike. As more and more companies realize the value of tenant coordination, those of us in the profession believe it is important to take this function to the next level by standardizing this practice within the industry.

The purpose of this book is threefold:

1. To give developers the tools to start their own tenant coordination departments.

2. To provide a basis for standardizing practitioners' skills.
3. To encourage professionals engaged in shopping center operations, design and construction or students completing school to consider tenant coordination as a profession.

Tenant Coordination as a Career Choice

Tenant coordination is a rewarding and unique career choice in a demanding industry. Large retail developers have had tenant coordinators on board for nearly 30 years and have set the standards for the skills and experience required of the successful tenant coordinator. However, today more and more small developers are seeing the need for professional tenant coordination, resulting in an increased demand. Also, there are tenant coordination consulting firms—many comprised of tenant coordinators who earned their spurs working for the country's top developers—who are always looking for the right, detail-oriented, firm but personable manager to oversee the construction and opening of new tenant space. If you're thinking about moving into tenant coordination, now is the time. Professionals who can fill this challenging and vital role are in demand.

1 Who Are Tenant Coordinators?

Tenant coordinators (TCs) bridge the gap between the development, leasing, construction and design teams and the tenants and property management. Simply stated, they are the professionals responsible for getting tenants open, in either new or existing centers, as quickly as possible.

As important as this profession has become to the commercial development industry, one cannot earn a degree in tenant coordination. In fact, in the shopping center industry, people do not go to school to learn this profession.

Tenant coordinators come from a wide variety of backgrounds: property management, architecture, engineering, construction or lease administration. The wider their variety of experiences in shopping center management and construction and in the types of projects they have managed or been involved with, the more versatility and hands-on product knowledge they bring to the development team. More and more tenant coordinators coming into the industry today have been trained in architecture and construction management.

Qualifications for tenant coordinators are generally specific to the needs of the hiring organization. However, at minimum, developers/owners tend to look for candidates with hands-on experience in construction, property management, architectural design or lease administration. Good communication and negotiation skills are a must. Understanding retail terminology and merchandising strategy is also a major plus.

What Do Tenant Coordinators Do for the Owner?

Landlords and owners rely on tenant coordinators to provide a dedicated source of information, communication and control to assist retail tenants and to protect the landlord's interests.

Tenant coordinators are the central point of communication between landlord design and construction teams and internal property management and operations. They create a layer of protection for landlords to ensure that the lease requirements are being met and that the tenant design team and contractors are building tenant spaces according to the landlord's specifications. These specifications range from store presentation and signage criteria to the quality of finishes and materials. Tenant coordination also includes the major functions of monitoring the way tenants tie into critical mall and building mechanical and electrical systems, installation of exterior signs and storefronts and protection of mall interiors. In addition, tenant coordinators are responsible for administering the lease between the time the lease is signed until opening, freeing up operations and management to handle their daily responsibilities without the frustration of trying to control tenant contractors.

Tenant coordinators also prove their worth by tracking details and administrative issues. They are dedicated team members and watchdogs for the landlord, ensuring that tenant plans and construction are going according to schedule, alerting leasing to potential fulfillment problems, and flagging problems with tenants that do not have the financial reserves or professional capability to meet the terms of their lease agreements. These valuable services can save landlords time and money by recapturing space early before it gets tied up in the default process and court systems.

Tenant Coordinators Work for the Retailers, Too

Providing a single point of information for tenant design, construction and operations teams can save a tenant and their consultants a lot of time and aggravation. Tenant coordinators become particularly invaluable on challenging projects with huge coordination issues or complicated building systems. In addition, by understanding and administering a landlord's lease agreement with the tenant under construction, the TC also ensures that the landlord lives up to his or her legal responsibilities.

Field tenant coordinators tend to have more construction experience.

They can often assess construction issues at a glance and assist tenants and their building contractors in creating workable solutions that save time and money. Tenant coordinators trained in lease administration are more likely to read and follow the terms of the lease and be quick to make sure that all deadlines and correspondence are met and issued in a timely manner. Tenant coordinators with a design background are more likely to enjoy reviewing tenant plans and assisting retail architects in creating a seamless meld of the tenant's unique style into the mall framework. Construction-background tenant coordinators can be utilized for reviewing leases, estimating and identifying unexpected costs to the landlord due to tenant prototype specifications.

Highly specialized departments can train staff already skilled in one of these areas to pick up expertise in other areas to assist the development and construction teams. Smaller developers are better off looking for people with more general background who can manage multiple tasks.

Tenant coordinators are becoming recognized as a powerful force. They have earned equal footing on project teams along with both project and construction managers. More and more experienced construction, design and operations professionals are entering this field and finding it a unique and rewarding career choice.

Regardless of the skills a tenant coordinator brings to the development team, the time to involve them is at the front end of the project, not the back end when it is time to turn the project or space over to the tenants. A tenant coordinator who is treated with respect as a full member of the development and construction team brings a wealth of experience to that team. They also bring the ability to project the result of decisions made in the near time to cost and time impacts at the end of the project, due to their experiences with openings.

2 | Putting Together an Effective Tenant Coordination Program

Perhaps you are reading this because you have come to the decision that you need someone to bridge the gap or manage the process between leasing (the deal) and property management (store opening). It is time to put together a tenant coordination program. This chapter is dedicated to assisting owners and developers to put together such a program. That program might mean an internal department, a single person hired to fulfill the function, or tasks to be fulfilled by people within the company that adds tenant coordination to their job responsibilities.

Although it should go without saying that the way the program is structured should be based on the projected needs and goals of the organization, that does not mean that many of us have the time to actually perform the research or have the resources to create a formal department. If not a department, then a formalized written program such as a listing of tasks might be what you need at this time.

> "The tenant coordinator acts as the landlord's liaison to the tenant regarding landlord's work and tenant's design and construction requirements with the primary objective of expediting store openings."
>
> BRUCE HARRELL,
> Director of Tenant Coordination,
> Simon Property Group

Tenant coordination is a support function in three primary ways:

1. It provides leasing with the architectural and construction expertise to negotiate the landlord's and tenant's work with respect to scope, schedule and cost.

2. It coordinates the landlord's and tenant's requirements with the landlord's design and construction team(s).
3. It supports property management in solving tenant construction issues.

Structuring the Department Internally

The first thing a company should consider when thinking about creating a tenant coordination program is to look realistically at their requirements and needs. When getting ready to create a program, look at your 5- and 10-year growth projection plans. If you say, "What plans?" put this book down and take the time to write a business plan. Creating and hiring for a tenant coordination program should take into account future growth. The people you hire today should be poised to assist your company grow according to your vision. If you are a small, aggressive developer, a formalized department with trained architects will frustrate you. Your needs will be different from a larger developer more concerned with a volume of one type of project.

Once you assess where you are and where you want to be, you can start putting your program and department together.

Large firms have tenant coordinators functioning as a separate departmental entity. Depending upon the firm, the department might be under the oversight of leasing, development, construction or property management. The philosophy of the department will depend upon the discipline that is overseeing it. Knowledge base tends to be aligned with more traditional disciplines such as architecture or lease administration.

Smaller firms might have one person working directly for the development manager or for the leasing team. Generally these people will have a more broad-based area of knowledge and skills but will handle less volume.

How to Find and Train Qualified People

Once you decide where you are and where you want to be, start looking for people who fit into your company's personality as well as its wants and needs. Small developers need to look for people who can multi-task under pressure and have a variety of skills. Formal education might not be as important, but the ability to handle field construction issues, talk to a building department or inspector and handle site work for outparcels as well as review plans might be more valuable.

Typical Tenant Coordination Departments		
Typical In-House Department, Large Developer for Malls and Lifestyle Centers (large volume of tenants, often multiple properties)	*Typical In-House Department, Small Developer for Power Centers, Neighborhood Centers and Lifestyle Centers (smaller volume of tenants, fewer properties)*	*Tenant Coordination, Outsource or Third Party for All Product Types (depending upon the needs of the department or developer)*
1. Architectural and sign review and approvals 2. Track status of plans, permit and construction 3. Answer questions for tenant design and construction teams and troubleshoot 4. Hand off to mall operations or field TC for construction oversight 5. Work as field representative during final days toward opening 6. Negotiate lease scope 7. Perform Construction Project Manager functions for landlord's work	1. Obtain tenant prototypical plans and specs and translate to landlord construction drawings for building and site as required 2. Lease negotiation, construction costs 3. Lease administration 4. Obtain approvals on plans with tenants 5. Oversee permitting process 6. Hire general contractor 7. Oversee turnover of store and associated site with all work completed as per the lease exhibits to store operations 8. Will visit site and troubleshoot problems and site-verify completion of work for tenants and landlord's contractors 9. Turn over tenant upon opening to property management team	1. Write design criteria 2. Review construction drawings 3. Fulfill administrative functions as designated by owner they are working for 4. Work as field associate overseeing compliance to landlord rules and regulations and adherence to approved plans 5. Field troubleshooting between tenant's and landlord's construction teams

Remember, you can always outsource. If it is more important to hire someone who has field experience, then use your architect or hire an outside firm to do plan review. Vice versa, if adherence to strict design criteria and lease administration is more important, then outsource field coordination to construction managers or assign field coordination responsibilities to a member of the construction team.

Tenant Coordinator's Qualifications

Professional and Educational Background: Architecture, Construction Management, Business Management, Real Estate

Professional Background:
- Tenant Coordination, Retail Developer
- Or Architect
- Or Construction Manager for retailer or retail contractor
- Or Property Manager or Operations Manager
- Or paralegal or lease or contract administration in a developer's construction department

Skills:
- Multitask
- Ability to effectively communicate and negotiate
- Strong sense of urgency, understands the importance of deadlines
- Personality meshes with a wide variety of people, including construction, leasing, store retail operations and mall management

Experienced tenant coordinators are hard to find. It is such a highly niched job function that it is a challenge to find people available to come on board. Until recently there was no standardization of skills. The International Council of Shopping Centers has instituted a Certified Development Design Construction Professional (CDP) Program which provides a method of testing and recognition in design, construction and development for tenant coordinators and their professional counterparts.

Experienced people in tenant coordination often move into construction management, consulting, design and operations and management and leasing.

Instead of looking outside the firm, consider hiring and promoting from within. A skilled operations manager can often make the transition to tenant coordinator. A paralegal interested in contracts and administration or a CADD operator could also make the transition. Be prepared to invest in their skills and complement them with outsourced help if needed. The wider variety of projects they are exposed to and the more hands-on experience they have, the greater value they will provide as you grow and expand into various types of shopping center product lines.

Creating Process and Reporting Systems

Creating a formalized process for tracking and reporting key milestones and activities is critical to fulfilling important administrative functions. If you have a strong reporting system that asks timely questions such as "has the tenant hired an architect," "is the space ready for delivery" or "have we a signoff in the landlord plans," then you can start to flag problems almost immediately.

Consider putting together a program that requires constant question-asking and -answering, which will trigger a responsible flow of communication between your team and your tenants, even if you do not hire one person specifically for the tenant coordination process.

Another important form of reporting is project tracking. Creating and maintaining forms and documentation that show where you are in collecting plans, approvals and construction status for tenants for multitenant openings for centers is key to the success of the grand opening. This is particularly important if you have multiple coordinators assigned to a project or different members of the development team who need to know where a project is at any given time.

Team meetings are also an important key to project success. Tenant coordinators should be included in the development and construction meetings, as they often hold the answers to some of the most important questions regarding landlord and tenant design requirements, scope and schedules. Whether trying to decide how to permit a group of buildings, size grease traps and water meters or determine realistic opening dates a year in advance, tenant coordinators can often answer pertinent questions from experience or know the right person to call for the answer. They should be brought into the project as soon as preliminary design is commenced. Tenant coordinators with operations backgrounds can be particularly helpful, especially if a property manager or mall manager has yet to be chosen, since they know what the operations team will need to get the center open.

3 | Professional Training for Tenant Coordinators

Currently, there is no "go-to" place to learn how to be a tenant coordinator, nor is there a prescribed curriculum. So what do tenant coordinators need to know and how do they learn? Here are a few suggestions on where to go to learn more to prepare yourself or a team member to step into the tenant coordination role.

Good tenant coordinators need to be well-rounded in a variety of disciplines. The more they know about each of these areas, the bigger asset they will become to their team. Ideally, a tenant coordinator should know how to read a lease, understand construction terminology and read schedules, read blueprints and integrate a tenant's systems into a new or operating center. Unfortunately, most people entering into tenant coordination do not bring all of these skills to the plate at one time unless they have considerable experience in the operations or construction side. Tenant coordinators tend to have strengths in one or two areas and learn the rest on the job.

Skill sets for well-rounded tenant coordinators include:

- Construction knowledge
- Operations experience
- Lease administration
- Design training

If you are looking to move someone into a position internally or are hiring someone to fill a position, determine if their major experience and strengths fit your most immediate goals and long-term growth. Training, outsourcing and support from other key staff members can fill in the gaps as personnel proceed.

For example, a firm taking over existing properties might need a tenant coordinator with a heavy operations background. Their candidate might be someone who has 10 years' experience in maintenance and has handled a lot of facility management work. That candidate has exposure to lease administration and understands basic construction. To support them, you can make sure they have administrative help to abstract leases as well as provide them with outsource support for design review. Future investment in more construction classes will give them confidence as they proceed.

Another example might be a firm that is experiencing rapid growth in building new power centers with a large percentage of big box users. Here the ideal candidate might be tagged as having a good architectural background in order to deal with the design consultants and interpret the requirements of the lease and tenant prototype drawings. An employer would supplement that person with a strong construction manager and a good tracking program for hitting key dates, and would provide training in operational systems and procedures.

Finally, a large mall operator more concerned about how a store fits into an established look for a center that is already operational might look for a design-trained person who is comfortable in dealing with an on-site maintenance team and who will oversee the construction for them. These coordinators will be able to translate the design requirements to store designers more efficiently and, in the case of large center openings or renovations, can be supplemented by on-site construction tenant coordinators who have more construction experience versus architectural and design training.

Construction Basics

Construction basics can be learned through a variety of sources. Several universities have full programs in construction management, including the University of Florida and Clemson. For those of us who do not have the time to get a degree in construction management, there are some other educational opportunities more readily available.

It is harder to get people trained in construction coming out of schools and universities to come on board as a tenant coordinator. Their degrees are highly sought after and they can command a high salary by working for large general contractors, or have more prestige by coming on board as a project manager. Many have not heard of tenant coordination as a construction management avenue and see it more as a coordination position versus a management one.

If you are going to transition into a tenant coordination position and do not have a construction background, one great source of construction education is in local apprenticeship programs offered through state community college programs. Along with trade information, they often teach classes in estimating and scheduling.

Another great source of additional training and education is through the American Builders and Contractors, Inc., which is a professional trade organization. Local chapters offer classes as part of their membership benefits. These classes teach the basics of construction management, scheduling and estimating, blueprint reading, OSHA regulations and construction terminology. If you are already trained as an architect or engineer, these classes will teach you how to produce and read schedules along with field management and production techniques. These are invaluable skills when you begin to start negotiating contracts with general contractors doing landlord's work on your behalf. If you are coming from an operations or administrative background, these classes will quickly immerse you in the area of construction management and give you a basic crash course in blueprint reading. This is also a great way to meet other people in the construction industry whom you could eventually recruit as part of your own design and construction resource team for future work.

Many states require licensing for general contractors. Taking classes through local construction schools that specialize in teaching contractors how to take licensing exams is also a valuable resource for local education. Along with teaching for the exams, many of these schools offer continuing educational classes with special topics of interest such as contractual law, lien waivers, and safety and operations.

Do not overlook resources available to professionals through our own retail industry. The International Council of Shopping Centers often provides opportunities through regional and national meetings to learn more about construction, design and lease administration. Center-Build is a yearly conference held by the International Council of Shopping Centers specifically for design and construction professionals in the shopping center industry. The conference focuses on industry work sessions while also recognizing design and construction achievement.

Spillover of construction- and project-management–oriented classes is now starting to be seen in other conferences, too. Panel discussions in specialty conferences often focus on how to put together a design team, how to find the right general contractor and how to make a private and public partnership work between municipalities and private developers.

The International Council of Shopping Centers offers a School of Development, Construction and Design every year at the University of Shopping Centers located at the Wharton School of Business facilities in Philadelphia, Pennsylvania. As the construction role within the retail industry expands, more and more courses are being offered that meet the needs of design, construction and retail tenant coordination professionals.

Tenant retail design and construction managers have their own specialty meetings and conferences that are open for shopping center construction managers and tenant coordinators to attend. Shopping center personnel who attend not only learn about the latest retail trends, but also they get an understanding of the unique terminology of retail merchandising and operations and the demands of store design related to the function of increased sales opportunity.

Please see the list of educational resources at the end of the chapter for more information on trade organizations, seminars and publications.

Management Know-How

Tenant coordinators who come in through the operations side of the retail industry have a big advantage in understanding how their role interacts with the leasing and management teams. Many operations people already have hands-on working knowledge of construction basics and are familiar with working with existing centers' mechanical and electrical systems. They understand the impact of tenant construction within the overall shell of an operating center and are sensitive to making sure that in their quest to get a tenant or group of tenants open, they generate the least impact on others already operating.

They also become valuable allies to property managers in place, who know they can depend upon these operations-oriented tenant coordinators to assist them by making sure tenants adhere to landlord rules and regulations and cause minimum disruption during the construction process.

Since these tenant coordinators are trained in management systems and think in terms of long-term maintenance and ownership, they also add value to the overall development and construction team because they see the gaps between design and construction and actual operations of the center when opened. They can often be relied upon, sometimes to the annoyance of construction teams who are primarily interested in getting space open but do not care about long-term maintenance as they will not be involved in it, to point out where future operations problems might occur.

Tenant coordinators with a design or administration orientation can become stronger in the operations side through increased educational opportunities in facility management. However, the best experience is to team your tenant coordinator with an operations person and send them into the field to job shadow. By giving them the experience of seeing how operations teams work and creating a teamwork environment, tenant coordinators without strong operations backgrounds or who rarely visit the field will be more successful by knowing who to call on when they do need assistance in a center or to spot-check a problem.

Lease Administration

Lease administration is one of the most important functions of a successful tenant coordinator. One who has a handle on what the lease is really saying and can translate that back to both the owner and the tenant in the quickest, most efficient manner can save the owners a lot of time and aggravation. Unfortunately, a lot of lease administration is done with the use of "legalese" and not tactfully, and what should be an added benefit can become a source of irritation. Owners who encourage good communication and tactfulness will end up in a better long-term relationship with their tenants on current and future projects.

Tenant coordinators with a heavy lease administration background tend to have a handle on what the lease really says. Often owners sign leases in good faith, not really recognizing what they are promising tenants. When they find out they have signed a lease that basically states 100% of all construction costs to a space is theirs and that their building has to undergo retrofitting to meet the tenant's specifications, they tend to argue and lose time, money, and integrity with potentially what could be an important tenant for this and other projects in their portfolio.

Unfortunately, tenant coordinators who come from a lease background tend to be the least qualified to handle and understand constructability and design issues, and need the most additional support in terms of staff members and outsourced consultants to assist them. The transition can be made, but it takes a big commitment from both the owner and the prospective candidate wishing to make the change into a new role.

Architectural and Design Basics

New tenant coordinators tend to come in through this area. They might have studied design but realize that their interests are more in working hands-on with people rather than sitting behind the desk and using CAD programs. Tenant coordination allows them to interface with people with like training and creatively solve problems. Since they are working in an ownership position and likely to be paid more than if they were working in an architectural firm, they see the tenant coordination role as being more advantageous than people trained in construction management do. They are more likely to be familiar with the role of tenant coordinators also.

Their background and skills make them invaluable in dealing with tenant store design professionals, who appreciate having the opportunity to speak with another design professional. They have more problems dealing with tenant construction managers, who would rather interface with someone who understands constructability and whose attitude tends to be more "let's get it done and we can change in the field."

As invaluable as their skills are, they too need to be supplemented with additional training. Sitting them down with a good lease administrator and teaching them terminology is invaluable. Supporting them with a strong written tenant coordination program and process where they track items electronically brings them up to speed quickly on the reporting and tracking process. They would also benefit from the experience of working in the field as an on-site construction tenant coordinator during a couple of openings or projects before being brought into the office. This gives them construction skills and understanding as well as exposure to maintenance and management needs.

Increased confidence in the design area can be obtained through reading retail design magazines and attending design conferences as mentioned in the educational resources section. Tenant coordinators without a formal background in design can get up to speed quicker by taking classes in blueprint reading and AutoCAD basics through some of the local community colleges and trade organizations.

Architectural design is one of the easier parts of the tenant coordination field to outsource. However, even with providing outsource support for your tenant coordination team, the tenant coordinators themselves still need to have enough working understanding of design and engineering to be able to effectively communicate with the design professionals paid to assist them.

Educational Resources

CONFERENCES AND SEMINARS
1. University of Shopping Centers, International Council of Shopping Centers, School of Development, Construction and Design, www.icsc.org
2. CenterBuild, International Council of Shopping Centers, www.icsc.org
3. Retail Construction Expo, www.retailconstructionmag.com

TRADE ORGANIZATIONS
1. Associated Builders and Contractors, Inc., (703) 812–2000, *http://www.abc.org*
2. National Retail Federation, www.nrf.com
3. Retail Contractors Association, (800) 847-5085, www.retailcontractors.org
4. BOMA, www.boma.org
5. CoreNet Global, www2.corenetglobal.org

TRADE MAGAZINES
1. *Shopping Centers Today*, International Council of Shopping Centers, www.icsc.org
2. *Retail Construction* Magazine, *The Journal of Architecture, Design, Construction & Facilities Operation, http://retailconstructionmag.com*
3. *Shopping Center Business* at *http://www.shoppingcenterbusiness.com*
4. *Retail Traffic*, http://retailtrafficmag.com

TRADE CERTIFICATIONS
CDP, Certified Development Design & Construction Professional, www.icsc.org

4 | How to Create an Effective Construction Exhibit in the Lease

One of the first lessons a tenant coordinator learns, when faced with a conflict of information or an unusual problem, is to ask, "What's in the lease?"

A smart developer will ask input from not only his legal team, but also his key department managers for suggestions on what they think ought to be in a lease. Lease exhibits need to be part of an ongoing review process, constantly being rewritten to keep up with the changes within the industry as well as the impacts of new laws and regulations on local, state and national levels.

It is just as important that the tenant coordination and construction management teams be a part of this process as it is for the legal, property management and marketing teams. The construction team is put into the position of having to interpret the leases, often secondhand before the deal is actually completed, if not immediately after the deal is done. Each team's experience, based on construction and schedule impacts as well as specific industry knowledge, is invaluable.

How to Write a Lease Exhibit

When it comes time to review a letter of intent and lease exhibit, it is often easier for tenant coordination to read the existing document handed to them by the tenant and analyze impact from that. However, when tenant coordination is asked to actually create their own exhibit at the start of a project, this is the ideal time to actually line out what you intend to give the tenants and on what terms. This is particularly in reference to national tenant leases or for small independent merchants. Larger stores tend to prefer that their own leases be used or modified.

Generally tenant coordination is primarily concerned with what is typically set aside as the "Construction Exhibit" of a lease. For tracking purposes they will also extract information on rent commencement, notices, insurance and tenant improvement funds. The bulk of what they need to know is generally pulled from a lease and put into a "Lease Abstract" form.

In order to write a construction exhibit, you need to have your own design criteria at least lined out. Determine what it is you realistically plan to give the tenants in your initial working drawings. Do you plan to come into the building with 120/208 or 208/480 volts? Do you intend to bring in just telephone conduit or are you going to make them use your telecom provider only? Also plan to address timing requirements by tying days from lease execution to when plans need to come in for review. This gives you a point-of-tracking reference that tenants can be put into default on for nonconformance.

Often the leasing and development team will not want to answer design or designated subcontractor questions during initial discussion due to timing. If you need a certain amount of leases signed before you can go into initial design or until the development team feels there is enough interest in a project to take it from initial design to construction documents and seek construction funding, you might have to try to anticipate what you are going to give and put enough flexibility into the wording of the construction exhibit to make sure that the tenant is held to future design criteria and/or construction documents that will be issued independently at a later date.

When it comes time to actually write an exhibit, create a "best practices" review. Take a look at existing leases in-house or get ahold of copies of construction exhibits from other companies and analyze them. Look for what gave you the best coverage in the past or the most flexibility. Draft some points you would like covered in the lease exhibits and hand them to the legal department. They are the ones who should actually write the exhibits.

Be aware that some of your points need to appear in other sections than just the construction exhibits. Days for build-out typically are part of the rent commencement process, so they might be included there, whereas insurance requirements and special notices for lease communication would appear in other sections.

What Information to Include

The more comprehensive the construction exhibit, the better the details are covered and the less room there is for argument and confrontation. As good as it sounds, it is often impossible for various reasons, such as timing on getting a project sold with leases having to be presigned or not knowing until you are halfway into a project the particular extraordinary demands of a site or a building department.

Information that should be included in the construction exhibit should not only cover design and construction requirements but also potential fees and use of designated contractors. Below are some suggestions.

DESIGN AND ENGINEERING REQUIREMENTS

This is the time to tell the tenants that you are looking for particular levels of finishes, setbacks into mall structures and types of signage as well as special mechanical, electrical and plumbing coordination requirements. Always refer them to your design criteria, which should be a separate publication, dated. This is also the time to tell them if they will be getting plans in electronic or hard copies. As more architectural firms go to CAD format, the expectation is that they will get all documents electronically and the stores base their design and cost budgets on that expectation. If your arrangement with your architect is otherwise, the tenant needs to know.

Occasionally the separate document referred to as the "Design Criteria" will need to be updated as you learn more specific things about the construction and operation of the center. Each time it is updated, it needs to be specifically dated so that you have a basis of reference if a tenant has a conflict on criteria or submittal. This puts the onus on tenant coordination to be extremely prompt in relaying significant design and engineering changes as a project proceeds.

DESIGN REVIEW TIMING AND SUBMITTAL PACKAGE

This is the area to line out exact expectations on what you need to do a review of and when. Tie tenant's submittal dates into the lease through reference to lease execution. That way, if they do not perform in a timely manner, you have a method of putting them into default to get their attention. Stores with multiple openings in a year will often assign their own level of rating on which stores are most important to open based on various reasons, including funding, fixture manufacturing, and stock market performances. Creating a lease commitment on when plans are due makes sure that you and they are both clear on what your expectation is and they schedule accordingly.

Specify what you need to get from tenants and do not be afraid to repeat it in your introductory letter to them. Typically tenant coordinators want the following:

Initial submission:

- Multiple sets of hard copies of the plans, depending upon the number of consultants Tenant Coordination wishes to distribute to
- Photos of existing stores or computer or hand renderings of new ones
- Sample or finish board, keyed to finish plan
- Sign submittal drawings from the sign company
- Mechanical information on tie-in to mall system, including testing information and specifications matching design criteria
- Electrical loads and summary
- Plumbing submittal showing connections to center-provided facilities as per design criteria
- Fire alarm and fire sprinkler plans or acknowledgment that they intend to use mall-designated contractors for design and build of systems

ENGINEERING

If there are specific engineering requirements the tenant needs to adhere to, try to tell them in advance. This can also be covered under the Design Criteria and should mention it. For purposes of connections and testing, the engineering section should also refer to the "construction handbook," which is a separate document from the Design Criteria. Companies make the mistake of referring to Design Criteria and not the Construction Handbooks which are used by the tenant contractors, not as much the architects. More often, it is the construction handbooks that will tell the tenant contractors how to tie into a system and when to call in for a operations observation of a tie-in or how to clean a system before tying it in.

CONSTRUCTION COSTS

Construction costs are generally upfront charges for certain items that the contractor for the tenant pays when they check in or become what is called a chargeback, where the tenant acknowledges that they will be responsible for that charge and agree to reimburse the Landlord at a later date.

If you know there are going to be certain costs associated with construction or that there will be or is a possible chargeback, line it out now.

Generally, upfront costs to the tenant's general contractor are known as check-in fees. Savvy tenant contractors will call the landlord and ask for these in advance. Those not used to performing in a mall or shopping center environment will not include these fees and will then protest to the owner about the cost of the work and try to pass these fees back. If it is not agreed to or acknowledged in the lease, the tenant will come back to the landlord and try to force him to roll back the fees or not charge them, and the landlord will be stuck with nothing to enforce or protect him. If fees are not set by the time the lease is written, refer to them as "fees related to on-site construction as per the Construction Handbook" or in some other legal format.

Typically tenant general contractor upfront fees are:

1. Security deposits for damage, refundable
2. Charges for temporary utilities such as power, toilet, phone or containers
3. Tying systems into landlord systems where the costs are known up front, such as electrical, fire alarm or telecom
4. Obtaining devices compatible with the landlord's systems such as fire alarms
5. Additional work that the tenant feels it is easier for the landlord to perform, since the landlord general contractor already has resources on-site to do it cheaper, such as concrete pourbacks
6. Additional work that the tenant needs but that the landlord wants to retain control of, since it will impact a building completion date or a warranty
7. Inspection fees for cleaning chemicals and pressure tests on cooling and heating systems

Some landlords use these fees not only as offsets to costs incurred, but as a source of revenue to support their on-site tenant coordination construction teams. If the fees are not reasonable, savvy tenants will catch them and protest.

Chargebacks are collected after the store opens as part of rent commencement or in figuring out what tenant allowance money is due to the tenant. If a chargeback is not referred to in the lease and the tenant wants to get work done, then a separate letter of agreement needs to be issued and signed by the tenant or landlord. Occasionally, as part of the lease, the landlord ends up taking work back on themselves due to extenuating circumstances. When this happens, the landlord needs to let the tenant know in advance as a matter of record. For instance, if the landlord is providing only metal stud demising walls and a tenant gets ready to open and the tenant on the other side has not started, then the landlord or first tenant might be forced to build the other side of the rated demising wall. At that time a letter needs to be issued by the first tenant and landlord if the tenant is going to build the wall, or a letter to the second tenant from the landlord stating that the adjoining tenant is being impacted and the landlord will build the other half of the wall and it will be charged to the second tenant.

It is a good practice to have everything in writing and tying back to a clause in the lease exhibit that allows you to do this so that the accounting department can track all agreements upon closeout if Tenant Coordination has been pulled onto another project.

Generally landlords charge back for plan review, awnings and signs and construction fees where the landlord's contractor is not third party to the tenant and wants to deal only with the landlord.

TENANT ALLOWANCES OR INDUCEMENT

If incentives or costs are going to be covered or reimbursed by the landlord, this needs to be addressed specifically in the lease. Often the construction exhibit is the best place to do this. These inducements or allowances often take one of two forms. The first is when the landlord is given a cash allowance or reimbursement for the tenant's work, generally known as tenant inducement or "TI" work. The second is when the landlord is actually constructing a portion or all of the tenant work, commonly known as "landlord's work."

Tenant inducement payments are part of a financial incentive or allowance draw program to reimburse the tenant for certain costs related to their design and opening of the store. Some inducement clauses specifically spell out what the money will be used for and can have caps. When you are working with this in a lease, make sure you take into account when these inducement payments or allowances will be paid and what supporting documentation will be needed to release them. This is an important thing to consider, especially if you are dealing with a lender who might have their own specific requirements for release of money.

Large stores or restaurants often request draws typically on a 30%, 30%, balance upon completion or a 50% and balance of completion schedule. Documents required by the owners' lenders to give them the funding to meet these draws generally include the following:

1. Architect's certification of percentage complete
2. Site verification by third-party bank examiners
3. Copies of full or partial release of liens, depending on state law
4. AIA document and payment applications with schedules with an affidavit of work complete to date

Landlords need to protect themselves from tenants who use these draws to subsidize their own construction or to purchase their equipment and fixtures or merchandise. Often they will come in aggressively demanding their money in advance of the draw and proper submittal of paperwork because they have overspent and do not want to go out of pocket or use a line of credit to fund their own construction and fixturing.

Occasionally tenants will attempt to draw upon allowances for work they have not ordered or fixtures and merchandise they do not intend to order, and then disappear. This will tie up the space for future leases until resolved, and the tenant contractor and landlord can end up in litigation.

When dealing with small operators or restaurants, tie their inducements for fixturing and merchandise to on-site verification. Also, be willing to work out deals with their contractors to make direct payment to them to keep work rolling and force a tenant to perform if there is a payment or cash-flow problem between the tenant and the tenant's general contractor.

Tenant allowance programs are usually easier to track and handle than "landlord's work" if the landlord is doing complete build-to-suits. Generally, most landlord's work is limited in shopping centers to minimum lease construction buildout requirements in order to get the tenant in while assisting other tenants in opening. Landlord's work falls into several separate categories, including black box, vanilla box or build-to-suit. Since every landlord's definition tends to be different, for purposes of standardization, we will be using the following definitions.

Black Box or Warm Brick

This is the minimum amount of work given. It is often referred to as cold, dark shell. At the most, conduit will be brought in from the landlord's riser or mechanical rooms for electrical and phone; sanitary stubs are in place; connections to landlord domestic water and fresh air and exhausts are available; and a sprinkler system, depending upon the municipality, might be installed with heads turned up. More sophisticated buildings with harder-to-reach operational systems will require additional connections. The tenant does most of the work.

Vanilla Box

This typically refers to a space that is modified to meet the terms of the lease negotiation but is not 100% built out. It generally means demising walls and stockroom walls are built, restrooms in place, rooftop units and electrical panel installed, ductwork run and ceilings installed along with a storefront enclosure and exterior and interior doors in. The tenant would come in on top to install additional partition walls, finishes and fixtures. Sometimes it is referred to as a *white box*.

Build-to-Suit

A build to suit is when the store is designed and built 100% to tenant specifications, including fixtures and finishes. The tenant will typically supply their own vendors for low-voltage wiring for computer, security and cash wraps and do their own interior signage package.

Freestanding Building

Another type of lease arrangement a landlord might have with a free-standing tenant is for the tenant to build their own shell and interior and the landlord will do the exterior site work necessary for the tenant to open, such as paving, landscaping and site lighting. This will usually occur when the building is part of the overall shopping center planned development and the landlord is responsible to the municipality for the buildings to meet certain design and construction guidelines as per overall design control, as well as maintain control of the lots.

Outparcel

When a piece of land is legally separated out from a parcel or sits on the perimeter of a shopping center, but is not necessarily conforming to the overall design plan of the center, it is called an *outparcel*. Outparcel tenants typically maintain control of their own parking and irrigation and site lighting controls and the land is delivered raw. Occasionally landlords will make arrangements to do the paving and lighting for the tenant after they build the building.

Designated Contractors

A clause stating that the tenant is obligated to use key designated sub-contractors can prove immeasurably helpful in protecting the landlord's systems and rights. Asserting in the construction exhibit that the design criteria and construction handbook are considered part of the working documents of the lease helps to ensure that the designated contractors specified by the landlord are used. Generally these contractors are ones associated with life safety systems or who protect major warranties for the envelope of the building and include fire alarm, fire sprinkler, roof, storefront, landing into landlord electrical distribution boxes and cleaning or certifying the cleaning and pressure-testing of tenant steam and mechanical systems before tying into the landlord's overall distribution for steam and chilled water. In large metropolitan areas where certificates of occupancy are never handed out since the building always has some section under construction, or where municipalities and landlords have struck permitting assistance deals due to a private/public agreement, expert permit expediters should also be specified so that the landlord has one person responsible for making sure all operating certificates are always current.

Since these subcontractors will be expected to know the protocol of shutdowns and startups, by requiring their use, landlords can rest more assured that their systems are protected and that other tenants will not be affected if systems are shut down without proper notifications. If a tenant knowingly elects to use another subcontractor and a problem results, then the landlord has the right to make the tenant fix the problem or bond against future warranty issues.

Insurance

Setting the stage for what insurance requirements are needed is a definite must in the lease. Make sure that you change this on a lease-by-lease basis so that small tenants do not get hit with unrealistic expectations. Also, if you are going to have a list of additional to-be-insureds, this is the section to either list them or state in conclusive language that it is the tenant's obligation to state them on the certificate of insurance. If no provision is made for this and your lender comes in with a requirement for it, you will spend a lot of time trying to collect updated insurance certificates and a lot of tenants who will flat-out refuse to do it.

How to Protect the Landlord Without Killing the Deal

Obviously the more a tenant knows in advance, the more they will want to protect themselves from additional costs by trying to put the onus of cost back on the landlord. If a landlord allows too much information to go out in advance, they take that risk. On the other hand, the more information a tenant knows, the better their plans will be and the faster their construction, since they have fewer unknowns to contend with. Landlords can protect tenants and themselves by requiring designated subcontractors to provide a price list to protect all parties from price-gouging.

Landlords can also protect themselves by requiring strict adherence to when tenant draws can be made and lining out in the lease what paperwork will be needed to get the tenant allowance released.

Another area landlords and tenants need to look at is tenant leases that refer to prototype plans that take precedence over all other items in the lease. By specifying which prototype is applicable and making the tenant responsible for costs over and above, the landlord controls costs while the tenant has a baseline of understanding on what changes can and cannot be made.

The landlord also needs to fully assess what impacts to their base building a lease will have before they commit to it. Sometimes an innocuous statement about the size of an electrical service, if not fully investigated in the field before signing the lease, can result in a huge amount of money due to having to retrofit an entire electrical room to make room for an enlarged service at a riser. The simple words "as is" can save a landlord a lot of money and time and put the burden of research and design on the tenant. If it looks like the retrofit is needed to make the deal happen, at least the landlord is forewarned and can try to make the increased cost part of his pro forma or tie it into operations versus leasing costs.

Fees

Fees pertinent to construction have already been mentioned above. However, occasionally other fees can crop up that management might make the responsibility of Tenant Coordination to gather. If these fees become their responsibility, then tenant coordinators need to assist themselves by insisting that these fees be spelled out in the lease with a date or timetable based on an execution date or opening when they can be collected. Some of these fees typically include special assessments for marketing and promotions, impact fees for water and sewer and security deposits.

Samples of Forms are included in the back of the book to help tenant coordinators or other staff members perform tenant coordination functions. These forms include typical construction and insurance exhibits, sample lease abstract forms, construction handbooks, and fees and design criteria samples.

In addition, a glossary of terms is included.

5

How to Produce Landlord Design and Construction Criteria

This is it! This is the time to start gathering information on your new project or redevelopment and put together an overall comprehensive design plan for what the owner's vision of the project is to look like. Or perhaps you already have an operating center taken over from someone else and you want to put the criteria into a formal guideline for new tenants.

Clear, easy-to-read communications guidelines in the form of a design criteria or manual and a construction manual can become two of the most important tools you can use to portray the overall design standard as well as communicate important mechanical, electrical and plumbing information to your tenants. Typically, the design criteria and the construction manual are two separate handbooks for new centers, due to the timing of getting the information out for design versus construction information coming in at a later date. However, after a center is open, the two can be updated and merged into one handbook for future tenants and will become an invaluable tool for them as well as your property management and operations teams.

Protecting the Landlord's Interests

Design and construction criteria should be a strong tool used to protect the landlord's interests. They should be referred to in the lease and considered part of the leasing documents for conformance to building design and management. The information they convey should be easy to read and formatted in a quick, nonlegalistic, bullet-point delivery.

Today's electronic society makes it easy for the landlord to supplement the manuals in forms that make it easy for tenant design teams to visualize the landlord's goals and translate valuable mechanical information directly to the plans for tenant contractors to read and implement.

Along with the handbook, a savvy Tenant Coordination team can produce CD/DVD disks with renderings or computer modeling of the center so tenant design teams can get a feel for the overall concept. The team should also provide lease outline drawings and storefront elevations of the specific space so that the tenant does not have to guess at what his store will look like and will understand where it sits within the center

Design criteria that assist architects and store designers in understanding how to conform and fit within the overall building design are essential.

and how it orients to the rest of the center's design.

Posting the design criteria on the Internet along with a plan room for tenant design teams to download MEP information can also be invaluable, not only saving time in design for tenants but also ensuring they are getting the right information to perform. Plan rooms are available through Buzzsaw.com and other plan production firms that can assist construction managers not only with gathering information and distribution of plans, but also posting project management updates for consultants.

By using these tools, landlords can save time in sharing their vision of what the design of the center will be and assist tenants in creating store plans that fit within that overall look, with less review time needed by the on-staff tenant coordination team.

Defining the Design of the Center in Easy-to-Read Style

Architects who are excited about their vision for a new center often tend to write in flowing, descriptive terms that would put Shelley and Keats to shame. For tenant coordinators, communicating that vision to tenants can become an onerous challenge. While it is necessary to include some of the poetic big picture vision of the design to the tenants so they can allow their imagination to grab ahold of the overall creative vision, the design criteria needs to allow only a small section dedicated to that and make sure the rest of it is factual and down-to-earth.

Your center design criteria should spell out as clearly as possible the landlord's expectations of types of finishes, signage and branding. Do not use words and phrases such as "tenants are encouraged to be creative." Tenants working within branded concepts do not want to be creative; they want to reproduce their heavily researched and proven design 100%. By giving them your expectations clearly, the tenants will understand what you want and precisely where they might need to change a look or materials to meet your specifications.

Some "play" was added to a children-oriented store, resulting in a more eye-catching and fun retail environment.

It is advisable to write and label different criteria for different sections of your center if the criterion varies. For instance, you should have one set of criteria for food court tenants and another for retailers. If you have different sections of a center built around themed courts, then tenants in each of those areas should also receive different criteria if there are different design and storefront requirements.

Architectural information spelled out to the tenants should help them define what you are looking for in terms of lighting, signage, finishes and storefront projections. The following are samples of what typical design criteria would call out for.

LANDLORD CONTROL ZONES

Do you require the tenants to adhere to special signage or lighting criteria in the front of the store? Perhaps you want special ambient lighting for after-hours shoppers in an entertainment-themed center for when theaters and restaurants are still open? Call it out in this section and define the zone, such as 5 feet from the exterior of storefront glass.

INTERIOR FINISHES

Are you an upscale specialty center and want only high-end finishes such as stone, natural wood and stainless steel and glass? Are you a community center and want to encourage independent stores to have a more professional look? The types of finishes you call out in this section will help the tenants to understand what you want.

These finishes will include flooring, fixtures, ceiling tile, wall treatments and exterior facade finishes. The following chart gives a quick overview of three types of centers and the differences in finish levels that might be acceptable.

Types of Finishes	High-End Specialty Center	Regional Mall	Community Center
Flooring	Wood, natural stone, porcelain tile	Ceramic or porcelain tile, wood or wood laiminates, carpet	Wood laminates, VCT, commercial-grade carpet
Ceilings	Drywall, specialty tin or metal	Drywall, 2 × 2 acoustical tile, open grids with painted ceilings	Drywall, acoustical tile
Fixtures	High-end wood, metal and glass, no laminates	High-end wood, metal and glass, laminates professionally produced acceptable	Professionally made fixtures required

Typically, landlords call out the following in their design criteria for store interiors:

- Type of flooring
- Electrical lighting package in terms of color and location
- Type of ceilings
- Type of store fixtures, including display cabinets and wall units
- Location of electronic equipment in relation to storefront
- Type of wall finishes

Spelling Out MEP Requirements at a Glance

Mechanical, electrical and plumbing (MEP) components of the design criteria should be spelled out in a quick, easy-to-read manner. Along with an overall description of the landlord systems, the tenant should be given information on the types of testing that will be required. Design criteria that go into extensive detail on types of pipe or conduit and how they are to be joined together are often ignored. Try to give the most information in a minimum manner. Request the information from your consultants in advance and after you format it into the criteria, have them review it to make sure it is correct.

MEP criteria for urban high-rise or skyscraper centers with immense cooling and heating systems and limited tie-ins to exhaust and fresh air will be much more detail-oriented than neighborhood centers where each tenant has a stand-alone design for a rooftop unit and an electrical meter base off the landlord's riser. If your design criteria do require the coordination of extensive MEP information, then landlords should consider outsourcing the conveyance of MEP information and review to an engineering team. This will ensure compliance to stricter utility requirements and protect sensitive landlord systems and environments.

Along with the MEP criteria, tenant coordinators who are able to ship out MEP plans directly to the store engineers will have a lot less frustration in getting comprehensive plans back. Often design criteria and lease exhibits get shipped to the owners and the architectural team but are not given to the engineers. By talking directly to the engineers, the Tenant Coordination team will know that the engineers understand the design criteria and will feel comfortable calling the tenant coordinator for information instead of trying to pull it out of other sources and getting the wrong information.

The following chart gives a quick overview of three types of centers and the differences in MEP information that might be conveyed.

Typical Tenant Coordination Departments			
Types of Systems	*High-End Specialty Center*	*Regional Mall*	*Community Center*
Mechanical	Closed circulating systems, high-pressure high-rise, limited tie-ins and extensive testing, limited availability to fresh air and exhaust	Closed circulating systems that require inspected taps by field team, limited tie-ins to fresh air or exhaust, or stand-alone rooftop systems feed spaces	Individually mounted rooftop systems
Electrical	Specific guidelines to overall watts; limited availability of power, will need connection into landlord distribution center	Specific guidelines to overall watts; limited availability of power, might need connection by designated sub into distribution box	Generally comes from landlord meter room or separate riser; might be limited availability of power due to riser size or transformer size

(continued)

Typical Tenant Coordination Departments			
Types of Systems	High-End Specialty Center	Regional Mall	Community Center
Plumbing	Shutoff valve in ceiling with limited use, no availability to upgrade the size of line for additional water flow	Shutoff valve in ceiling with limited use, limited availability to upgrade the size of line, might be submetered	Typically independently metered, can upgrade size of water line and meter if use changes, subject to impact fees
Fire Alarm	Information on type of fire alarm system, location and compatibility of devices and if there is a designated contractor	Information on type of fire alarm system, location and compatibility of devices and if there is a designated contractor	Information on type of fire alarm system, location and compatibility of devices and if there is a designated contractor
Automatic Sprinkler Protection	Information on tie-in locations, existing plans and designated contractor	Information on tie-in locations, existing plans and designated contractor and shutdown requirements	Information on tie-in locations, existing plans and designated contractor or shutdown requirements
Telecom	High-rises might have own telecom room and service provider	Might be designated provider, or tenant provides wiring and equipment and runs back to central distribution points in landlord rooms	Pedestal from local provider to landlord distribution area or to tenant space; tenant provides equipment and wiring back to distribution area or direct to pedestal
Type of information conveyed to tenant and their design team	Recommend landlord engineering team convey information to tenant architects and engineers and review information from tenants to ensure tenant utilizes only	If extensive coordination with landlord systems required, generally in multi-level center, then engineering team conveys information and review. If single-story mall with	Shell plans with MEP info showing any tie-in locations, a roof framing plan and MEP plans showing any existing equipment or landlord-provided equipment. If it is

Types of Systems	High-End Specialty Center	Regional Mall	Community Center
	what is available and provides direction to general contractor for testing and tie-in compliance	mostly stand-alone systems, the MEP plans and roof framing plans can be conveyed. Shop drawings for sprinkler system might be available.	an existing center, then tenant field verification must be required.

Storefront Criteria

Malls and specialty centers often present the toughest challenge to store design teams on how storefronts are to blend in within the neutral pier modeling. The more information you give tenant design teams on how their storefront should be designed, the easier it will be for them and your review and construction team.

Encourage interactive storefronts . . .

For interior centers or centers where the tenants are building the storefronts, provide information supported with sketches from the plans showing the landlord's expectations of how the storefront should line up with existing bulkheads and piers. Criteria for projecting storefronts and recessed doors should be spelled out, including what the landlord wants for a transition between landlord surfaces and tenant.

Even if the landlord is providing the storefront, there can still be information that design teams need to know so that they can figure out how to lay out their fixture plans and transition their flooring.

Community and neighborhood centers present less of a challenge to

Bring the store outside to draw shoppers inside . . .

Creative signage can add a modern twist to an old-fashioned storefront.

tenant design teams. Inevitably, some of your tenants will request a storefront change to better meet their store layout and design needs. Typically storefronts in new centers are under general contractor warranty. If a landlord's tenant coordinator approves a change in the storefront configuration, they need to make sure that the tenant contractor protects both the tenant and the landlord from loss of warranty. The best way to do that is to make the landlord's storefront subcontractor a designated subcontractor.

Oversized graphics create a lifestyle message that supplements a simple sign band and identifies at a glance the store's marketing position.

If it is an older, established center with no warranties on the storefront and the tenant requires a change in storefront, then the landlord should make it clear in the lease that storefront warranty on installation belongs to the tenant. Over time, store operations people will report problems with storefronts, not realizing that their contractor installed it. Hav-

Do not hesitate to provide specific tenant criteria when writing the design specifications. A requirement simply for 90% glazing at the storefront can result in dramatically different storefronts as shown in this store.

Tenant coordinators at upscale centers are often challenged with the task of convincing tenants to upgrade their already successful branded looks to fit within a rigorous design criterion. At this center, Godiva stepped up charmingly to the challenge.

ing it stated in the lease reminds all parties that the storefront became the tenant's responsibility.

Another subject that should be addressed in the storefront criteria is use of grilles and electronic surveillance equipment. Lifestyle and entertainment theme centers are going to discourage these, whereas community centers will not care as long as they do not infringe on landlord structural systems. Make sure you tell the tenant what is or is not acceptable up front. If you do not want grilles and you know a tenant, such as a jewelry store, typically wants one, put it in the lease outright. There are various types of

"The mall storefront criteria are a good place to bring up the use of varying types of electronic surveillance equipment. The good, the bad and the ugly should be discussed here."

Martha J. Spatz,
Senior Vice President Architectural
Services, Urban Retail Properties Co.

electronic surveillance equipment used by retailers to help prevent merchandise loss. Generally landlords are going to encourage use of less obvious equipment, as they want shoppers to feel like they are in a friendly environment.

Signage Criteria—Keep It Simple and to the Point

For years landlords have debated about how tightly they should control the tenant signage criteria. Landlords with community centers interested in an integrated look and dealing with a variety of small shop tenants might insist on a uniform sign program, with all the signs the same size proportionately and similar in color and letter font. Although landlords are becoming more sensitive to branded logos as more national tenants populate their centers, you will still see uniform signage in some areas, particularly if it was part of the community approval for the center, limiting size and color.

More and more, sign individuality is accepted and even desired by landlords, particularly those interested in entertainment-type concepts in their centers. A landlord with a lifestyle center is going to encourage something larger and entertainment-themed, whereas a landlord with a neighborhood convenience center is going to be happy as long as a tenant does not exceed size requirements and use or not use a raceway as designated.

Design criteria should have a separate section dedicated just to the landlord's expectations on signage, both exterior-mounted and interior. Those criteria should indicate the size allowed as well as colors and means of fastening, types of reveals and trims, and a sketch showing backing in place if it does not extend along the entire storefront. The criteria should also call out if the sign needs to be under landlord control or on a store timer.

The following chart gives a quick overview to three types of centers and the differences in signage criteria that might be conveyed.

"Can" signs can be creative and fun.

Think outside the sign band. Successful projects encourage and allow tenant signage creativity in the signage manual or criteria.

Types of Signage	High-End Specialty Center	Regional Mall	Community Center
Exterior signage	Halo-lit, concealed neon, sandblasted glass, metallic leaf, routed signs with push-through letters	Halo-lit, concealed neon, sandblasted glass, routed signs with push-through letters, individually mounted, channel letters, tied into landlord's time clock, no raceways	No box signs, individually mounted channel letters, raceways acceptable if painted to match facade, professionally produced and installed
Interior signage	Dimensionally designed and artistic signs; translucent posters on lightboxes	Professionally made, no handwritten signs, no running LED reader boards visible through storefront	Professionally made, no handwritten signs

Creating a Construction Handbook

Construction handbooks are also specifically written for a project and contain information pertinent to the tenant's general contractor. These handbooks are then given out to tenant contractors when they are bidding work at the center and again on check-in to the superintendent, who sometimes is not given the handbook by his or her estimating department.

Some of the topics a handbook should cover include:

- Maps—location of center and building and utility departments
- Check-in procedures
- Contractor responsibilities and paperwork
- Preconstruction services—landlord-provided services to tenant contractor
- Contractor's on-site work
- MEP requirements
- Exterior elevation signage
- Work practices and general housekeeping
- Designated contractor—information
- Utility contacts—information
- Insurance guidelines
- Permit pickup procedures

- Sample forms
- Occupational license information
- Contractor information form
- Construction rules and regulations acceptance form
- Space acceptance form

CHECK-IN PROCEDURES

This is a list of all the items the tenant contractor needs to provide to the on-site tenant coordination or operations team before construction can begin.

Typically these items include:

1. Copy of the Certificate of Insurance
2. Copy of building permit
3. In states or municipalities where applicable, copy of the Notice of Commencement, stamped indicating it has been filed
4. Construction deposit
5. Contractor prepaid fees
6. Landlord and city-approved drawings
7. Emergency contact list
8. Subcontractor list
9. Lease premise acceptance form indicating space has been walked and accepted or what might be outstanding for completion by landlord's contractor
10. Construction rules and regulations signature form acknowledging receipt of a copy of the construction handbook
11. Construction schedule

CONTRACTOR RESPONSIBILITIES AND PAPERWORK

This information tells contractors what the landlord considers their responsibility to do or provide, either as part of their relationship with the client and the landlord or due to common construction courtesy. These items can include field verification, code and ADA requirements or disclaimers; bonding requirements as per the lease; lien rights; information on storage, deliveries and tenant employee hiring; mailing and shipping addresses and express and construction delivery dropoff and pickup information; use of service corridors or back house for deliveries, trash and storage; dumpster location and protocol; parking and loading zones and special pass and hours of work requirements; mall security information; and information on getting special equipment in such as cranes, scissors and boom lifts and concrete trucks or mixers.

PRECONSTRUCTION SERVICES; SERVICES PROVIDED BY THE LANDLORD TO THE TENANT CONTRACTOR

This information gives the tenant contractor the how-to on how to get utilities for construction, including power, phone, water and gas. It also contains information on existing systems for fire protection and shutdown protocol, dumpster location and use and toilet room locations.

CONTRACTOR'S ON-SITE WORK

This lays out the expectations for tenant contractors on how to construct their store within the framework of the structure. These rules will change if the center is open and operating. This section is the area that defines whether contractors can install barricades and when they can work, who to report theft and break-ins to, whether banners or signs are permitted, prohibited attachment of work to landlord structures, work hours, noise and dust control, and safety and fire regulations during construction.

MEP REQUIREMENTS

This section can complement the design handbook by giving out specific information on what the landlord will or will not accept. If the landlord does not want romex or requires site inspections on VAV box hookups or grease trap connections, this is the place to state it.

EXTERIOR ELEVATION SIGNAGE

This section can also complement the design handbook by spelling out in detail when exterior signs can be installed and if there is a special procedure for installation or equipment that is needed. An outdoor operating center might require trucks equipped with stabilizing wings to have plywood under them and have cones and barricades placed around them if installing in public areas. Indoor centers might require after hours installation and only behind barricades.

DESIGNATED CONTRACTORS

If you have certain contractors that are allowed on-site due to warranties and shutdown procedures, even if this is already mentioned in the design criteria, mention it again in the handbook. The use of these contractors is important enough to mention several times in various places so that tenant's contractors cannot tell the tenant they did not know about them and try to have the tenant force the landlord to accede.

Typical designated contractors might include roofing, storefront, fire alarm, fire sprinkler, and electricians.

WORK PRACTICES AND HOUSEKEEPING

Rules and regulations that relate to common courtesy between the landlord, the landlord's general contractor and the tenant and their contractor can go in this section. It should include information on use of service corridors and common areas during construction; waterproofing on interior spaces if required by the landlord; labor harmony; protection of others' work from damage and theft; use of hard hats, safety gear and clothing; access panels and allowance for the landlord if they need to get into the space to get to a base building system; coordination of other tenants' work that might cross through the store; proper labeling of base building as well as tenant operational systems such as gas lines, electrical services and rooftop units; care of exterior work already in place, including landscaping, neutral piers, finished floors; no hazardous material storage; and fire protection on-site and particularly during welding.

Sometimes, just to emphasize their importance, some construction manuals will have a separate section on specially prohibited work and practices. This list of items might include storage of combustibles in concealed non-sprinkler areas, imposing loads on building structure without landlord's approval or making penetrations in floors or fire walls without approval of landlord and coordination with surrounding tenants.

A special notice should also be inserted in this section allowing for corrective work that might need to be performed by the landlord if a tenant abuses a privilege or neglects to clean up after themselves.

UTILITY CONTACTS—INFORMATION

A list of the local utility providers can be inserted in this section along with addresses, phone numbers and contact names and requirements. If pre-power is available through the municipality, this is the ideal place to put that information also. By making this information a separate section, it can easily be pulled out of the handbook and e-mailed or faxed to the utility coordinators and managers for tenants who set up accounts, who might not be interested in the rest of the handbook information.

INSURANCE GUIDELINES

This is also an appropriate place to remind the tenant contractors that they need to submit a certificate of insurance. Place a list of the additional insureds to be covered along with information on who receives the copies of the certificate. This information will often be requested separately and can be formatted to be independently e-mailed or faxed to contractors and their insurers.

PERMIT PICKUP PROCEDURES

If the tenant contractors are responsible for obtaining the permits after they have been approved, a separate how-to section can be immeasurably invaluable to helping them understand what they will need and where they should go. This will save the operations and Tenant Coordination teams from having to answer these questions repeatedly.

SAMPLE FORMS

A section designated for providing sample forms the contractor will need during construction and inspections can also be helpful. Some of these forms can be collected in advance from the municipality and attached with explanations on how and when to use them, such as permit applications, contractor licensing requirements, automated inspection systems, revisions, pre-power, requests for temporary and permanent occupancy forms. Forms for roof access, sprinkler shutdown, landing of equipment into landlord electrical distribution and fire alarm systems and loading dock access can also go in this section.

OCCUPATIONAL LICENSE INFORMATION

A separate section for tenants and their operations people on how to apply for and get a business license is often appreciated by the tenants themselves, especially when they have not opened a store in that municipality before.

CONTRACTOR INFORMATION FORM

A form asking basic contact information about the contractor should be inserted. This form should ask for contact names, emergency phone numbers, addresses, e-mail addresses and so forth. This form becomes a handy point of reference for the management and operations teams once the tenant coordinator is no longer involved in the project if there is a store warranty or construction issue in the future. A separate list requiring contact names and numbers for the store subcontractors can also be invaluable.

CONSTRUCTION RULES AND REGULATIONS ACCEPTANCE FORM

This form is for the superintendent to sign upon check-in confirming the date of the work start, the acceptance of paperwork as being complete or outstanding and that they have read and understand the rules and regulations.

SPACE ACCEPTANCE FORM

This form confirms the status of the store upon turnover. It should include a list of all of the items owed by the landlord as per the lease and a place to note if the required work was complete at the time the store construction manager or superintendent walked the store with the landlord's representative. This form helps protect the landlord by having the tenant contractor and landlord's representative agree if work is complete or damaged so that both have an established baseline on what might still need to be completed or what was subsequently damaged during tenant construction.

After the Center Is Open, Merge Your Manuals

Once the new center is open or if you are writing a manual for an open and operating center, the design and construction criteria can be merged into one handbook. This handbook will have the appropriate tenant co-ordination and operations contacts and will need to be updated with information pertinent to how the property management wants construction conducted in an open and operating center.

Some of the issues and additional forms that will need to be inserted include shutdown requests for fire alarm and fire sprinkler systems, roof access forms, barricade design approval forms and requests for security badges. Operating shopping centers will generally require construction during nonoperating hours and special arrangements will need to be made if access through another tenant is needed. Some centers will let contractors work during the day as long as they stay within the demised premises and do loud, noisy work at night or on Sunday mornings before adjoining tenants open. In addition, they will not be able to park in front of operating tenants and have to take deliveries before and after the stores open.

6

Plan Review— How to Streamline the Process and Make Effective Comments

Plan review of tenant's submittals is one of the primary functions of most tenant coordinators. However, the time involved and the number of submittals and follow-up actions that must be made also make it extremely tedious and time-consuming. It is not a job for the cowardly lions of this world, afraid to make decisions, encourage creativity or think out of the box. On the other hand, it is not the job for people who shrug off details and have no sense of urgency.

An effective submittal and review program does not need to be terrible and tedious. It does need to be easy to administer, quick to respond to and full of stopgap and tracking procedures to make sure that all parties are efficiently communicating with each other, that important information is being shared and passed on and that landlords and tenants both feel that their interests are protected.

Timely Plan Submittal

The best way to ensure timely plan submittal and subsequent review is to put it into the lease with easily identifiable milestones. Making it a commitment ensures that the tenant will be paying attention. If they are doing multiple openings and their staff is swamped and if you do not have your submittal time tied to a lease date, they will overlook you in meeting their other, more pressing obligations. Then your Tenant Coordination department will have to waste more time trying to reach the right people and convincing them you really need their plans to meet your opening dates.

Stores that create an interactive environment for their customers encourage them to come in, stay and shop.

In centers where you do not have a grand opening involved, the easiest way to do it is to tie it to a turnover date. By stating that they will have rent commence 30, 60, 90 or 120 days from the day the space is turned over to them, then even if they are not ready, you will get money coming in.

If you are doing a grand opening of a block of stores at once or have square footage tenant occupancy clauses where tenants won't pay full rent until a certain amount is actually open and operating, you would want to tie the submittal process to the lease execution date.

In some cases, providing both gives you a fail-safe to ensure timely submittal as well as a sense of urgency for them to actually get your final sign-off and get into the permitting department to build.

Where you are dealing with mom-and-pop independent operators, make sure it is clear in the lease that the submittal has to be from a certified architect and engineer. If you are really uncomfortable with an operator, make sure you include kickout clauses so that if they do not proceed with the design and construction phase, you can tag it early and get the space back without having to wait until the delivery and commencement dates start.

Tracking Reports

It does not speak well of the industry in general that our big box operators feel compelled to do the reverse to the developers. Their leases will spell out the time we have to review and respond back to them or we will be deemed to be in default or to have simply accepted the plans "as approved" since we did not respond.

Typical types of reviews as per center type:

Type of Center	Power Center, Big Boxes	Regional Mall, Grand Opening	Community Center, Already Operating
Landlord documents or criteria	Landlord sends lease outline drawings and shell criteria	Landlord sends design criteria, base building plans and lease outline drawing	Landlord sends lease outline drawing, access to space info, design and construction criteria and any as-builds
Submittal package	Prototypes received from tenant	Construction plans, signage and finish board	Construction plans, signage and finish board
Typical type of review	Landlord reviews for lease conformance and gives to architect to put on own plans	Landlord reviews and comments	Landlord reviews and comments
Follow-up process	Will be specified in lease	Generally not specified, sense of urgency on landlord required	Generally not specified

Whether dealing with the tenants or them dealing with us, it is extremely important to have a good tracking system in place so that dates are watched and not missed. If they are missed, they need to be acknowledged and proceeded upon with urgency.

One of the easiest ways to do this is through electronic calendars programmed to give you a couple of days' warning when critical deadlines are approaching. Tenant Coordination managers who spend a lot of time in the field are better protected by in-house support or administration that is watching these critical dates for them.

The type of deals you are doing in a center will help you arrange how to set up your reports. If you are a lifestyle center with build-to-suit big box users, your reports will hinge on the dates when you receive prototype plans from the tenants. Malls or centers with specialty stores will base their reports on lease execution dates. Where there is a large opening involved, typically the opening date will determine the plan review timing and process, and working back from that, submittal dates will be plotted out and tenants informed of when they need to get plans in.

Information typically included in these reports includes:

Type of Center	Power Center, Big Boxes	Regional Mall, Grand Opening	Community Center, Already Operating
Process kickoff date	Date prototype received	Date plans received	Date plans received
Submittal package	Date architect cut loose	Date plans reviewed, returned and status	Date plans reviewed, returned and status
Typical type of review	Date plans sent to tenant for review	Review for design criteria, storefront in relation to center, mall systems	Review for conformance to criteria, quality of materials and if they are conforming to available utilities
Follow-up process	Date tenant responds to landlord, proceeded with back-and-forth until tenant accepts landlord plans	Generally not specified, sense of urgency by landlord required	Generally not specified
Sign-off	Sign-off required by the tenant on landlord's plans adequately reflecting what will be built for them	Sign-off required by landlord	Sign-off required by landlord

Quality Review Time

Usually it is not a matter of not wanting to provide a quality review as much as finding the time to do it. Tenant coordinators managing several projects at one time often have the hardest time because they have to mentally shift gears to make sure they are communicating the right information. That can get extremely tiring.

There is an old saying, "Start off in the means you intend to go on in." This means to not even accept a package for review unless it is 100% complete upon submittal. The problem with that is that in our need to expedite or to get pertinent information needed to coordinate other tenants' work or our own, we ignore our own rule and take things piecemeal.

Overall, the best practice is to try to get things in all at one time from one source. It certainly is more efficient for tracking, keeps the attention focused on one area and makes best use of our consultants who might be participating in any reviews with us.

Some companies impose review standards upon their own teams. Their goal is to provide a benchmark to their tenants of what the standard review time is so that the tenant knows what to expect and can plan accordingly. While this seems efficient, it might not always be feasible. The tendency of a time-pressed tenant coordinator would become akin to a bureaucratic machine that uses multiple stamps to cover themselves or automatically rejects to buy time. This does not mean you should not use stamps or reject; in fact, you should. What it does mean is that if the formalized approach is more important than the partnership of encouraging creativity and solving problems, then tenant coordinators and the developers they work for have become part of a machine that does not truly partner with their tenants or treat them with the same creative approach with which we want them to address their stores in our centers.

In other words, we become our own worst enemies.

What quality review time does mean is taking the time to really look at plans, call when we have questions, encourage new and alternative finishes and methods of construction and be willing to take an occasional risk on something different. It also means telling a tenant why you won't approve something, respecting branded images and occasionally be willing to fight for the tenant if you think they have a good idea even if it is against the specified criteria or puts them under undue hardship for some reason other than costs.

Here are a couple of tips to help tenant coordinators find quality time to review plans.

ESTABLISH A SCHEDULE

Make it a known policy that you set aside from 2:00 P.M. to 5:00 P.M. daily for plan review. Do not accept meetings or take calls. Dedicate that time only to the tenant whose plans are in front of you and recap immediately any conversations you have had with them in the form of handwritten notes on the plans or a note to file or written response by letter, transmittal or e-mail.

WORK A DIFFERENT SCHEDULE

Instead of working 8:00 to 5:00 daily, work 10:00 to 7:00 two days a week and use the hours after everyone else has left to review drawings. This is particularly helpful if you are on Eastern Standard Time, as you can use the last two hours to deal with West Coast clients. You can do the opposite if you live on the West Coast and deal with eastern design and construction teams.

CONSTANT COMMUNICATION

If you accept plans that are not complete submittals, acknowledge on your transmittals back what they still owe you as a standard practice. Withhold 100% approval of the entire package until everything is in and reviewed.

PRE-REVIEW

Have someone else on your team pre-review plans and communicate back to the tenant in advance what is missing. Tell them that you will not do the review until all items are together.

CREATE STANDARD STAMPS OR RESPONSE FORMS

Once you work on a project for a while, you will tend to have the same comments over and over. Save time by having these on a desktop file. Open that file when reviewing and delete what is not appropriate, adding additional comments as needed. When finished with the review, it is an easy cut and paste to your comments and saves you a lot of writing and recording.

> *"Streamline your operational portfolio plan reviews: a cut-and-paste library of notes covers 90% of your comments."*
>
> GREGORY R. GUNTER
> Vice President
> 3rd Works

DO NOT REVIEW FOR CODE

Why accept the liability? This is the architects' and engineers' responsibility. You do not have to read every detail; just make sure you tell them up front you are not accepting the liability or responsibility.

REQUIRE SITE VERIFICATION FROM THE TENANT INSTEAD OF DOING IT YOURSELF

Why accept the responsibility? If you are dealing with new construction where field conflicts affect changes that might not be on your shell drawings or if you have a store renovation and no one knows what is under sheetrock or floor covering, put the onus on the tenant general contractor as part of due diligence. Field conditions are usually not discovered until shop drawings commence, and most experienced general contractors and subcontractors can handle this more efficiently than we can.

DIRECT COMMENT ON PLANS

Make sure all your comments are on a set of plans that get handed to the tenant's general contractor in the field as well as to the tenant's construction managers and owners. Make them responsible through the field coordination process to be aware of your comments and construction rules and regulations. This way you can spend less time in the office reviewing plans you have seen several times, nitpicking for exact data, and more time reviewing other projects. In order to do this, you will need a strong field team or pair of eyes in the field to assist you.

Information to Provide in Advance

One area where you can save time in review is through making sure the tenant design teams have the most thorough information package they can. Upon being notified by the tenant who their design team is, arrange to ship out shell plans, as-builds, design criteria, utility information and any testing procedures you have available. The more information they have and the better the quality, the more effective your tenant coordination efforts are.

"Remember your compatriot on the tenant side juggles a host of store openings for dozens of projects. Streamline their procedural hurdles, and you'll be their ally."

Gregory R. Gunter
Vice President
3rd Works

SHELL PLANS
The age of CAD and electronic drawings has made this so much easier. The problem? Not all landlords want to invest in a contract that allows their architect and engineers to do this electronically. Occasionally you also run into design teams that will not let go of their plans electronically because of their own internal policies. Landlords who hire design teams and make arrangements in advance for electronic transfer will get tenant plan submittals back more quickly and will spend less time and money on reproduction and shipping costs.

AS-BUILDS
Property managers who hold onto tenant plans are worth their weight in platinum, gold and silver combined. When it comes time to turn the space over to a new user, these plans are invaluable and can save everyone time, money and effort. Keeping as-builds in electronic format is making this more feasible, as less time and room are needed for file storage and retrieval.

DESIGN CRITERIA
Specifications on what the landlord is looking for in terms of design and mechanical systems should be sent out promptly to the tenants.

Often there is a lapse between what is published and what is actually happening in the field. That information can be updated into the design criteria occasionally or it can be shot over as part of a separate file. Transmitting this information electronically can also save the tenant design team time, as they can pick up lease plans, rules and regulations and LODs right out of your file. Some malls have started posting their criteria on Internet sites or plan rooms, which can also save time and money. Once a center is open, combining the design criteria with the construction rules and regulations becomes an even more effective tool for not only the design and construction teams, but also operations teams and subsequent tenant coordinators who only work on tenant construction at that center occasionally.

UTILITY AND MEP INFORMATION

The more the engineers know about what is available and where connections are within the building or premises and about your installation and testing systems, the better the quality of their plans, your review time and ultimately the cost of construction for tenants, who have fewer surprises.

DESIGNATED SUBCONTRACTORS

The quicker you get information out on who the designated subcontractors are and what procedures to follow with them, the less review time will be needed to make sure mall property and systems are understood and protected.

What the Community Is Looking For

If you know the permitting department will be looking for certain criteria, why not provide a list of them in advance? Just make sure that the tenant design team understands that you are doing this to assist, but it is still up to them to make sure they understand the code.

Usually community "hot buttons" become more available as more and more tenants go into review and you start hearing comments back from them. If possible, strike up an arrangement with the community plan reviewers and ask to be put onto the comment dispersal list as a matter of course. That way you will know exactly when a tenant submits, what the reviewer's comments are and when comments were issued. If the tenant's design team is arguing with the reviewer, this could hold up the permit and thus jeopardize your tenant from opening in a timely manner.

You will also know if the problem is due to a landlord issue and can re-act quickly. This is especially important if you have a lease clause that says you are obligated to assist a tenant in the permitting process or if you need a tenant to get open quickly because of a co-tenancy requirement.

Typically some of the hot topics communities look for are required number of bathrooms and access, life safety issues, ADA issues, structural loads and fire wall types and sealing penetrations.

Protecting the Landlord's Property

This is worth mentioning repeatedly because it is another one of the prime functions of a good tenant coordinator and coordination team. As much as we might want to assist tenants with design and construction, it is one of our prime duties to make sure we look after our employer.

Ensuring that life safety issues are met, that penetrations are tight and sealed and that other tenants and the public are not impacted or endangered; protecting sensitive mall systems from contamination; meeting development agreements and requirements; upholding lease standards; protecting structural integrity and watching out for dangerous practices are also part of tenant coordination oversight. These items can all be addressed through proper comments during the plan review process.

LIFE SAFETY
Tenant coordinators need to make sure that barricades are installed; tenant contractors adhere to proper OSHA standards; and chemical storage, welding and flammables are properly stored, conducted and handled.

PENETRATIONS SEALED
Call out and require work standards and practices that should work to protect the landlord and other tenants in the future by having the right waterproofing and sealing done during the construction process.

WATCHING FOR DANGEROUS PRACTICES
Require proper barricades and work practices be called out to the tenant contractor in the plans so that they understand the impacts and account for the costs during the bid process to their clients.

PROTECTING SENSITIVE MALL SYSTEMS AND FINISHES
Anytime a tenant has to hook into a system that affects multiple tenants, there is going to be inconvenience. Make sure that designated contractor info is called out if they control the process or that the proper

shutdown sequence is spelled out exactly. Also make it clear that dust control and access over sensitive finishes should be coordinated with the right operations and construction people in your plan review comments. Make sure the tenant contractor also has a copy of the plans calling this information out.

ASSISTING IN-PLACE TENANTS

Calling out procedures to protect surrounding tenants from inconvenience and noise is also a good standard to have noted in the plans. It gives the operations or on-site tenant coordinator additional means to enforce proper work procedures.

MEETING DEVELOPMENT AGREEMENTS

Often deals and arrangements are made with the municipalities that impact tenant coordination and tenant work. When we know about these agreements, we should be conveying them in both written and verbal manner to the tenant design and construction teams. Some of the related issues that tenant coordinators typically run into will be no parking or delivery regulations, noise control, no after-hours work, no banners, limited signage opportunities, restricted light levels and enforced heavy landscaping in areas in front of tenant storefronts and signs. Often these regulations will run afoul of promises made in the lease. Try to insist that tenant coordination have an opportunity to review a lease, looking for these items as well as construction exhibits.

UPHOLDING LEASE STANDARDS

This can go both ways. Sometimes we are forced to make sure tenants meet the letter of the lease. Sometimes we are forced to make sure our own construction and management team meets the letter of the lease. Regardless, tenant coordinators are often put into tenuous positions because of their duty to the landlord and tenants.

If a tenant prototype says to use a specific type of assembly or product, there is usually a good reason and we need to make sure our architect and contractor live up to the specification. If the lease says no banners, then there is usually a good reason and we need to make sure our tenant abides by it.

PROTECTING STRUCTURAL INTEGRITY

We hire engineers and architects to design buildings that can withstand certain loads and pressures. To maintain that integrity we often have to make sure that tenants and their contractors understand that the impacts they are going to make will have a cost, including additional engineering. When in doubt, bring in the experts. This is one liability no construction team member or tenant coordinator should want to knowingly take on.

Often, tenant coordination is just common sense put into practice. By calling out expectations in terms not only of finishes and fixtures and materials, but also life safety and best construction practices as much as possible in advance, the fewer problems you will have in the field and the more quickly tenants will open.

7 | Landlord's Work from Plans to Construction: How to Meet the Obligations and Expectations of the Lease

After months of negotiation and hard work, the leasing agent is done and Tenant Coordination is handed a paper document that sums up a contractual relationship. Depending on how difficult the negotiations were, the history and relationship of the people involved and the financial nature of the project, that paper lease already brings with it a load of obligations and expectations that tenant coordinators are expected to wade through and know quickly.

In other words, it can be like stepping into the proverbial minefield.

Taking the emotions out of the document and determining what the actual obligations are is the first step in making sure that the landlord's role in meeting the expectations of the tenants is fair and understood. Tenant coordinators who have to ask their leasing agents on a constant basis "But what was your intent?" need to report back to their development team that the document is not supporting the landlord's interests enough for them to be able to simply pick it up and move forward with no surprises.

The Lease Provisions That Govern the Process

All lease provisions govern, otherwise it would not be a contractual document. However, some lease provisions are of more importance to tenant coordinators than others. The first thing a tenant coordinator should do is read the lease and look for certain key points. Some tenant coordinators will post-note those clauses; others will abstract them into key tracking documents of forms in the shape of a lease abstract. Generally the lease abstract that a property manager prepares is not going to pick up on the same points as tenant coordination would.

LOCATION

Look for the location of the center and identify for quick reference by suite number or address. This little piece of information will be one of the most frequently asked questions you will get.

SIZE AND CERTIFICATION REQUIREMENTS

Note the size and any specific requirements for certification noted in the lease. Do you need to have a certified letter sent? What regulates the form of measurement? How do you handle disputes?

DATE OF EXECUTION

Check the signature page and see what date the lease was actually signed. This piece of information often triggers other important dates. It also serves as a double-check to make sure you have a signed document and are not working prematurely off of something that might still be modified.

LEASE/RENT COMMENCEMENT DATE

This is usually the first thing tenant coordinators look for. It tells you the expected date for opening the store. It is occasionally disguised under or tied into days for construction terminology also.

DAYS FOR CONSTRUCTION

See the lease/rent commencement date; sometimes days for construction stands alone. Days for construction becomes even more important when you are opening a number of different tenants at one time but have staggered deliveries based on what they feel a reasonable amount of time is for them to actually open a store.

A few words of warning are appropriate here. Just because the lease says the tenant has 120 days to open does not always mean they intend to take 120 days. If a tenant is motivated to get a certain amount of stores open within a private timetable, such as those driven by firms on the stock market, they might need only 60 days to do it. If you deliver based on 120 days and do not have the shell and landlord areas complete on the exterior and they decide to do a 60-day buildout in order to include your store location in the block of stores they need to open that quarter, you could have a problem here. If you intend to deliver in advance of shell completion, always check with the tenant construction manager and let them know in advance so that if there are any conflicts with actual opening dates, you know and can make some financial decisions.

On the other hand, if the tenant intends to open only a few stores a quarter and you intend to have a grand opening and want as many stores open as possible, let them know. Sometimes tenants can shift store opening dates around to assist, particularly if they are excited about a center opening in your market. Also, occasionally other new store locations run into problems, and if they can move yours up into a more aggressive timetable, you end up helping them out.

DELIVERY AND BLACKOUT DATES

There are usually very specific clauses in leases addressing these items. Delivery is typically established by counting back the anticipated days of construction from the anticipated lease/rent commencement date, unless a specified date has been established. If you need to send out a pre-delivery and/or delivery notice, you need to note it. Also, you need to note if there are dates when they will not accept delivery or will not open. Usually blackouts are timed to protect store resources so that tenants are not expected to open during their operationally busiest times of the year. These blackouts also preclude retailers from being required to open without having the appropriate amount of merchandise because of the buying and shipping times required for seasonally sensitive merchandise. Landlords need to be sensitive to this, since it is an important part of the retail merchandising industry. Requiring a store not fully stocked or operational to make a grand opening or seasonal sales period can be detrimental to the long-range health of the store, as customers will question the store's and center's viability if they do not look fully stocked.

For instance, children's clothing stores will not want to drain resources during spring merchandising, back-to-school sales or holiday sales. Craft stores are often busy in the summer and again in the holiday season between November 1 and December 31. In the United States, most chain stores will not open from the end of October until after the New Year. Other countries would have similar merchandising season impacts based on the religious and cultural traditions of their marketplace.

CONSTRUCTION EXHIBIT OR WORK ORDER

Sometimes this is as simple as "space as is." At other times it refers to a complete set of prototype plans and a full specifications book. It is the second most important thing the tenant coordinator should look at, and the complexity of what is owed to the tenant according to what it states will govern the business relationship of the tenant construction manager and the tenant coordinator and development team.

Unfortunately, this is the section where a lot of promises are made by the development and leasing team without recognition of the full impact of what they are committing to. When Tenant Coordination starts to create working drawings and present construction bids to meet these demands, it becomes the number-one area of anger and frustration: the landlord not understanding fully what he agreed to and the tenant not understanding why the landlord is not living up to the obligations he signed up for. This is the one area that tends to cause the most internal frustration between development and Tenant Coordination teams and Tenant Coordination and the tenant's construction teams.

Also, depending upon the nature of the project, the construction exhibit can also contain specific information related directly to the design and construction process, such as construction insurance, plan submittal, temporary office and hiring information and labor harmony. Leases that require outparcels might also have specific information on site work completion that will need to be noted.

PLAN SUBMITTAL AND REVIEW DATES

Landlords have begun tying plan submittals to lease execution dates so that they have a means of committing tenants to work schedules. By tying these dates to something solid in the lease, there is also a means of being able to put tenants into the default process if they do not comply or if they do not want to move their store opening up to meet the landlord's opening schedules.

Also, tenants use these dates to make sure landlords are participating in timely review and submittals of their plans so that tenants can plan their own resources for opening stores.

UTILITY PROVISIONS

The responsibility for who provides utilities and pays impact fees and when utilities get taken over by the tenant are often stated in the lease. Since these can become serious points of contention, they need to be noted so that the tenant coordinator can see at a glance what their responsibility is to the tenant and tenant's construction team.

SIGNAGE REQUIREMENTS

Tenant coordinators usually have sign approval rights for facade signs on behalf of the landlord. If there are certain looks or locations agreed to, they will usually be shown in a lease exhibit. Signage requirements can also require Tenant Coordination to assist in obtaining or locating temporary signs and in coordinating monument and pylon signs.

CO-TENANCY

Co-tenancy usually requires that a certain percentage of total square feet or specific tenants be open for some tenants' rent to commence or for tenants with these agreements to go from partial rent to full-rent payments. If certain openings are not happening on a timely basis, for whatever reasons, tenant coordinators need to notify the development or property management teams who are forecasting income.

EXCLUSIVITY REQUIREMENTS

Tenant coordinators watching construction and merchandising on-site need to be aware if a tenant is putting merchandise into their store that is prohibited due to an exclusive arrangement with another store. Since other leases will preclude this, it needs to be flagged immediately and sometimes legally to protect the landlord from possible litigation from stores with exclusive arrangements.

Although occasionally you can see it and note it in the tenant plans during plan review, more typically the signs that this might be about to happen will be seen by literally watching tenant display and graphic package installations. Most stores guilty of exclusivity infringement tend to be small mom-and-pop or independent operators that often do not realize the legal implications. Since they tend to be the most independent-minded, they also are the hardest to control. An example of this would be a small bakery that decides a few tables and chairs and a lunch sandwich business would be a nice extension to their business, not realizing they have now become a conflict to the landlord, who has an exclusive with a larger national sandwich chain.

NOTICE REQUIREMENTS

Tenant Coordination needs to call out anyone who needs to be sent or copied on notices of special correspondence for quick reference. This is usually hidden in a separate section of the lease, but not always. This is particularly important when default and delivery notices go out. Making sure everyone is properly noticed ensures adequate protection to landlords from tenants who state that they have not received information as per the lease.

TENANT ALLOWANCE OR INDUCEMENT CLAUSES

Tenant allowance or inducement payment information can be found either in a separate section of the lease or in the construction exhibit. Along with clauses on these allowances, there should be a written protocol on when they become due and the paperwork process needed to obtain them.

Since a lot of these allowances are paid out through part of the construction draw process by the landlord, they need to be supported with adequate documentation as required not only by the landlord, but also by his bankers or lenders. This documentation is to ensure that the tenant has paid their own consultants and contractor obligations so that the landlord does not end up paying twice, once to the tenant for work and then again to their general contractor because the tenant did not pay them. It is important that timing and documentation be spelled out in advance so that the proper sequence is clear to all parties. Tenant coordinators who are applying for releases on tenant allowances and inducements through the draw process need to be in tune with the accounting team so that when an allowance is due, the tenant coordinator can actually get the money in a timely manner so that the landlord himself does not go into default of the lease.

If the lease does not lay out the draw and payment procedure, Tenant Coordination needs to flag it and let the tenant and leasing teams know as soon as possible in order to avoid conflict.

CHARGEBACK REQUIREMENTS OR ALLOWANCES

Some developers like to play with the idea of making tenant coordination self-supporting or a profit center. Usually tenants will strike these clauses from the lease. However, if there are some chargebacks to cover standard coordination plan review or to do additional work on a tenant's behalf, this should also be noted. Look for administration fees and note them also.

CONSTRUCTION INSURANCE

Note any special requirements, found either as a stand-alone clause or in the construction exhibit.

Below is a sample of a "Lease Abstract" for tenant coordination, showing items that are for tracking purposes, handy to have all in one form.

TENANT ABSTRACT
SMITH'S TOWN STORE

Tenant Name: Smith's Town Store, LLC

Address: Smith's Town Store
2300 Regency Place Park, Suite 3500
Atlanta, GA 30326
Attention: Real Estate

Others for Notices: Joseph Brown, Esq.
Brown, Group and Jones, LLP
1500 Peachtree Center Avenue, N.E.
Atlanta, GA 30303

    And

James Adler
Construction Manager
2300 Regency Place Park, Suite 3500
Atlanta, GA 30326

Size: 3,000 sf, size certification not required unless requested by tenant within 5 days of delivery.

Location: J520

Date of Execution: 3/20/05

Lease Commencement: The first to occur of 90 days from the day of delivery or date tenant opens.

Delivery Information: Pre-delivery notice due 30 days prior, delivery notice day of delivery.

Plan Submission: Within 30 days from lease execution. Landlord has 10 days to respond and comment. Tenant has 15 days to address.

Landlord's Responsibility: White box, see construction exhibit.

Utilities: Upon delivery.

Signage: No pylon, mall directory allowed, coming soon banners allowed.

Exclusivity: None.

Tenant Inducement or Allowance $120,000 evidence of work satisfactorily completed, reasonable evidence all work is paid for, all liens satisfied or waived, open one month, tenant not in default, estoppel, tenant in good standing.

Chargebacks: Landlord has right to charge back for signage directory, awnings and additional work as per requested by tenant with 15% administration fee.

Approvals: Tenant can install satellite, landlord to approve location.

Blackout: Tenant not required to open between August 15 and September 15, November 1 and January 15.

Closeout: Landlord and tenant must walk space 10 days after letter sent out; LL has 15 days to complete outstanding items—tenant must give LL list within 30 days.

Pre-delivery notice required	Date sent	Delivery notice date required	Date sent
30 days	6/1/05	7/1/05	7/1/05

Date Plans Submitted	Reviewed	Date Approved or Commented
4/17/05	Rejected 4/25/05	Final approval 5/9/05
	Revised received 5/2/05	

Construction Contact	Architect	Contractor
James Adler, 404-650-0054 call	Priscilla Smith ABD Design Team 3679 Pine Road Orlando, Fl 32765 407-366-4099	Joe Smith, superintendent 2349 Central Parkway Fort Walton Beach, Fl 32845 850-660-2536

Permit Submittal	Permit Number	Plans Approved	Construction Start	Date of CO
Made 5/15/05	PO50496	6/25/05	7/3/05	9/20/05

Issuing Proper Documentation

One of the most important jobs of Tenant Coordination and lease administration is to make sure that the proper paperwork is issued in a timely manner and as correctly as possible. These documents create a paper trail for tracking submittals and approvals as well as store deliveries, which eventually kick off rent commencement.

Tenant Coordination also needs to make sure that all parties as stated by the lease to be notified are properly done so and collect substantiation of receipt if they need to.

These documents tend to include delivery notices, start and stop work notices, copies of insurance, delivery of surveys, title and geotechnical paperwork and notices of failure to perform. Standard forms for each should be established.

If a tenant coordinator spends a lot of time in the field, then critical office support in lease administration is necessary. If various consultants are used, tracking of their paperwork and documentation is also needed.

Once documents are issued, they need to be kept in a central file for quick reference. Copies should be sent to the proper other departments that also need to be tracking for their own process, such as property management and accounting.

Communicating with the Tenants, Tenants' Agents (Architects, General Contractors), Management and Construction Teams

The more effectively a tenant coordinator communicates what the landlord's role and expectations are to the tenant and their design and construction team, the better the results will be in getting timely and correct submittals and proper turnovers of space.

Tenant coordinators should contact the tenant design and construction managers as soon as they receive the lease if they have not already been in contact. Call them up and introduce yourself and exchange contact information. Let them know where you stand in the process of getting them open and ask what their expectations are of you. If you are in the field more than in the office, make sure they know so that they do not get frustrated expecting answers at the push of an e-mail "Send" button.

> *"Tenant coordinators should keep in mind that whatever their qualifications and background, they are foremost the landlord's representative."*
>
> BRAD SMITH
> Director of Retail Tenant Coordination
> Forest City Commercial Group

Arrange to get pertinent plans, drawings and design handbooks to the design team immediately so that the design process can start.

When dealing with the contractors, a key sign to how knowledgeable they are in dealing with retail construction will be the questions they ask you at the start of the conversation. If they ask for handbooks, construction deposits and fees and designated subcontractors, you are probably dealing with a knowledgeable contractor. Occasionally some contractors and subcontractors are barred from projects due to bad work practices, theft or nonconformance with mall construction rules, and most store construction managers do not mind getting legitimate input of this type. If a lease allows for approval of a contractor, then make sure the construction manager lets you know who they are bidding to so that you can give them input of this type before they sign a contract.

When communicating with a tenant's design and construction teams, tenant coordinators need to remember that the tenant's team does not work for the landlord. Landlords should not put themselves in the position of causing the tenants to pay additional costs for work unless there is substantial documentation to show the work is required, such as in the design criteria, noted on reviewed plans or in a widely distributed construction handbook. Tenant coordinators should make sure that the tenant design and construction managers are copied on correspondence to their consultants so that they are aware of all issues out of professional courtesy. Landlords and tenant coordinators should also expect the same professional courtesy in return and tenant construction managers should not communicate with the landlord's own design and construction teams without also first alerting the tenant coordinator or copying them.

Landlord designers and contractors doing work for a tenant coordinator as per a tenant's plans and specifications should be made aware that no substitutions on specified items will be allowed without notifying the tenant coordinator, who will need to ask permission from the tenant design and construction team. Landlords who allow changes in specifically stated items in plans and prototypes referred to in the lease are in violation of their lease unless proper permission is requested from the tenant. Tenants who wish to make changes should also recognize that every change has a time and cost impact to the landlord and that they need to give reasonable notice of an intent to request a change and accept liability for delivery impact if needed. Tenant coordinators need to make sure all parties understand this and are in compliance and in communication with one another.

Follow-Through Is Critical

Part of the tenant coordinator's role is to make sure that follow-through on all issues is made and all parties informed so that decisions impacting others are communicated. A tenant coordinator who operates in a vacuum, not alerting the construction team of impacts of a lease to their shell construction or not telling a tenant that their architect is not meeting proper submittal requirements, is not fulfilling the role they are most critically needed for, coordination. A good tenant coordinator will be balancing many balls in the air at one time. They will also be constantly looking to the future to protect their tenants and the landlord from obstacles that will hinder store openings and rent commencement.

Conflict in the construction field is inevitable. Tenant coordinators who have good records and photo documentation will be of better support to their development team when it comes time to figure out what the problems are and how to solve them. Tenant coordinators with personalities that allow them to handle the egos of both the tenant and the landlord construction and design teams will have more success in resolving issues before they turn into potential lawsuits.

Effective communications, strong tracking systems and proper administrative support will help to make the tenant coordinator more effective in making sure all parties are aware of where people sit in the planning, approval and construction process as well as what impacts to successful store openings are out there that the landlord and tenant can control.

8 How to Choose and Work with White Box and Build-to-Suit Contractors

For many tenant coordinators, one of the most challenging parts of their work is actually getting the landlord's commitments built and delivered. This is where a solid construction background becomes useful. A tenant coordinator who has worked as a construction manager for a developer or retail general contractor is more likely to deliver store buildouts faster and less expensively.

Since tenant coordinators work with a variety of projects on their owners' and tenants' behalf, over time they become more versatile in understanding the demands of various retail products. Their field experience also teaches them what potential problems to look for and how to troubleshoot. Quicker, more efficient construction means faster delivery to tenants and more value to the development team when stores open early or on time.

The Demised Premises: White Box, Vanilla Box, Etc.

One of the first questions a tenant coordinator will ask when handed a copy of the letter of intent or a construction exhibit is, "What am I delivering"? In Chapter 4, we learned that the most common categories for delivery were black box or warm brick, vanilla box or white box, built-to-suit, freestanding building or outparcels. In this chapter we are going to be talking about hiring contractors primarily for white box and build-to-suit work. Occasionally tenant coordinators do have to hire contractors for work involved in the other categories.

BLACK BOX, COLD DARK SHELL, SHELL CONDITION OR WARM BRICK

Black box, also known as cold dark shell, shell condition, or warm brick, is usually the minimum amount of work given to a tenant as per the lease. Typically the electrical and telephone conduits and connection points for base building utility services are in place as part of the shell construction. In some cases, a storefront is provided at exterior centers. The tenant is expected to take the space as is and start construction. Tenant coordinators must make sure that the connection points for utilities are in place, the space swept clean, the storefront complete as required and the space accessible to a retail contractor to start work.

Occasionally tenant coordinators run into construction clauses that require something atypical or additional in terms of delivery that require some modification of the shell (usually in utilities) from the rest of the black boxes, as an example, adding a low-pressure gas line or running electrical feed from a riser into the space.

If the shell is still under construction, it is better to have the base building contractor handle this work so that there are no conflicts with ongoing completion of work for shell completion or problems with warranties of work. This work will often have to be permitted through the local municipality and can be as challenging to perform as a full build-out due to site demands, such as adding a grease interceptor or running new ductwork back through multiple spaces to a fresh air tap.

If the work needs to be done in an operational center, coordination with the management team is essential. Tenant coordinators who can use the construction resources of the management team or who have a small group of contractors who know the center and its operations team and utility systems will have more success in getting this often demanding work done.

Even though the space requires additional work of some scope, since it is not a complete, ready-to-move-in buildout, it is not white box work. Sometimes it is referred to as a modified black box.

VANILLA BOX OR WHITE BOX

The terms *vanilla box* and *white box* are often used interchangeably, depending upon the tenant coordinator, development team or architect you are talking to. This tends to cause a lot of confusion in the industry. It also gets permitting departments at municipalities confused, as they don't understand the intent of the work and worry about unauthorized move-ins by tenants.

For purposes of this chapter we are going to refer to them as white boxes. White boxes are typically spaces that are modified to meet the terms of the lease negotiation but are not 100% complete. White boxes might contain all the components of a complete store such as demising walls, stockroom walls, ceilings, restrooms, complete and operational mechanical systems and lighting, but they usually need the finishes and fixtures to be installed as part of the final opening.

Once the white box is complete and delivered to a tenant, the tenant or their contractor would need to come in with a separate permit, such as a fixturing or occupancy permit, and install their flooring, fixtures, low-voltage point of sale and telephone and security systems and signage packages. Their permit is typically what gets the store actually inspected and approved for official occupancy by the municipality.

BUILD-TO-SUIT

A build-to-suit is when the store is designed and built 100% to tenant specifications, including fixtures and finishes. Although the tenant might supply their own vendors for low-voltage wiring for computer, security and cash wraps and signage, it is generally work performed under the landlord's contractor, and when complete, the store will have passed all inspections for occupancy and can be stocked and open for business.

FREESTANDING BUILDINGS AND OUTPARCELS

Tenant coordinators are called upon often to complete landlord site work for freestanding and outparcel work. Site work needs to be designed, approved and permitted just as interior work does. Site work on existing centers can be particularly challenging, especially if the tenant's lease calls for taps into existing utilities that require disruption of services to others.

This type of work can also be a challenge on older, existing properties because the original site drawings have often disappeared and design of existing underground can't start until drawings are located and as-build locations are verified.

Whenever possible, tenant coordinators should try to work with the original civil design and construction team. If that is not possible, contact the local utilities and ask for help, as they often have as-builds they can get you copies of.

The types of work tenant coordinators typically run into in this area include bringing utilities to specific points at the pad to meet the tenant's design criteria, completing paving, sidewalks and landscaping or tearing out and upgrading existing pipes and lines to meet a bigger demand than originally expected in the initial civil designs.

Responsibilities—Landlord Versus Tenant

Even with the structure of a lease document or construction exhibit to support you, it is amazing how determining whose responsibility is what still ends up being the biggest source of contention and conflict between the development and tenant design and construction teams. Many a developer and tenant coordinator have been surprised by the final interpretation of just a couple of little words that seem innocuous enough during the initial reviews of the lease clauses.

Development teams, when reviewing lease exhibits, need to be on the lookout for things that indicate that additional documents might impact the lease agreement. Some of these clues include statements such as "per tenant's prototypes and plans" or "tenant plans to take precedent." Unfortunately, this leaves a lot of room for gray and often is the biggest source of frustration to a developer who realizes that he has given more than he intends or that he has impacted his shell or site work completion because he was not paying attention to everything in the lease. Usually these clauses are tucked into the construction exhibits or delivery clauses. When a landlord uses a tenant's lease form, he needs to be extra vigilant on this.

Once a lease is signed, it is a good idea for the tenant coordinator to actually read the lease immediately and then call the tenant construction manager or design manager and discuss mutual expectations. If a coordinator is missing critical information or if there is a problem with mutual expectations, it gets flagged early, before the leasing team moves on to other things.

Once the expectations are discussed, the tenant coordinator needs to get the lease translated to working construction drawings, which need to be approved by the tenant and by the municipalities. Approved drawings can then be sent out to general contractors or site contractors for review and bid.

Sending Plans Out to Bid

When doing work for retail tenants, tenant coordinators would be well advised to deal only with experienced retail tenant contractors. Experienced retail contractors who understand how to work with retailers and speak their language save tenant coordinators a lot of time in construction and turnover.

Typically, most tenant coordinators will request that a complete set of construction plans be sent out to a coterie of preferred contractors.

The rule of thumb is to solicit three bids, although some tenant coordinators might prefer to do more while others will work with one general contractor for a while and only occasionally bid as a check to make sure pricing remains fair. If you typically use the same three contractors over and over, if your budgeting allows for it, make sure all three occasionally get jobs. If a general contractor is always bidding but never gets work, they will move on and you can lose a valuable resource.

When the plans go out to bid, it is helpful to include a copy of the pertinent lease exhibits and marked-up site plans with location to the contractors so that they know what is expected and where the space is. Arrange to have keys available to them at all times so that you do not have to be constantly arranging to meet them or call on your operations or mall manager and disrupting their schedule.

If it is a build-to-suit on a big box or complicated site work, a pre-bid conference might occasionally be required with the tenant construction manager. This can be risky and you will want to make it clear that any work contracted is through you, not them. Otherwise the tenant construction manager could call your contractor directly and order work that you might not feel is your responsibility, and you would not know until the bill is presented.

Expect to get calls from the contractors asking questions for additional information. These calls can be directed to your architect or engineer, but you should always be copied on them, as the information they are requesting might be pertinent to items left off the plans that the other contractors will need to know about or reflect a deficiency in the plans.

Always put a time limit on when you expect bids back in. Plan to follow up several times to make sure contractors are working on them and have not decided to drop out, in case you have to find another bidder.

How to Revise Bid Packages Based on New Information

Occasionally information found out during the initial bid uncovers critical information that results in a plan redesign or a major change in location of equipment or a utility. It is often easier and less risky to issue an amended plan or addendum rather than to try and analyze each bid and determine if the general contractor has included the new information. If this happens, alert each contractor that a revision is coming and for them to re-price. Although this takes time, it is easier to have apples-to-apples bidding than being across the board with a lot of unknowns.

If there is a disparity in bids between contractors, ask for the subcontractors' pricing and see why. Occasionally one subcontractor or contractor will pick up something that the others have left out that could have a huge impact on the success of the project. This is usually a red flag that needs to be explored and picked up on to protect the developer or owner.

Some construction managers believe that if a tenant contractor does not uncover something in his bid and his contract is accepted, then he should be expected to hold to his price. While that is an acceptable method of doing business in construction circles, it is not always the most beneficial, and contractors can usually find their way around it.

Contractor Qualifications

When looking for a new contractor to work with, tenant coordinators should always seek out experienced retail contractors. Look for contractors who can present an extensive list of references from other landlords or from tenants. Make sure you check on them personally. Questions to ask include have they ever been sued by a landlord and why, if they have missed a construction completion date and why, who their preferred subcontractors are, what their operational structure is and what their insurance and bonding structures are.

Also ask who the superintendent will be and make sure that the GC does not have them spread too thin over several projects. Ask to meet the superintendent, and if you do not feel that he understands the job or will be comfortable working with you, suggest the general contractor replace him or look to another general contractor. A good superintendent can make or break a job and can often compensate for poorly designed plans, an irascible building inspector or a weak construction project administration team. A good superintendent who also understands and gets along with your center's operation or construction team as well as the tenant's operations people is worth more than their weight in gold and will impact the success of the delivery of the store and future relations with that tenant.

Writing a Contract

Once a contractor is selected, it is time to work out the details of the arrangement and write a contract. Tying contracts to specific performances and completions can help to ensure deadlines are met in a timely manner. Tenant coordinators also need to be aware of their own internal payment structure and process and convey that to the general contractor so that no problems with timely payment and floats of cash will interrupt the work and turnover process.

While it is always preferable to use your own contract form, not all tenant coordinators have the luxury of having their own contract administrator to assist them. Some tenant coordinators have their architects review the contracts also to try to make sure they are covered in all aspects of the work to be completed.

One thing tenant coordinators and construction managers also need to keep in mind is that just because a contractor had the lowest bid, does not always mean he is the wisest choice. Contractors often use low bids to get a project, especially if the plans are weak and have a lot of unanswered questions. They know that they will make up the money in change orders down the road. This is another reason why bids should be looked at critically when they come in and reviewed and analyzed thoroughly, especially if there is a large disparity in price.

Tenant coordinators need to be very careful when dealing with pricing issues with competing contractors. If there is a huge disparity between contractors, call them up and talk to them. You do not have to tell them what the problem is, but you should ask them about what they were taking into account. If it is sufficiently important enough to warrant telling the other contractors in order to make sure the bids are equitable, then you can make that call. At all times, tenant coordinators must act in as fair and equitable a manner as possible to avoid accusations of unfair practices.

Supervising Your Contractor

Once the contract is awarded and the permit secured, it is time to get the work done. Tenant coordinators who visit their sites on a regular basis, sometimes unannounced, will be able to keep a better eye on the project and communicate accurate status back to the developer and tenant construction teams.

Hard-working construction superintendents appreciate owner's representatives who are willing to help troubleshoot and who are willing to assist them in getting the owner-supplied materials and vendors in when needed to complete their work in a timely manner. They do not appreciate owner's representatives who interrupt work flow, make changes without backup or consideration of schedule or do not respond to questions on required materials or deliveries.

On large build-to-suits, the tenant coordinator should also be available to meet with the contractor and his subcontractors on a regular basis to go over construction and answer questions, and be prepared to intercede with the tenant and architects if additional information is needed.

Tenant coordinators and construction managers have to always take care to not appear to be dictating a means and method or interfering in a contractor's business operation, or they risk being sued by the contractor or being held liable by outside parties if serious construction deficiencies are found in the future, such as a structural collapse of a wall.

If draws are required throughout the process of the project, then the tenant coordinator owes it to the contractor to assist him in making sure they are paid in a timely manner in order to keep his own work moving. Sometimes that means calling the contractor and reminding them that they need to provide their required paperwork in a timely manner to your accounting department. Other times it might mean making sure the accounting department has requested in advance any construction draws as part of their requisitions.

Tenant coordinators who treat their construction contractors as valuable members of their team will end up with better-quality buildouts, delivered on time and budget. It is worth a substantial investment in time and effort to build those relationships and honor them.

9 Store Design and Construction—When and How to Step in to Assist Independent Tenants

Talk to any major developer's construction and tenant coordination staff and chances are good that they will tell you the toughest tenants to open are the independent ones or the ones commonly referred to as the mom-and-pop retailers.

The large tenants and the nationals have construction professionals to assist them. They are experienced in rolling out multiple units, have adequate financing and know the ropes. The independents do not have the knowledge and experience or the direct access to competent design and construction professionals.

While they do not have the money, the know-how or the time, they probably do have a brother-in-law or son in the business and are relying on unsophisticated help to make their dreams happen. Chances are they will fail before the doors have opened or the landlord has even collected rent.

Yet these are also the tenants many of us need and want in our centers. They add spice to our centers, providing unique one-of-a-kind stores. They give our homogenized centers the local feel and talent we want, ground-

High-end looks, as typified by this Steinway store can often be based within very simple white boxes. The use of incandescent lighting, marble and decorator touches makes this simple white box store look elegant and inviting.

ing our centers into the community. They are also sources of invaluable information, helping our property management and marketing teams understand what the real pulse of the community is. With luck and good care, they can grow into successful, solid long-term business partners that can eventually expand into our other centers.

Spotting Potential "Trouble Tenants"

Experienced tenant coordinators know quickly when they have a potential problem tenant on their hands simply by the answers to certain basic questions. Some of these questions can and should be asked in the leasing process, and if they are answered negatively, the tenant should be encouraged to go back and rethink their business plan or sometimes not even allowed to sign the lease, no matter how badly a space needs to be filled.

Here are some key questions to ask independent operators.

DO YOU HAVE A BUSINESS PLAN?

Without a business plan in place, there is no long-term commitment to growth and no financial support in place other than what is coming out of someone's own pocket or life savings and retirement funds. A well-thought-out business plan shows a commitment to the long term, proves business know-how or support and demonstrates the potential for strong management of a successful idea.

> *"When working with independent retailers, suggest they use or provide the services of a professional merchandiser. A local merchandiser can help give a tenant a professional look and improve productivity with visual presentation."*
>
> Nick Galloro
> Director Retail Tenant Coordination Services & Technical Services
> Oxford Properties Group

WHY ARE YOU GOING INTO THIS PARTICULAR BUSINESS?

If it is a new venture, find out why he is going into business for himself. Many entrepreneurs have a romantic dream of being their own boss and buy a franchise or open their doors not really understanding how demanding retail and service industries are. If you like their idea and they have adequate financial support, make sure you provide some kickouts in the lease to protect you in case they can't make it and need to close their doors. Innovative landlords in specialty centers or with hard-to-lease spaces used to do percentage rent deals with this type of tenant. This is less common now, and more of these tenants are put into specialty leasing category programs instead to help incubate them into new businesses. Ask these tenants if they would be averse to using a professional merchandiser to assist them in the setup of their store prior to opening for business.

As baby boomers start to retire, we are starting to see a trend toward opening up small specialty retail stores as a retirement income or hobby. Some of these new storefront businesses are quite viable, backed up by aggressive marketing campaigns easily done through Internet activities.

Be careful of businesses that are lightly disguised knockoffs of other successful ventures. Their potential lawsuit can become your problem if you are not adequately protected in the lease if they cannot pay rent or if you are accused of being a partner.

Watch out for new tenants who have strong, angry personalities. No matter what you do, they are going to be a challenge. Sometimes the best decision is to walk away from a certain tenant profile, no matter how strong their finances and proposed plan are. Tenants with a history of jumping from center to center often do so due to litigation, not paying rent or not being good tenants. Landlords who walk into relationships with tenants like these are taking the risk of tying up space and employee manpower without the benefit of actually being paid full rent.

WHY DO YOU WANT TO OPEN IN MY CENTER?

If this is a second or additional outlet for a tenant, chances are he is already on the road to success. His idea is solid, tried by fire already, and he is expanding. The questions you ask him will be different than what you ask the first-time operator. From this tenant you will want to know

When the department store boutique operator Joseph Abboud decided to create a flagship store, they chose The Shops at Columbus Circle in Manhattan. Creating a store concept that portrayed their branded image, which could be used for future replication in other centers, was a challenge for the tenant's operations team. The results were stunning.

why he is choosing your center. Find out if he really has the resources to expand out of his own operations, and make sure he is not using you or a potential franchisee to leverage his growth plans. Make sure you are protected with lease clauses on approval of who he can sublease his space to.

New ventures who answer that they want your location due to market research, proximity to major transportation systems, or an established customer base are demonstrating that they have already done their due diligence and probably know more about you as a landlord than you realize.

WHO IS YOUR ARCHITECT? GENERAL CONTRACTOR?

If the tenant answers they have a brother-in-law in the business, think twice. This means they plan to "cheap" their way through the construction process. If you are giving them a white box, there is still a certain element of professionalism and design you expect to see. Tell them that as part of the lease, they will be expected to present to you a professionally designed floor plan along with a list of all of their fixtures and suppliers and a professional finish board. By providing this information the tenant will have made their intentions known and understood, with no surprises for either party.

HAVE THEY CHECKED WITH THE LOCAL MUNICIPALITY TO SEE WHAT THE OPENING PROCESS IS?

The tenant who tells you they are just going to "move in" has already demonstrated that they have not talked to the right people. Most municipalities have a mechanism for making new retail tenants pull the proper permits so that they can inspect their spaces for life safety and ADA violations. If a tenant opens without the proper authorization, chances are they will close quickly and you will be left with a damaged reputation, a code violation and no rent.

If the leasing team feels comfortable that they have a potential winner and decide to sign the lease, it then becomes the role of the tenant coordinator to become involved with the tenant and monitor their process. Independent tenants can take a lot of hand-holding through the entire process, and if at any time the tenant coordinator runs into a problem, they should feel comfortable in pulling the leasing team back into the process to keep the tenant in line.

Store Design

If the independent tenant is getting an old store to renovate or a black box, insist that they hire an architect promptly. Give them a list of local architects who will also provide engineering services as part of their fees. Small architectural firms or independent architects who specialize in retail and who are on a friendly walk-in basis with the local building department are often a good choice for entrepreneurs to work with. They can provide the hand-holding experience they need, along with the professional expertise you want to actually get these tenants open.

Since they work locally, know the codes and know the center's rules and regulations, they can be of immense benefit to entrepreneurs quick enough to realize their benefits.

If a tenant is getting a white box, there are still certain permits they are going to need to allow them to open within the municipality, which might require fixture and floor plans. As the landlord, you also want to have the right to see what they are proposing to build out and finish with, particularly if you have tenant design criteria other tenants have to hold to or if there is a level of expectation demanded by the community. Require those tenants to provide you with floor plans, sketches, computer renderings and finish boards along with a list of fixture suppliers. These plans might not require an architect's services, but at the minimum you should try to require a professional store designer's signature on them.

On no account should a restaurant or café owner be allowed to set up shop without also providing you a detailed kitchen plan and list of equipment so that you can make sure they have adequate fire protection and grease and sanitary removal as well as facilities for cleaning. Also ask for a schedule of maintenance.

Construction

Landlords need to be even more demanding regarding getting information on who is handling the tenant's construction when it comes time to start construction.

If a tenant is getting a white box and is simply painting, laying flooring and putting in fixtures, letting them handle it themselves might be sufficient, and only a few site visits might be needed to make sure work is proceeding along in a satisfactory manner.

However, if any type of construction work is required to get a store open, insist on seeing the company profile and qualifications of the tenant's general contractor. In fact, write it into the lease that you have the right to review and reject their choice of contractor.

Many entrepreneurs plan to save opening costs by doing the work themselves or through family members who might be contractors or in the business. These people might have an interest in construction, but unless they are fully licensed and covered with insurance, they usually end up costing both the business owners and the landlord more in lost revenues as well as repair and damages to structures than saving the tenant money.

Experienced tenant coordinators can usually pull out a litany of botched projects and nightmarish structural damages caused by mom-and-pop tenants who try to wing their way through the construction process. If you do allow an independent to do their own work or use a family member, plan on having a presence in the space daily and be prepared to take over the work or put the tenant into default.

Budgets for Independents

There is no magical number an independent tenant should spend to get open, although they will often be quick to ask you how much it is going to cost them. Since they carry no weight in getting multiple stores open, they usually have limited bargaining power in getting good rates from contractors, who might see them as being more of a risk than even you do.

As part of the leasing process, ask to see the construction budget. Many of these tenants have heard stories about how landlords can pay for their buildouts, and they expect it. If you feel that you want to take the risk in doing this, provide a limited build-to-suit instead. That way you know the work is done professionally, and the tenant cannot come back and ask for reimbursement for substandard work.

If you really want to acquire this tenant as part of your merchandising mix, there are some ways that landlords do this that might be of benefit to your development team.

MALLS AND SHOPPING CENTERS

Unique, one-of-a-kind tenants will often get referred to the specialty leasing departments of large developers. These tenants will end up in cart or kiosk programs. Successful ones eventually can find themselves in traditional stores within a relatively quick time. The mall owners and developers actually go into a joint business venture with these entrepreneurs, teaching them how to become successful retailers while benefiting from the unique merchandise they can bring to their center to make the mall look local.

LIFESTYLE AND SPECIALTY CENTERS

These types of developments benefit from unique, one-of-a-kind tenants even more, especially gift stores, boutiques and cafés. The reality is that many of these unique retailers will look for renovated, established downtowns first instead of a unique specialty center unless they feel the benefit the developer can give them in increased exposure is there or the developer is willing to give them more in construction assistance. If you want these types of tenants in your specialty center, consider giving them assistance not only with construction, but also with signage and joint advertising programs.

COMMUNITY AND POWER CENTERS

Community and power centers that are owned by real estate investment trusts or pension funds tend to allocate a budget for upgrading a certain amount of space each year to meet code. If you are managing space for them, consider tapping into spaces that you know need to be upgraded and arrange to put these tenants into them as white box users, providing their own finishes. Since the space needed to be upgraded and is part of the cost of doing business and tenant finishes can be easily removed, this provides a win–win for landlords and tenants you are willing to take a chance with.

NEIGHBORHOOD CENTERS

If you own a community center where you have some old space that needs some updating but is generally up to current code, consider putting your mom-and-pop tenants in there and encourage them to reuse the space and materials already in place. Some creative business owners can do a lot with what we would just tear out.

Assisting "Problem Tenants"

No matter how well you try to protect yourself and your potential tenant against problems, there will be times you have to step in and assist them. With patience and care, problem tenants can be helped through the opening process and eventually open successfully.

Common problems independent tenants run into include losing financing or running out of money, hiring inferior architects and contractors, running afoul of local municipal rules and regulations and not meeting franchise requirements.

FINANCIAL PROBLEMS

Tenant coordinators and operations managers charged with construction oversight will be the first to spot this. If they notice that work stalls or they start getting calls from contractors and subcontractors about not being paid, there is usually a finance problem happening.

Demand a meeting with the tenant and ask what is going on. If your suspicions are confirmed, you can let the construction days clause in your lease continue and then put them into default, initiating eviction, or you can simply ask them to give back the premises. If you decide you want to assist them, then you can get involved in their construction and restructure the financial terms of the lease for more long-term financial return, as part of their rent payment, to cover the cost.

Generally, once a landlord decides to assist financially, he will want to make sure that the tenant's contractors are being paid. Some landlords actually direct their tenant coordinators to take over the construction process. Others choose to make payments directly to subcontractors and contractors, pending verification of completion of work by the tenant coordination team.

DESIGN CONSULTANT PROBLEMS

Occasionally tenants choose consultants who simply cannot or do not get the plans done in a timely or affordable manner. In today's age of CAD drawings, a common sign that a tenant might be about to run into this problem is when the landlord receives hand-drawn plans or floor plans without supporting mechanical, electrical or plumbing plans.

If the plans are not sufficient for a full review in regard to not only design criteria compliance but also to utilization of existing base building tie-ins or reference to landlord systems tie-ins, call the tenant and flag him that you have concerns about his design team's ability to perform. Architects and consultants who refuse to visit new store locations to site-verify existing connections and call tenant coordinators to ask them to "tell them where things are" usually raise a flag also.

Another sign that an architect or consultant might be a problem is if they call the tenant coordinator and start to argue with them about what is being provided as per the lease or through site verification. Occasionally architects and engineers are handicapped by clients who do not give them adequate information to do their job and then find that they have undersold their services and try to get the landlord to assist more. Argumentative consultants who demand more information or insist on being shown spaces on their terms are likely to cause problems throughout the length of the job for tenant coordinators and eventually their clients.

If you flag potential problems with design consultants and the tenant chooses to proceed with them, then a decision will need to be made by the individual tenant coordinator on how willing he or she is prepared to be to assist this consultant, at the cost of slowing down the tenant's work or having a tenant miss a key opening date.

CONTRACTOR PROBLEMS

Construction problems can come through a variety of sources, some related to the quality of the supervision the contractor provides or the financial resources of the firm itself. However, when dealing with small operations or mom-and-pop stores, your problems won't necessarily be due to the quality of the general contractor, but rather to the lack of one altogether.

Independent operators, especially those starting their first business, want to do as much as possible themselves to save money. If you are giving them a white box, this is feasible. If they have work to do that includes electrical or structural, they need a contractor.

Insist on seeing their contractor's qualifications and company profile. Visit the store often. Make sure to meet the superintendent and find out the scope of his work. If the owner has an arrangement where they will do or furnish a certain amount of work themselves, ask the superintendent for a schedule and watch the construction to make sure the tenant is providing the materials and labor the superintendent needs. Also make sure the tenant and contractor do not try to save money by bypassing any landlord-designated subcontractors or required procedures by working when they don't think others will be paying attention.

If, despite your efforts, the tenant starts to run into trouble, try to determine if it is the tenant's fault or if it is due to the contractor. Generally owners are at fault if they do not live up to their end of the agreement by furnishing owner-provided materials, equipment or services in a timely manner or by not paying their bills or signing change orders. Sometimes it is a combination of several factors, usually related to money. Tenant coordinators can start calling the owners to nag them more to make sure they are providing the contractor with the materials to finish their work. If the owner is behind in payment, you might have to step in and make some financial arrangements to assist.

If the contractor is at fault, find out why. If it is due to no or poor supervision, the tenant might have to become more active in being on hand to make sure things are happening. If the contractor is not performing due to ineptness, the tenant coordinator might have to ally with the tenant to force the contractor to perform or assist the tenant in removing the contractor from the job and finding another way to finish the work.

Taking Action Against Problem Tenants

Tenant coordinators are often the first to flag a problem tenant for property management. If a tenant cannot get their plans in on a timely manner, refuses to hire a competent consultant or contractor or is consistently argumentative over issues in the design and the lease, chances are they will continue to be a problem.

If you start coupling these experiences with work stoppages, excessive damages to the building and structure and telephone calls from contractors or subcontractors complaining about nonpayment of work and liens, you definitely have a problem tenant in hand.

More and more leases are allowing for kickouts for landlords as part of the construction process. Make sure your leasing staff is aware of your problems and even gets involved if needed. Keep logs of contacts and problems and make sure the proper notification system as per the lease is met.

If a tenant does not perform or cannot, especially once the days of construction have passed, then start the lease default process. The sooner you get rid of a problem tenant and take your space back, the quicker you can get someone in who will add value to your project.

Often business decisions are made to continue working with tenants who cannot perform, and then the parties eventually end up in the courts. The more entrenched they are, the more it will cost your management team to get rid of them and your leasing team to replace them with a valuable and successful tenant. Over time, tenant coordinators can help their property managers and developers spot these tenants and make decisions that will save the cost of stretched-out litigation.

The Rewards of Working with Independents

Assisting an entrepreneur to develop, open and grow a successful retail business can be very rewarding to a tenant coordinator and property management team. Along the way, the luxury of developing long-term friendships and business partnerships also develops. These tenants bring unique merchandise and services to our homogenized centers as well as strong community flavor.

Independent operators also bring solid business insight and unique perspectives to the management of our centers that national store managers might not have. If a tenant's personal livelihood is at stake, they are going to take more interest in the promotional aspects and community life surrounding your center and be more likely to participate in them, bringing you the benefit of additional marketing and promotional opportunities based on their energy. Property managers can rely upon these tenants for a bird's-eye view of what the pulse of the community is as well as feedback on day-to-day operational issues in their centers and insight on what other tenants are doing. This can be especially helpful to property managers running multiple properties who cannot always visit each one on a regular basis.

In addition, if treated with respect by you as the landlord, these tenants will often bring you other prospective tenants and will also approach you first if they decide to expand.

Although the cost in manpower and time can be higher to help get them open, the long-term rewards can be beneficial to landlords who take the risk of seeking and encouraging independent operators.

10

Effective Landlord and Tenant Communication: The Lease Is Signed; Let's Get the Tenant Open for Business

Perhaps it is the nature of the business, but it seems that the landlord–tenant relationship always seems adversarial. While much of this can be blamed on unequal expectations or a different interpretation of the lease, most simply comes down to poor communication and a lack of respect for the other's role in the store opening process. Frankly, most retail tenant construction teams simply do not understand the tenant coordinator's role in the store opening process due to a lack of consistent training of tenant coordinators within the retail business. Tenant construction teams will often take the offensive and try to establish the ground rules from the front because they feel they have been negatively impacted by landlords who have not lived up to their obligations in the past.

Tenant coordinators who understand this and work to establish open, honest communication with their tenants while still maintaining the difficult balance of protecting their owners' interests will have more success in assisting their tenants to open than others who assume purely adversarial roles from the start.

Timely Introductions

Let's face it: We usually do not speak the same language as our tenants. We do not even interpret the leases the same way. The merchandising rollout dates, fixture locations and signage programs that are important to our tenants just cause us aggravation when they want to stick signs in windows, which is prohibited by community standards, or create blackouts for opening that run contrary to our goal of opening a new wing in time for the holiday season.

The storefront tie-ins that we insist on for ease of mall maintenance or the use of designated contractors to protect our system and roof warranties or our insistence on certain signage programs cause them just as much aggravation as they try to drop a store that represents their branded image into one of our spaces.

Once a lease is signed, tenant coordinators who pick up the phone and call their retail counterparts and say "let's talk" are often met with stunned silence. On the other hand, tenant construction managers who show up on-site and walk through long lead times for items required as part of landlord-required work are also met to surprise.

Tenant coordinators who request introductions to the tenant construction team from the start will have much more success than those who send out letters and simply sit back and wait for information to come in.

Opening the Dialogue

How to open the dialogue? Pick up the phone and call. Introduce yourself and tell the tenant contact that you have a copy of the lease in front of you and want to ask them some questions. Tell them that you want to make sure that you understand what they are looking for, and in return, you want to share what you will be doing with them to assist them and what your role is on the development team.

> "Break the ice. Send the tenants a welcome package and then do the unthinkable: Pick up the phone and make contact. After that, e-mail can rule."
>
> GREGORY R. GUNTER
> Vice President
> 3rd Works

Exchange contact information and backgrounds. Occasionally you will find that you know people in common or have worked on other projects before, and a common ground can be established. The types of questions asked and the information shared will depend upon the type of project you both will be involved in as well as the sophistication level of the construction manager. A construction manager handling a big box that opens 15 stores a year will be a lot more to the point and concise in telling you what they expect than an independent store operator with multiple locations who relies on his design team to project-manage his stores through the design and construction process.

Some of the information pertinent to the tenant coordinator from the tenant will include such questions as:

- Who is your architect or designer?
- Have I received everything related to your prototypical plans so I can start my own plans?
- What are your expectations of me and my team?
- How do you interpret turnover in the lease?

Information that the tenant might want from the tenant coordinator can include:

- What do you look for in design review?
- How long do you take?
- How often are you on-site?
- Do you have any feedback on what the community will look for in plan review and permitting and how long will it take?
- Do you have any pictures or renderings you can send me so I can see how to fit my prototype into your overall mall setting?

Talking Each Other's Language

The biggest criticism most tenant coordinators get from store people is that tenant coordinators do not speak "retailese." While this criticism is unfair in the sense that the demands of tenant coordination working for a shopping center or mall developer require a different skill set, it is one that needs to be treated with respect and considered. Tenant coordinators who take the time to learn the language and demands of the retail business will be more sympathetic to their tenants' needs and requirements and can even assist their small operators in becoming better retailers. In addition, they will better understand the demands of the retail operation and design teams and can help their developers make more retail-friendly decisions not only in the design of the centers, but in their opening and operations, too.

Tenant coordinators can take advantage of retail design and construction seminars and expos to learn more about the retail side of the business. Retail events such as the CenterBuild Retail Design and Construction Conference and Retail Construction Expo, not only provide trade show opportunities to learn the latest about store designs, but also a chance to network with the retailers and to learn more about their business. The International Council of Shopping Centers also provides opportunities for members to learn more about the retail industry through trade magazines and publications. The Marketing and Management I and II series also teach special classes in retailing, and a portion of the ICSC certified marketing and management exams focuses on retail terminology. Study guides for these exams can be made available to tenant coordinators who wish to learn more.

Subscriptions to retail trade magazines can also help tenant coordinators learn more about our retail counterpart's methodology and needs.

When to Step In and When to Stay Out

One of the benefits of understanding retail requirements and needs is that it gives tenant coordinators a better feel for when problems are occurring or will occur. It also gives you a better means of determining if and when you should step in during the store design and construction process and give more input or make an additional demand.

Tenant coordinators who do not understand branded images and merchandising will be more insistent on adhering to mall criteria that might not be retail-friendly for their tenants. This inevitably leads to conflict. A knowledgeable coordinator will understand when a demand is unrealistic and will work with the tenant to come up with a win-win compromise.

Tenant coordinators who insist on speaking in legalese instead of retailese also run the risk of creating adversarial relationships that result in litigation. Smart communicators pick their battles wisely and tactfully. By understanding what words trigger misunderstanding, tenant coordinators can help their development team more successfully negotiate through the dangers of construction delays and broken lease promises.

Negotiating

Successful tenant coordinators know how to negotiate. They know when to push for a point or a "look" and when to step back and accept less. As all good negotiators know, you have to let the other person feel like they have won something. If you truly understand retail and its needs, it is easier to determine what your tenant needs to truly feel like they have won something.

Generally, retail tenants who have a lot invested in their branded image will look to preserve that as much as possible. Other tenants who are operationally heavy will look for concessions that allow their management teams to come in and function with the least amount of involvement or restrictions with the developer's team. Retail tenants who are listed on the stock exchange might be more interested in getting a certain volume of stores open than merchandise sales or image requirements. They will be more interested in what you can do to help them get open within their allotted time period.

> *"Remember horse-trading? That's what a good tenant coordinator does."*
>
> GREGORY R. GUNTER
> Vice President
> 3rd Works

Resolving Conflict

Every tenant relationship is going to have conflict of some sort. That is the nature of the business. Whether it is interpretation of the lease, a contractor not meeting a schedule, a landlord dealing with a natural disaster or a municipality withholding a critical inspection based on landlord work, there will be conflict. Tenant coordinators who realize that and work to not only assist the tenant through the issues, but also to manage their own development and construction teams' reactions, will eventually end up with a store opening.

Here are a few tips for resolving conflict.

KNOW YOUR LEASE

Tenant coordinators need to know the lease and have it available for reference. However, they also need to be careful to not appear to be legalistic. When problems occur and the lease needs to be consulted, research the lease in advance as much as possible. Allow the tenant to tell you what they are looking at in the lease also. By allowing them to do this, you are acknowledging their rights and often will see a way to negotiate through an issue instead of antagonizing them more.

Make sure you really understand what an issue is before you start blasting a tenant or quoting a lease. Often what you think is the issue will not be once you start to talk.

KNOW YOUR TENANT

The retail industry is a small industry and our reputations often precede us. When you start to talk with a tenant, learn about their store, method of operations and the people you are dealing with. Find out if the store is retail- or real estate– or stock market–driven. Find out what their hottest retail seasons are and what type of projects they like to open in. The more you know about them, the more you can configure your arguments for your point of view to a standard they will understand.

RETURN PHONE CALLS AND E-MAILS PROMPTLY

We all get busy, particularly tenant coordinators who are opening a large number of stores at one time and are under tight time restraints. On the other hand, our store counterparts are also busy. Many of them are handling store openings and renovations over extended territories and are constantly on the road dealing with contractors and operations teams. Try to return their phone calls and e-mails quickly. Let them know if there is a better time for them to reach you and set up phone appointments if needed.

When you do get ahold of them, don't waste their time unless you sense they are relaxed and want to talk. Be quick and concise while demonstrating that you are willing to listen. Follow up all conversations with notes, action or e-mails and keep a log of them.

BE HONEST AND FAIR

Tenant coordinators walk a fine line trying to protect their owner's interests while still assisting the tenants to get open in a quick, timely or efficient manner. The more honest and fair you are, the better the trust and the more likely you and your tenant counterpart are to work through problems and conflict.

Tenant coordinators will deal with the same design and construction teams again, and the tenants will remember those who played fair and square the next time they work together on another project.

KEEP EXCELLENT WRITTEN RECORDS

Tenant coordination requires extensive use of tracking reports and communications within the development team. These reports can flag the development team when potential problems are occurring in the design and construction process. These reports can become backup support at a later date if for some reason litigation results.

Tenant coordinators who also invest in newsletters or group e-mails keeping tenants and their design and construction teams informed of issues on-site provide an invaluable service that can help expedite a store opening and control costs as well as delivery expectations. The more challenging the on-site coordination issues, the more invaluable this can become. It also becomes a support or backup to the development team if a retailer states no one told him about something and you have proof of constant and regular communication even if it is through group dispersal.

When finished with a conversation with a tenant on something relating to or changing a lease point, make sure it is recorded in writing so that if it comes up again down the road, the property management team can see what happened and what was agreed upon. This is particularly helpful if there is money or a delivery date involved.

Tenant coordinators should also photograph and record issues and conflicts in the field and share these with the tenants. If there is damage or a constructability issue, a tenant coordinator should contact the tenant involved by phone or e-mail and let them know there is a concern. A follow-up letter or memo relating the incident or concern, supported with photographs, will help immensely in making sure the damage was repaired or paid for long after the store is open and the financial accounting and closeout have begun.

Finally, it should go without saying that certain documents in and of themselves are milestones to the landlord-tenant relationship. Delivery notices, estoppel agreements, letters of chargeback and tenant allowance requests and settlements should all be in written form and filed carefully for ease of reference.

KNOW WHEN TO BRING IN THE BIG GUNS

Sometimes, no matter what you do to try to work out a problem, you can't. That is when it is time to willingly concede and bring in the big guns. Occasionally tenant coordinators find themselves in the uncomfortable position of having to throw themselves under the wheels of a cart and ask a tenant to put them on notice for nonperformance in order to get their own development team to pay attention. While this is a regrettable tactic and often ends up causing the coordinator more grief, it might be the only tool available to save the developer from himself.

If a tenant is not performing and delivering plans or living up to the criteria of the lease, the first person to alert should be the leasing agent who brought the tenant to the table. Savvy leasing agents know that it is easier to rent a happy tenant multiple spaces over the long term than to be doing a series of one-of-a-kind leases perpetually. They treasure their hard-won relationships with the tenant leasing and real estate departments and like to be told when problems are developing so that they can assist or are at least aware if they hear directly from the tenant.

Often it is not leasing that needs to be brought in to assist a tenant, but property management. If a tenant needs a concession for extra hours of construction or to bring in some equipment through a mall opening during mall operational hours, tenant coordination will need to intercede for the tenant with property management. If the mall operations team is not cooperative, then the tenant coordinator might need to go above them to request assistance.

By learning about your tenant's needs and what drives them, when it comes time to negotiate a compromise, you will be more likely to find their hot button on what they are looking for and can find a compromise that will help you both realize your mutual goal, which is to open the store as soon as possible.

11 Field Coordination— How to Assist and When to Enforce

Tenant coordinators serve to fill two functions in the field. The first is to protect the landlord's interests by making sure tenant contractors are abiding by the center's construction rules and regulations and to protect mall systems and finishes. The second is to assist the tenants and their contractors by troubleshooting and helping them solve problems.

Occasionally these two roles conflict, and tenant coordinators have to work out solutions that keep construction moving while still protecting the landlord.

Tenant coordinators need to keep in mind a key point about their role in the design and construction process: the quicker they can get a tenant open, the quicker the tenant and the developer are making money. Sometimes it is difficult to balance the demands of when to help a tenant by letting their contractor bend rules versus when to stop them and risk an impact to a critical opening date.

The following guidelines can help you make a decision:

- If a decision impacts a critical landlord system, building structure or member or life safety, stop them.
- If a decision impacts another tenant, slow them down and coordinate on their behalf.
- If a decision impacts a mall finish that cannot be repaired easily, stop them; if it can be repaired easily and you have the means to charge them if they do not, keep them going.

- If a decision results in nonadherence to critical mall design criteria such as storefront connection to neutral piers or tie-in to a bulkhead, stop them.
- If a decision results in a noncritical change to mall criteria that enables the store to maintain its branded identity, keep them going.
- If a decision results in a cost to the store owner, stop them until they have approval unless you are willing to eat the cost yourself or have adequate financial protection through wording in design criteria or lease; let the tenant know immediately in writing.
- If a decision is the result of an impact from ongoing landlord work or noncompletion of landlord work, step in to assist them immediately.

Working with Tenant Contractors

Tenant contractors are sent in by the tenant to perform the function of building out their store at the least cost and in the quickest time possible. Experienced tenant coordinators can spot qualified retail contractors from the start by the questions they are asked during the construction bid period. Contractors who ask for the mall rules, associated fees and deposits and the designated contractors list and if the mall is closed or open shop (unionized labor) generally know what they are doing.

Occasionally tenant coordinators run into tenant contractors who assume that the coordinators are there for their convenience and try to use the tenant coordinator as a runner to show space or assist with permitting issues. While many tenant coordinators will try to help because they want to get the store open as quickly as possible, this usually pinpoints a contractor who is going to be labor-intensive and require a lot of hand-holding.

Tenant coordinators will also run into contractors who want to argue with them about rules and regulations, system testing or use of designated contractors. This should be a red flag, as it often indicates they are inexperienced contractors who have bid the job too low before doing all of their homework and instead of going back to the tenant, want to bully the landlord into assisting them out of their money crunch.

Tenant coordinators should express their concerns to the tenants as quickly as possible and make sure they document their interactions with the tenant and their contractors immediately when these sorts of red flags go up. If there is concern about a potential contractor due to their business reputation, the tenant should also be notified as soon as possible. Landlords are writing into their leases more clauses to protect themselves against these types of contractors by using clauses that refer to labor harmony, approval of contractor and use of landlord-approved subcontractors.

Over time, tenant coordinators will start to build relationships with contractors whom they see on multiple jobs. These contractors also share information about the tenant coordinators with other contractors. Tenant coordinators who are fair and honest and try to solve problems in a positive manner will be rewarded by mutual respect from some of the best contractors and seasoned superintendents in the retail field. Tenant coordinators who accept bribes, business trips, payoffs and gifts subject themselves to loss of credibility when protecting the interests of their employer.

When a tenant contractor checks in on-site, the first meeting he should have is with the tenant coordinator, or with the field supervisor from the operations team if the coordinator is not on-site full-time. During this meeting, the superintendent and field coordinator should walk the store, find the landlord rooms the tenant needs access to, walk the mall to find the construction entrances and review the mall rules and regulations. If there is a critical system to tie into that testing has to be done on or that a mall-designated contractor is involved with, that is also a good time to discuss what needs to occur. It is a good idea to have the superintendent and landlord field representative read through the construction rules and regulations together and have the contractor sign a piece of paper that he has read them and understands what they entail. Often the construction firm's project manager or estimator will come in and will want to do this in advance because they have not picked their superintendent yet and want to get started. Since they will not be the ones actually performing the work in the field, insist on the superintendent being there.

As part of the space walkthrough, it is also a good idea to have a space acceptance and sign-off form handy. Review the utility point of connections to make sure they are in place, look at the space for any damage on landlord-provided items that might need to be corrected or completed and double-check the condition of existing doors, surrounding mall finishes, tile and landscaping. The benefit to assessing and logging the condition of things likely to be damaged, and mutually agreeing upon the condition they are in, is that a lot of conflict and finger-pointing will be avoided later on in the job.

Field Supervision

The on-site landlord's representative or tenant coordinator needs to stay in contact with the contractor on a regular basis after the check-in. Periodically walk the store to make sure the construction rules are being abided by and to see if the superintendent has any questions or problems. Also ask them for a look ahead on their schedule and see if they need help with getting your designated contractor into place or if they are being supported by the owner of the store or their project managers by getting the materials and services they need in a timely manner.

Tenant coordinators who are watching the tenant's work and see that owner-supplied items from the tenant are not being supplied or provided in a timely manner need to get involved to make sure the owner is paying attention to the job or to make sure that they have not run into cash flow problems.

Often there will be conflict between retail contractor project managers and tenant coordinators because the tenant coordinators will go over and around them to get the job done. While tenant coordinators often feel justified in doing this because the job was not finished quickly enough or because the superintendent is not getting support from his firm, there still needs to be a respect for the contractor's means and methods of construction. Tenant coordinators who come in and start to take an active construction role can be perceived as running the job and thus sharing liability if a problem occurs. Sometimes it is better to take a less active role to push a job to completion and just make sure the paper trail is strong, with open communications directly to the tenant, who should be the one pushing their own contractor.

Troubleshooting

Tenant coordinators or operations managers charged with overseeing tenant construction tend to look for certain key items that impact either the tenant's work or the landlord and their building, finishes, shared systems or other tenants.

Some of these issues include life safety, protecting sensitive and critical building systems, protecting mall finishes, protecting structural integrity, sealed penetrations, looking out for operating tenants' interests, coordinating entering other tenants' spaces, assisting mall operations, meeting developer agreements, upholding lease standards and watching for dangerous practices.

LIFE SAFETY

We tend to think of this as part of the fire marshal's responsibility. However, while a store is under construction, it is the contractor's responsibility to protect the public as well as their own subcontractors and personnel. Alert landlords want to feel comfortable that the contractors are doing that.

Urban centers present unique staging and coordination issues for landlord construction teams. Staging can be extremely challenging not only for construction issues, but also for the protection of extremely expensive and unique finishes of both the landlord and the tenants.

Tenant coordinators need to make sure that barricades are installed; tenant contractors understand that they are expected to adhere to proper OSHA standards and that chemical storage, welding and flammables are properly stored, conducted or handled. As the landlord, we are not directly contracted to the contractor and cannot dictate their means and methods. However, we can insist that they be responsible for making safety a priority while on our site.

If we see a possible violation we should immediately contact the superintendent and insist the problem be corrected immediately. If they persist in letting the problem continue, we need to document it and make sure the tenant knows they have what we see as a potential problem. If the possible violation could result in loss of life or damage to a mall structure or system, then we have the right and responsibility to close the work down until they correct.

PROTECTING SENSITIVE MALL SYSTEMS AND FINISHES

Anytime a tenant has to hook into a system that affects multiple tenants, there is going to be inconvenience and risk of damage.

Whether it is hooking into a fire

Staging shot, The Shops at Columbus Circle while under construction.

alarm system or shutting down a sprinkler riser, tapping into a chilled water or steam system or landing wire into a distribution panel or shutting down a transformer, it is going to impact someone else, somehow. Tenant coordinators and mall construction and operations teams who are sensitive to this and take the time to communicate with other tenants that might be impacted will have a lot more success in getting future work done.

Staging issues are not unique to urban centers. This lifestyle center under construction has two general contractors working on two separate buildings.

In addition, if a mall-designated contractor is not doing the work, then make sure you are on-site to witness that the work was done properly or insist on a certified inspection or testing report. You also might be needed in case of an emergency that might entail a longer shutdown than intended, which impacts other tenants.

PROTECTING BUILDING FINISHES AND ACCESS AREAS

Often tenant coordinators, especially field representatives, are called into traffic cop and enforcement roles. Sometimes it is funny; other times it can be potentially deadly or dangerous.

Common mishaps depend upon the center. In enclosed centers, tenant coordinators and operations teams watch out for damage to mall neutral piers, planters and landscaping, mall flooring, roof damage, improper connections and testing for tie-ins to critical mall systems such as fire alarm and chilled water and shoppers tripping over debris or improperly run electrical cords.

In open-air or community centers, tenant coordinators and property managers would look for damage to storefront systems and back doors and frames, damage to irrigation heads and landscaping, damage to sidewalks, curbs and asphalt, roof damage, improper penetrations to exterior facades for signage, damage to EIFES systems, debris being hauled out of stores while customers are close by and trip-and-fall hazards from improperly run electrical cords and hoses.

Even landlords working with outparcels need to keep a keen eye on the tenant contractor. Damage there can be to asphalt roads, sidewalks and curbs, irrigation systems and landscaping, paint overspray, uncoordinated shutdowns to transformers on a loop causing other stores and

Tenant coordinators all have war stories from their own experiences from mishaps in the field. Some experiences from the author include:

- Painter spilling black paint onto a finished marble floor from three stories up
- Welder having a temper tantrum because he was stopped from using a main electrical distribution room in a mall food court as a spot to do his welding
- Standing on the roof of a freestanding building with a contractor and watching news team helicopters cover a fire caused by his welder not doing a proper fire watch
- Wiping up hydraulic oil spills with the chemical equivalent of kitty litter on new asphalt just prior to a grand opening of a multiscreen movie so we could get traffic through
- Telling a tenant to remove his low-voltage subcontractor because they were not in labor harmony with the local unions and the electrical distribution center to an entire wing had been shut down.

businesses to go dark during operating hours, and people illegally entering construction sites that have not been properly barricaded and signed.

PROTECTING STRUCTURAL INTEGRITY
We hire engineers and architects to design buildings that are to withstand certain loads and pressures. To maintain that integrity we often have to make sure that tenants and their contractors understand that the impacts they are going to make will have a cost, including additional engineering. When in doubt, bring in the experts. This is one liability no construction team member or tenant coordinator should want to knowingly take on.

SEALED PENETRATIONS
It does not take a lot of water to ruin a beautiful finish on a floor below or destroy the electrical systems for an entire wing.

It does not take a lot of caulk to ensure that a fire stop is properly sealed.

It does take time and vigilance to make sure that the work is done properly. Often tenant coordinators do not have that ability. By putting procedures and extra eyes in the field to assist, construction and management teams can enforce policies that avoid future tenant maintenance and operation problems by having the right waterproofing and sealing done during the construction process.

LOOKING OUT FOR OPERATING TENANTS' INTERESTS

Most malls and centers have policies that contain loud and excessive noise to certain hours of the day so as not to impact other tenants and customers. They should also have policies that make sure that tenant contractors protect mall finishes, contain their work behind barricades, haul debris and bring in supplies after hours and sweep daily for dust control. This work becomes even more critical when a center is under renovation with existing businesses being kept operational. Extra steps to protect those tenants and their customers through the use of barricades, temporary access roads or tunnels with additional signage and lighting, and dust guards and barricades might be required. A strong communications program with other tenants while undergoing major renovation and construction programs can help alleviate some of the stress to all parties involved, including operations, store management and construction. That role of communications support can fall upon the tenant coordinator.

COORDINATING ENTERING OTHER TENANT SPACES

Occasionally tenants need to get through or into another tenant's space in order to complete their own work. Extensive coordination might be needed, and the tenant coordinator needs to be right in the middle of it. Mixed-use properties or tenants stacked on top of each other especially have these problems. However, malls, with limited system connections, also run into this. This can be one of the most critical things a tenant coordinator has to do and usually involves conflict of some kind eventually.

Depending upon the complexity of the work, try to put all parties together to review the extensiveness of the work and discuss when it can be done and the contractor's means and methods of doing it. If a landlord does not have a "right of access" clause in his lease, there is a strong possibility he will not be able to get the work done if it results in too much delay or trouble to another tenant. Make sure that any new conduit or ductwork being brought through the space does not impact the other tenant's public areas or critical mechanical areas if possible. For instance, don't route electrical conduit with feed for a large tenant without knowing if a future overrun pit for an elevator is going to be placed right over where the conduit is. If the space impacted is not built or a design approved, then try to get a set of as-builds for the file so that when a new tenant comes in he will know what critical items he has running through his space that would not show up on your building construction drawings.

If the work is minor and two contractors are working side by side, often the best thing to do is to introduce them to each other and suggest they settle it between themselves. Tenant contractors who work multiple projects run into this all the time, and the superintendents can often make these problems go away easily between themselves.

ASSISTING MALL OPERATIONS

When a center is operational, it makes good sense for on-site tenant coordinators still involved with opening other tenants to become friends with the operations team. Mutual respect for each other and stepping in to troubleshoot when a problem occurs that might be related to a tenant either under construction or recently open can assist the operations people, who might be backed up trying to get the center open or coping with large demands of dust and traffic control during an ongoing renovation. Eventually, after the bulk of the tenant coordinator's work is done and they are only doing a few tenant spaces in a center, that relationship built earlier will help the coordinator, as the operations team will become their eyes and ears for ongoing work.

Tenant coordinators who treat the property management team as their clients and who think ahead to what the operational methods and problems will be when they hand over a store to them are invaluable members of the developer's management team.

MEETING DEVELOPMENT AGREEMENTS

Often deals and arrangements are made with the municipalities that impact tenant coordination and tenant work. These arrangements are not always passed on to the tenant coordination team in a timely manner and can cause hardship for our tenants. When we do know about these agreements, we should be conveying them in both written and verbal manner to the tenant design and construction teams as well as the contractors. These arrangements tend to be more common when public money is involved, such as partnerships or redevelopment programs. If you are going to be involved in one of them, ask up front for the developer's and planning agreements.

These programs also tend to get a lot of public and media scrutiny, so be careful to make sure that you are always on guard to enforce or complete them. Some of the related issues that tenant coordinators typically run into include:

- No parking or delivery regulations
- After-hours work limitations and noise control
- No banners and limited signage opportunities
- Certifications and agreements on site work before centers or access roads can open or light signals are turned on
- Restricted storefront or parking lot light levels
- Enforced heavy landscaping in areas in front of tenant storefronts and signs
- No on-site trailer storage or hiring facilities

Often these regulations will run afoul of promises made in the lease. Try to insist that Tenant Coordination has an opportunity to review a lease looking for these items as well as construction exhibits.

UPHOLDING LEASE STANDARDS

This can go both ways. Sometimes we are forced to make sure tenants meet the letter of the lease. Sometimes we are forced to make sure our own construction and management team meets the letter of the lease. Regardless, tenant coordinators are often put into tenuous positions because of their duty to both landlord and tenants.

If a tenant prototype says to use a specific type of assembly or product, there is usually a good reason and we need to make sure our architect and contractor follow the specification. If the lease says no banners, then there is usually a good reason and we need to make sure our tenant abides by it.

Insisting all parties live up to their part of the lease bargain can be a challenge, and if the tenant coordinator does not have the support of his development team, conflict and lawsuits will result.

WATCHING FOR DANGEROUS PRACTICES

The role of an on-site tenant coordinator can often be compared to that of a policeman. If we see a person working on a scaffold without being tied off, we need to report it. If someone insists on welding without adequate protection, we need to stop it. If a tenant wants to hook into a live distribution center without a licensed electrician responsible, we need to deny them. That is the type of work we are hired to do. Often, tenant coordination is just common sense being put into practice.

When Things Go Wrong

The first clue a tenant coordinator will have about the quality of a contractor is if they call and ask for a copy of the construction handbook and developer fees. Experienced retail contractors know to do this.

Sometimes problems happen where least expected . . .

Years ago a large national tenant had their own in-house construction firm that was apparently involved in a long-term feud with store operations. The tenant dissolved the department, leaving a lot of subcontractors without direction or payment.

They proceeded to make claims against the property for non-payment even though the tenant was open and viable. Fortunately, the landlord had insisted the tenant follow lien law procedures and was able to protect themselves from lawsuits.

The second clue is the type of questions they ask and the tone of their voice. If they ask if they have to use unionized labor, it could mean they are an experienced contractor running down a list of questions or it could also mean that they have not signed union agreements and are trying to figure out how to do the work without them. Listening carefully to the questions and to the tone of voice will help tenant coordinators offset some future tenant–contractor problems.

Tenant coordinators can also stave off problems by insisting that they receive a copy of the contractor's insurance and licensing in advance. If the tenant or the contractor cannot provide this, or if they "borrow" someone else's license, there is a possibility the contractor is not qualified. Be aware, though, that retail contractors who work multiple spaces for large chains often have relationships with other locally based contractors, and it might be the local general contractor's license and occupational license you eventually receive. If you run into a problem, as far as you are concerned, your contact is still the owner and the contractor who has the contract with the owner, no matter who holds the license on the permit.

States that have lien laws require a certain amount of protections for contractors to ensure that they get paid by their clients. These same protections can ultimately protect the landlord also by alerting him if a tenant is not paying their contractor or trades or if they are paying them and the contractor himself is withholding payment. Landlords need to pay attention if they start getting a lot of calls from subcontractors not being paid. Chances are they have a problem with either the tenant or the contractor, or both.

Landlords use designated contractors to protect both delicate building systems and warranties and to minimize construction damage impact on other tenants and management. If a landlord knowingly allows a tenant contractor to bring in and use someone else and there is damage to a building system, the landlord can risk losing his warranty protection from his base building general contractor. If a tenant insists on doing this and a landlord allows it, then a letter should be sent out stating that the landlord has agreed to it, but the tenant will be responsible for all warranty-related issues from that point on.

Good, experienced retail contractors do not usually take this risk. Contractors who do have either not done full due diligence and are trying to save money or have sold their work and signed a contract on a lump-sum basis and are trying to negotiate lower prices with other subcontractors to put more money back into their own pocket as profit. Once the tenant realizes what is happening and the risk he is taking, he will usually come back and make the contractor use the proper personnel unless someone's ego has become involved.

Tenant coordinators can also spot potential problems by insisting that they get copies of construction schedules in advance. It is best to insist you get this from the owner, but usually it is the contractor themselves who produce it. If the best you can get is handwritten or drawn, take it. It is usually a sign of a small operation, but does not mean that they will not perform admirably. However, having a guide to what the contractor and tenant expectations are will help you in flagging potential problems when you go on-site to visit jobs and you will need to alert them, especially if the work is for out-of-town tenants or tenants with construction managers who are extended over multiple projects and cannot visit regularly to spot problems.

When problems are spotted, such as improper construction procedures, poorly executed taps into existing utility connections, work slowdowns or labor problems, call the tenant construction contact first. The contract is between them and the contractor, not you. It is the tenant's responsibility to make sure the contractor is working in a safe, appropriate manner, and they need to direct the contractor.

If a contractor is doing something dangerous and you have to issue a stop work immediately to protect lives or structure, stop the superintendent and call the tenant next and inform them of what is happening. The last thing tenant coordinators usually want to do is stop work, since our goal is to get tenants open quickly and efficiently. However, if there is any threat to life or structure and systems, it is our responsibility to protect the landlord and public and the tenant's needs become secondary. Back up the incident in writing, either as a fax or e-mail to the tenant or as a note to file. Most professional contractors who work in multiple centers will respond immediately, many with a call directly to you after their client has called them.

If the behavior continues, issue a second warning and then a third, in writing. Once a third has been issued, a business decision to require

> ### *A heads-up to landlords doing big box work . . .*
>
> Contractors who are hired by the landlords themselves to do big box work on a build-to-suit basis have a different set of closeout criteria they need to adhere to. Usually performance of this related work and production of backup written materials is tied to rent commencement. General contractors who do not build this into their own internal closeout procedures with their subcontractors are impacting their client's ability to get rent paid. While this forces developers to pay them quicker, it also puts the developer into a nonconformance to lease position with the tenant, since it typically takes several months to close out a project. Items that will impact rent payment and closeout include punchout work, warranty books as built drawings and training of operations teams in critical operational issues.

removal of the contractor from the job might need to be made, which could cost the tenant and the landlord revenue and rent.

If a contractor does something to damage a facility, another tenant's property or the work and possessions of another contractor or member of the public, make sure it is documented with photographs and in writing and distributed accordingly. If a claim needs to be made against insurance, start the process immediately instead of waiting until completion of the job. It is much easier to get things resolved while the contractor is still on the project instead of waiting until after they have left.

Closing Out the Job

When a contractor indicates they are ready and wish to leave the job, tenant coordination needs to gather information and paperwork for the files and conduct a final walkthrough with the tenant contractor.

Closeout packages should include a copy of the certificate of occupancy, copies of test reports and certifications, letters of payment or satisfaction from mall-designated contractors, a final list of subcontractors and contact numbers and an "as-built" set of plans. More landlords are requiring the as-builds in CAD format due to storage limitations. The Time Warner building in Manhattan uses CAD as-builds as part of their "look see" program into tenant operations for use of chilled water and steam delivery.

Release of tenant allowances and inducements are a "big stick" that landlords have to occasionally use with their tenants to get the closeout paperwork. Tenant coordinators need to avoid getting into screaming matches with aggressive tenants who demand their allowances without paperwork being completed. Make sure a letter goes out in advance telling the tenant what the closeout or allowance procedure is and then give them periodic updates of what is outstanding. By doing this the tenant will become more motivated to assist in making sure you are getting what you need in a timely manner.

The final walkthrough should occur before the tenant opens, if possible. Some landlords insist that the tenant construction manager or store manager participate. Critical things to assess include labeling of required access panels for the landlord base building systems, storefront completion and approval of quality of work within the neutral piers and landlord tile, repair of landlord finishes, landscaping or asphalt that the tenant has agreed to do themselves, cleanliness of all staging areas, hallways and truck courts and adequate completion of all areas within any landlord control zone.

Once all work is satisfactorily completed, the tenant contractor's deposit should be released. Unfortunately, some landlords have gained a reputation for using this money as a means of additional income, and tenants are becoming leery of signing leases with this clause, as the contractors add it to the cost of building out the stores. Without the ability to collect from this, sincere landlords are forced to become more restrictive on what tenant contractors can do, which results in slower openings overall.

Tenant contractor and landlord relationships can often end up being mutually rewarding. Landlords who treat their tenants' contractors with respect and work with them to complete store openings in a cooperative manner will be rewarded with quicker rent commencement.

12 Dealing with Local Government: Using Local Know-How to Assist Your Tenants to Open Quicker

One of the most effective ways a tenant coordinator can help their tenants in opening more quickly is by effectively smoothing out the permitting and opening process for them. Tenant coordinators who take the time to get to know the local authorities of the centers they are handling and who understand the process and systems of approval and inspection can save considerable time and frustration for their tenant's design and construction teams and ultimately create value for the developer by getting stores open earlier and rent commenced.

Developers who take it a step further by negotiating a special permitting and inspection program in advance and by creating and maintaining a friendly and professional business relationship with the local municipality's staff can create a win-win environment. These relationships have to be built on long-term trust and word of honor, and developers who allow team members to try to bully their way through the process or to break their word on promises made will lose time and money when trying to open.

Understanding Local Codes, Building Permitting, Municipal Staffing and Timing Issues and Response

Each municipality overseeing the jurisdiction of public safety and building construction has its own unique system of taking in requests for construction and reviewing, permitting and inspecting work. Typi-

How do municipalities control growth?

One way municipalities do it is by not staffing up their planning and permitting departments. The community might appear to welcome you with open arms, but if you walk into a tedious bureaucracy of paperwork and an entanglement of "that's not my department" attitudes, you might have walked into a "no growth, slow growth" attitude.

If the "no growth" attitude is simply due to not enough assets, some simple assistance might be appreciated. This can include ideas such as:

- Offer to assist through providing on-site facilities or upgrade their operations equipment
- Hire special inspections teams
- Hire licensed architects to pre-review plans for local standards before submittal
- Create permit application packages
- Recommend local expediters and runners who are friendly with the municipality
- Control inspections during openings by funneling them through one coordinator

If the "no growth" attitude is political, more heavy artillery might be needed. How to combat it?

- Enlist the help of pro-growth politicians
- Create a good community public relations and/or communications plan
- Advertise in the local small independent newspapers to create excitement that you are coming soon
- Put staff members onto local community boards in volunteer positions
- Hire politically connected planning firms and professional expediters on the upper administrative level

cally a development team will be dealing with several governmental entities on one project, including:

- Building department
- Life safety and fire
- Engineering department
- Water authority

- Board of health
- Planning and land development
- Commissioners and town councils
- Downtown development or community redevelopment agencies
- Environmental engineering
- Land management, state or federal

Some of these authorities might be small departments consisting of only a few people, while others have huge regional overview and in-depth governmental oversight and review. Taking the time to truly understand which entities you are working with and what their requirements are can be an immense challenge. This has led to today's proliferation of engineering and planning firms that concentrate specifically on permitting issues from other governing authorities aside from the actual municipal building department.

Usually by the time a tenant coordinator comes on board, most of the groundwork for the site work established through the efforts of the civil engineers has been completed and the main issues tenants will need to be dealing with are primarily building. However, tenant coordinators operating with lease agreements in stand alone out parcels and free-standing buildings within huge approved and engineered planned developments will still need to know what additional approvals will be needed aside from building.

One of the first things a tenant coordinator coming on board should do is get to learn the local players within the municipality. Depending on the amount of time the tenant coordinator has and their role in the project, they can start to figure out the "who is who" through some simple preliminary legwork. A major thing to realize is that just because a

---

What is the biggest challenge for developers?
Understanding the bureaucratic mentality.

By nature, developers and their teams are entrepreneurs. Their "let's do it" attitude is diametrically opposed to the bureaucratic systems of most governmental regulatory agencies.

The best way to get a project permitted and run?

Create a long-term public–private relationship where both parties can work with and talk to each other as a project is initiated, permitted and built. Sometimes these relationships are officially created; sometimes developers have to find a way of creating the relationship unofficially.

staff member has a title behind their name that does not mean they are the real "player." Often the most helpful individuals are the ones who are in the least conspicuous positions. Those are the people a savvy construction manager and tenant coordinator really wants to identify and cultivate.

Investigative legwork can include walking the site with development team and general contractor construction managers and superintendents and watching them handle inspections called in, meeting with the staff members of the permitting departments and authorities and asking to be introduced to the people you will be interfacing with the most, dropping by the local authority offices and gathering up paperwork and watching people interact, and calling local contractors and architects already working within that municipality and asking them for information.

Tenant coordinators need to realize that most of these authorities are created to act as public servants, and they operate on bureaucratic systems designed to protect the interests of the people within the community. Over time these systems take on a unique life of their own, and the biggest challenge to a development team is getting to understand the system and playing within it enough to know how to get things done. Special favors and requests can be asked for only if the relationship has already proven strong and trustworthy.

Understanding the actual approval process is also invaluable. Tenant coordinators need to find out what type of paperwork actually needs to be submitted to the local permitting department and assist their tenants by giving them checklists and copies of any paperwork that they have that might be of assistance. A permit application package can consist of copies of the permit application itself, legal description, site plans, contractor licensing requirements, letters of authorization and approval and applications for business licenses and occupational licenses. Along with the paperwork, an understanding of the various departments it will go through, the amount of time it typically takes and instructions on certain key things the municipality looks for is helpful. For example, Florida has strict wind load and zoned structural tiedown and bolting requirements, whereas California has seismic requirements. Tenant coordinators can get a better handle on assisting their tenants by requesting that the local plan reviewers copy them on comments when issued to both the tenant and base building architects. By reviewing and seeing what comments are most commonly made, over time coordinators can assist other tenants to get through the review process much more quickly by passing on what will be looked for to the tenant architects in advance. Creating sample details and putting

---

Tip for a Successful Opening

If you are opening a lot of retail space at one time, name one specific permit expediter as a designated contractor and put it in the lease that they must be used. Architects and national firms tend to have their own expediters and might resist using your preferred contractor unless you put it in the lease.

Also, if the tenant does have a national relationship with an expediter, tell them to hire your designated contractor as the "runner," which allows them to use your designated contractor while still maintaining their long-term relationship with their own expediter. Most national expediters do not send someone down but look for a local runner, so you have actually helped them as well as yourself. A runner is a delivery person who actually knows the right people within a department to hand paperwork and checks to, ensuring timely receipt and processing of critical items, but who would not know code requirements.

---

them in the design criteria or e-mailing them to the tenant architects can also expedite this process.

Permit Expediters

A talented permit expediter can move a job through the most complicated system quickly and efficiently. The trick is to find one who understands construction and code versus one who is just a "runner." A professional expediter trained in construction and engineering who has the ability to pick up the phone and reach the right person to solve a problem can take a project from stalled to light speed in moments. The problem is that they are hard to find and expensive, and most developers don't want to bother finding one, depending upon their contractor or team to "figure it out."

There are certain municipalities where it is a given to not even attempt to start a project without one on board, such as New York City and Boston, which use certification programs. Due to language, culture and controlled growth attitudes, other areas where a good expediter comes in handy include South Florida.

Since expediters cover a lot of territory and many are just runners and are not trained professionally, how can you find a good one if you decide you need one?

- Ask the permit department for names of good expediters. They legally cannot recommend, but if there is someone they like, they will find a way to let you know.
- Ask other developers who helped them out.
- Hire a planning firm; they often have their own expediters on staff or do their own running.
- Hire a small, established and well-connected independent architect to do it for you on a project-specific basis.
- Ask a contractor; some have their own people on staff who can do it for you.

Plan Review

Another area where a tenant coordinator can help a tenant open earlier is by assisting them through the plan review process. Along with giving them a permit application package and information on what plan review will be looking for, ask for the process number. Many municipalities have automated permit approval programs that a tenant coordinator can follow along with the tenant design team to see where the plans are in the approval process. If something stalls or a tenant coordinator notices a problem, sometimes they can assist on expediting things by picking up the phone and calling the tenant or by calling the plan review department themselves. Busy bureaucracies have been known to lose plans and permits, and a savvy coordinator who watches for this can often pinpoint exactly who has it and tactfully ask why it is still sitting on their desk.

Tenant coordinators who have situations where tenant plans need to be reviewed in a hurry and who have a solid relationship with the local plan review department can also assist their tenants by calling the plan review team to request their assistance in order to get the plans reviewed quicker. Special arrangements for overtime review can be made through some building departments also.

Tenant coordinators can also set up meetings between the building officials and the tenant design and construction teams to do a pre-review so that items that will need correction can be caught in advance. This is especially helpful on projects involving complicated life safety systems or assembly uses such as multiscreen theaters and large health clubs.

Many tenants now have clauses written into their leases allowing them to kick out of a lease if they cannot get an approval in a timely basis. Tenant coordinators and development teams need to make sure they watch for those leases, know the submittal dates and get actively

A Relationship for the Long Term with Municipal Employees

If we have to tell you how to do this, you are probably already in trouble. However, here are a few tips:

1. Send thank-you notes when someone takes the time to assist you or give you information, along with your enclosed card.
2. When someone really goes out of the way to assist, send a thank-you letter to their boss. Make sure it is sincere and cannot be interpreted as a thank-you for bypassing a code or standard.
3. Call or visit just to say hi, not just when you are in trouble or need help.
4. Call with a "heads-up" if something is coming down the pike, such as a huge plan coming in for submittal.
5. Make sure your own applications are as complete and accurate as can be.
6. Intercede. If a tenant architect or contractor wants to argue with the local municipality, get into the middle of it. Make sure the tenant's team understands that the relationship with the plan reviewer or inspector is of key importance to you and that while you are going to help them resolve problems and get open, you are also going to maintain that relationship and expect them to honor that.
7. Supply information that makes plan review or inspections life easier, such as a comprehensive list of addresses, tenant names and permit numbers, or maps of store locations
8. Send carefully selected gifts that can be shared with others and do not appear as bribes, such as a platter of cookies. Many people think they can bribe their way to success. In today's business environment, this is sometimes more dangerous than successful.
9. When you send gifts, don't do it when everyone else does. Forget getting lost in the holiday season crowd and send boxes of Valentine hearts or shamrock cookies instead.

involved in assisting the tenant to get the permit so that the lease clause does not get utilized.

Tenant Coordination's Relations with Local Authorities

Depending upon the setup of the tenant coordination department, this is an asset that many development teams cannot call upon. Large developers doing a lot of in-fill might not have the time to allow their tenant coordinators to invest in a long-term one-on-one relationship. In that case, it is more likely that the local center operations team will be the ones to communicate with the building department on a regular basis. Tenant coordinators might be more likely to ask the help of their operations manager or find someone locally to refer to their tenants to pick up as an expediter.

Smaller development teams that tend to do more projects in a concentrated geographic location are more likely to have staff members on board who have direct relationships with local authorities. In many cases, after a center is open, it might be specifically the tenant coordinator who is the only one who does have that relationship and might find themselves utilized for more than just traditional tenant coordination activities.

Developers who are opening a center should make sure that a member of the Tenant Coordination department does establish a direct relationship early. Although the main permitting activities would be done as part of the building base construction permitting, the tenant coordinator should be involved to some extent so that when it comes time to start getting tenant plans or big box and white box landlord work permitted, they are already known to the plan review team, know the system and have credibility as a player on the team. Generally, since Tenant Coordination is usually one of the last to leave a project, it is the Tenant Coordination relationship that ultimately turns into the longest-lasting one and sets the tone for in-fill construction in the future, even if ultimately handled by the on-site management and operations team.

A coordinator knows they have a good relationship with the local authorities when they are the first notified of potential problems, even if they are base building–related. How do you get to that "first-call" relationship? Constant communication and commitment.

Many people make the mistake of contacting plan review only when there is a problem. However, like any relationship, by making the effort to open a two-way door through constant contact and communication, a professional relationship can turn into a profitable one for all parties involved. With care and skill, sometimes these relationships turn into a long-term relationship with mutual respect, which is a huge asset for any developer to have in a member of his staff.

Other authorities that tenant coordination usually establishes and maintains long-term relationships with include:

- Board of Health for restaurant plan approval, typically done for separate inspections for food service tenants to open

- Fire Department for permitting involving life safety, fire alarm panels and systems and sprinkler modifications
- Municipal utility departments, since there might be impact fees or credits for water and sewer usage involved
- Planning and zoning for sign and banner approvals
- Zoning for code violations and open permits or for approval of liquor licenses

Timely Introductions

The best time for tenant coordinators on new projects to meet authorities that will impact them and their tenants' work is at the beginning stages of a project. Unfortunately, most tenant coordination teams are not brought into a project until the base building is ready for turnover to tenants.

If your development team intends to follow that process, assign one lead coordinator to be a member of the development team and take a consultant role by sitting in at meetings so that the tenant coordination team is aware of who all the players are when they join a team. The lead coordinator would also be tasked with meeting the municipalities and authorities in advance and setting up operations standards and agreements specifically related to tenant coordination work, such as putting together application packages, approval letters, coordinating special inspection teams and learning the specifics of working within the application and approval process of the jurisdiction so that this information is being conveyed to the tenants.

Developers make the mistake of thinking their construction and project manager can do this work, not realizing that the operational skills of the Tenant Coordination team are often completely different and the information they need to function effectively should be coordinated directly.

Setting Up Meetings

When things seem to stall or a tenant just does not seem to "get it," it is often appropriate and necessary for tenant coordinators to request and set up meetings with the plan review team or the head of inspections and the tenant design and construction associates.

When setting up a meeting with plan review, if it is just one specific discipline needed (such as zoning or mechanical), call that reviewer and tell him what you would like to do and ask when would be a good time to come in. Bring just one or two people with you and sit down with the reviewer.

If the problem seems more widespread, call the head of plan review and explain the problem and request a meeting to be set up with multiple parties. If there is a particularly touchy subject involving one reviewer in particular, you might want to call them separately and let them know what you are doing so they will not feel like you are going over their head.

If the issue seems to be more of an inspection one, request that the contractor call in for an inspection. Then call the inspector separately and tell them that you have requested an inspection and that when they get there you will be joining them to review the issues. Sometimes they will give you a range of time when they plan to be there so you do not have to wait all day.

If it is a problem that cannot get solved in the field or is more far-reaching, involving several inspectors, call the head of inspections and request a meeting. It is better to request these meetings early in the morning, before the inspectors go into the field. At the end of the day they will be tired and will want to go home.

Communication of Issues

Usually in dealing with any governmental official it is always a good policy to be polite and to the point, unless you know them extremely well. Do not waste their time or attempt to argue with them. If you do request something that requires that they operate outside their established operational system or routine, do not assume a precedent that will allow you to do it again. Systems are like rules and are created to be maintained to protect others. In order to break the rules and systems, you have to know the boundaries and then request the favor in a reasonable and safe manner.

Do not ever put your licensed consultants or contractor in the position of requesting a deviation from code unless you are prepared to assume 100% liability or get involved in what could be a long, drawn-out battle over code or community standards with a higher jurisdiction than what you were originally dealing with, such as the department of environmental protection, the state code and licensing departments, regional water authorities or the federal government.

Realize that even if you come to an agreement on something and put it in writing, since you are dealing with a bureaucratic system designed to protect the people, it is always subject to change if someone within the system feels that the safety or property of the greater good, the people, is endangered. An argumentative attitude can cost a developer much more in the long term.

13 Urban and Mixed-Use Challenges for Retail Tenant Coordination Teams

Skyscrapers and multistory mixed-use developments create a special set of challenges for retail development and construction teams. Mix those challenges with an intense urban environment and the Tenant Coordination and development teams have major hurdles to overcome that require close scrutiny as well as a strong communications and design program.

In urban mixed-use developments, the retail component of a project is typically the most complicated piece of the overall project, requiring planning at the earliest stages of the development. This is due to the number of tenants with different design and construction requirements locating into one component, like a complicated jigsaw puzzle. Opening of a mixed-use project will require the retailers to design and construct their respective spaces while the development is at the peak of construction. In order to successfully open an urban or mixed-use center at one time, the entire project must open together. The developer's focus on the overall project's critical path may not always have what is best for the retailers in the retail component in mind. The importance of a tenant coordinator is paramount at this juncture.

A tenant coordinator should ask the following questions when considering how they can add value to these types of mixed-use coordination challenges:

- How can a tenant coordinator add value to a mixed-use developer's overall project planning?

- When should the retail tenant coordinator be added to the development team?
- How can the tenant coordinator tailor typical industry standards to this specific and demanding type of project?

Design Criteria

Mixed-use design is critical due to the relationships of the components of the different uses being stacked together. Retailers traditionally want as much street access and visibility as possible, with very little base building systems and columns impacting their space. In addition, each of the different components within the entire building requires its own unique type of support systems, which can impact the other uses. For example, residential components require security and restricted access, whereas the retail section will want on-demand loading dock access and easy back-of-house accessibility to their spaces.

"A mixed-use project design incorporates many identities while keeping the overall project design integrity. While National Tenants want to maintain their respective identity, to successfully fit into the overall design concept of a project they may have to be encouraged to creatively think out of their typical box, literally. Likewise, the developer also has to keep his retailers' needs in mind during the design phase."

SEAN JOHNSON
Vice President
The Related Companies

Since many of these projects share central operating systems such as loading docks, vertical transportation, technology rooms and mechanical distribution and electrical rooms, it is essential that the retail coordination team have as much information as possible in advance in order to share with their tenant design and construction teams the design requirements in mechanical, electrical and plumbing.

Many of the retail components of mixed-use projects are designed as just one part of a community within a building, and the élan of being in a premier project also requires strict adherence to a center's design criteria. These criteria are impacted not only by the development team's expectations of quality, but also by structural and mechanical support for components of a building 3 to 50 stories high. This demands extremely comprehensive design criteria and the availability of tenant coordination teams to answer demanding questions by design teams that want to get their drawings right the first time to save money for their owners.

Design criteria that are supplemented by visual renderings, illustrated details and photographs can become even more helpful to tenant design teams as they try to picture how their client's store is going to sit within

the framework of your building. More and more developers are making computerized renderings and architectural and mechanical CAD files in electronic or Web-based formats available to their tenants.

TELL THE STORY

Successful design criteria should tell the developer's story of what the retail component of the project is going to look like. This story should help motivate the design teams to create unique touches for their clients' image that help meld the tenants' look into the landlord's vision. While this can be a tough sell when you are dealing with huge national chains and their own branded images

Mixed-use and stacked retail centers create a host of their own unique challenges, such as how to have tenants working over the top of each other without impacting the stores that might be further along in construction above or below them.

and requirements, it can also be successfully accomplished through open communication and flexibility of both the tenant and landlord.

ARCHITECTURAL SPECIFICATIONS

How do you want to have the tenant's store connect into your bulkhead? Do you have a particular request for where the doors sit and how your tile bumps into theirs? What is the type and quality of the finishes you want? Do you have a special merchandising control zone? Are pop-out windows encouraged? Is there a unique signage requirement? What are your waterproofing requirements?

The design criteria need to spell it out. The more detail and the better the visual aids, the easier it will be for the tenant's architectural team to understand your vision and requirements, and the less time you will spend trying

"Tenant Coordination teams on very high-end centers should consider putting together a material board of acceptable finishes as a baseline. They can also stockpile samples of landlord finishes to send to tenant design consultants to help them visualize how their materials will look next to the landlord's and to encourage them to step their level of finishes up if needed."

SEAN JOHNSON
Vice President
The Related Companies

to assist them or their contractor at a later date. Take the time to put together practical working suggestions and components to the design criteria that supplement the flowery prose. The more detail-specific you are, the less time you will spend in answering questions and reviewing drawings.

MECHANICAL REQUIREMENTS

Multistory buildings share mechanical systems that limit how much chilled water, heating hot water, steam, fresh air intake, exhaust and domestic water and power are available. It is extremely important that the tenant's design team gets as much MEP information as possible and that they understand that if the tenant's demands outstrip what is available, getting more is not always an easy or cheap solution.

Tenants were encouraged to take advantage of the overscaled store heights to create visual merchandising opportunities.

On projects where the coordination of the mechanical, electrical and plumbing systems and distribution are critical due to limited availability or strict controls, insist the design team have their engineers contact you separately. Explain to them the project and get them as much information as you can on what is being provided as per the lease and building design to the tenant. Also get to them specific requirements on life safety, communications and technology and systems testing. Send them files for the entire retail component and guide them to where to look for their electrical and mechanical distribution connection points. Do not assume the owner or the architect will give them the information you provide; often these things go in a file because the leasing agent or store owner does not understand the importance of what they are being presented.

The more tenants are stacked and the smaller the footprint of the building, the more challenges tenant coordinators will have in finding available connections and supply for power, fire alarm, air and exhaust for tenants. It becomes even tougher when tenants start coming in and asking for more than what was originally planned for or allotted to their space or when other tenants have already completed their work, and routes to conduit or pipe and duct to additional connections have been shut off.

It is essential that developers take into account during their project planning how they are going to get additional power and air to tenants and where they are going to run conduits and pipes. They need to plan not only for second-day management contingency, but also for over-runs during the initial construction. Developers also need to make sure that the leasing team is aware of how much power and utilities are ac-tually available before each construction exhibit is written so that they do not give away what is simply not available.

CONSTRUCTION ISSUES

Vertical stacking creates a unique set of demands on tenant design teams. They have to figure out where to put elevator pits and overruns, kitchen grease traps and underslab plumbing over your public areas and in relation to the tenants above and below them, as well as landlord me-chanical and technology rooms and fire-rated stairways and halls. The quicker you catch these conflicts in the design phase, the easier the con-struction demands will be on the tenant and you later.

Make sure the tenant design team not only gets the standard lease outline drawing, but that they also get the floor plans of the space above and below them. They need to understand what type of tenant is adjoining them and the status of that tenant's construction and de-sign. Their plans also need to be subjected to a full review not only for design adherence, but also for construction impact on others.

Some landlords prefer to do review when the plans are 100% complete. However, in cases where tenants will be impacting others due to vertical stacking, pre-review of initial floor plans in person between the tenant and landlord design and construction teams looking for construction conflicts and hits is invaluable. Additionally, request the tenant's design and construction schedules. Tenant schedules are based upon their re-spective design, pre-purchasing and construction team availability. They do not take into account that the tenant below them may close their ceil-ing before underslab utilities or structure are going to be installed for their own design. By comparing adjacent space schedules, you can save time and money for all parties included within the coordination.

Tenants who insist on buildouts that will require additional coordi-nation through other tenant spaces or extensive protection of landlord common areas or sensitive mechanical and electrical systems need to know in advance so that they can include these protection and con-struction costs in their budgeting. If these issues are not called out in advance, the tenant will try to put them back on the landlord or the landlord will lose valuable time, tenant goodwill and resources in solving field conflicts that arise later.

The more information sent out in advance and called out for during the design phase, the better will be the ultimate relationship between the tenant and landlord.

Coordination of Moving Materials and People

One of the first questions a savvy contractor will ask the tenant coordinator is, "How do I get my material and tools into my space?" In a

high-rise location with limited loading dock and elevator access, this is a major issue that can cost the contractor and his client money and time. Developers need to create a vertical transportation plan for getting materials in and debris out.

If many stores are opening at one time, then a loading dock supervisor who books all elevator and dock times is essential. If the unions are involved and the developer does not have a signatory relationship, then the base building contractor or a primary tenant contractor might need to supply this key person to schedule deliveries. Tenant Coordination needs to make sure that the tenant contractors and store operations people are notified of and made responsible for using the proper channels for booking time and getting items in.

Urban- and galleria-style centers can create unique challenges for tenants, such as how to integrate second-story retail with stairs and accessible elevators.

Occasionally special challenges will arise that require creative solutions to getting material in. The more the burden of getting furnishings and materials is placed on the tenant's contractor, the better. Qualified contractors are assumed to have looked for these issues when putting together their bids and doing their site verification and as such are responsible.

However, if their solutions impact other tenants or base building construction or operations, tenant coordination needs to be involved to protect the interests of other tenants and the landlord.

Experienced tenant coordinators who see some of these problems in advance and notify the tenant's design team can often help save the tenant time and money. However, no matter how conscientious and experienced you are, no one is all-seeing, and coordination issues will arise.

Construction Coordination

Developers need to be flexible in getting tenants with underslab or structural component requirements, such as restaurants or stores with elevators and staircases, started earlier. Giving the tenants additional time and incentive to start earlier without early rent commencement can help find and alleviate a lot of coordination issues. If a developer's construction team can do something to lessen impact or conflict between two tenants or in a critical common area or mechanical room, then it might even pay for the developer to do the work themselves and charge the tenant back. In the long run it will save both tenants and developers money and aggravation.

On-site tenant coordination needs to be extremely vigilant in walking through tenant spaces while under construction and making sure all connections to major building systems are correctly done and tested. They need to watch contractors to make sure no more than what was allotted to the tenant is used in utility allocations. Since many of the systems the tenant contractor is tapping into might impact delivery of steam or water 50 stories up, it is extremely critical that tenant coordinators demand and get testing results before any system is opened up into the landlord's main system. Tenant coordinators also need to make sure all above-ceiling air passages for building smoke exhaust and air exchange are not blocked by tenant construction

The support and camaraderie union members display for one another can make them a challenge for development teams to work with. Tenant coordinators have a responsibility to their own construction team to make sure that their tenant's contractors can work harmoniously in any environment, whether union or not.

and that required plenum openings that need to be built by tenants are done so with the properly rated dampers and grills.

On-site tenant coordinators need to make sure the contractors are building structural components as per approved design and that they are not putting undue stress on building components or penetrating fire-rated rooms and stairwells without proper approval and repair. If they see something that makes them uncomfortable, tenant coordinators can put a halt to the work and insist on a member of the architect's team coming to inspect the work and signing off on it.

Development teams that provide additional support to their on-site tenant coordination through on-call engineering and architectural presence for troubleshooting can save a lot of time and money for both themselves and the tenant. These team members can provide support in identifying and helping solve issues in the field that can be related back to the development team for approval or to the tenant's team as a suggestion in solving a buildout problem.

Urban projects tend to have municipal funding and union involvement. Tenant Coordination teams need to watch and make sure that there is labor harmony in the store locations and buildouts. Incompatible labor can shut down construction on an entire site, resulting in delays to the overall project.

Stacked retail components, particularly restaurants with kitchens and tenants with restrooms, need to abide by strict waterproofing standards. Testing to make sure that wet areas do not leak over finished tenants, common areas or mechanical rooms below require intense coordination, and the Tenant Coordination team needs to be involved to make sure it is done correctly. The contractor doing the testing must have access to all spaces that could be impacted by a leak from his space as well as the proper emergency cleanup materials and personnel on hand before he does his testing. Tenant Coordination needs to ensure that he is properly coordinated and observe the tests.

Tenant Coordination also needs to be involved in coordination issues when tenant construction impacts others, such as needing access to or through another tenant space or in a sensitive landlord room or common area. Tenant Coordination should introduce the superintendents of tenant contractors working over the top of each other, as well as in adjoining spaces, and be prepared to host coordination meetings if needed. They also need to be constantly patrolling landlord rooms and space and insist that the tenant contractors adequately protect those areas when working above or in them.

Unique Issues

Particularly issues unique to urban and mixed-use centers include no or limited parking, limited building access for deliveries, various mixed-use components all fighting for access and staging at the same time and central building technology systems with limited outside access.

LIMITED PARKING

In many urban areas, this is not a problem, since public transportation is an option and the labor is used to utilizing it. Savvy subcontractors and contractors used to working in that municipality will figure out quickly how to get their gang boxes and manpower in and their delivery vans out of there without causing too many problems.

However, in areas of the South and West where in-fill construction is now becoming big and there is no public transportation, this is a major problem for developers. One creative solution would be to look for an empty lot close by for construction parking. Another would be to bus labor in and require deliveries of tools and gang boxes within special time limitations.

ACCESS FOR DELIVERIES

This is a particular problem for urban projects, which can easily have semi trucks stacked several blocks long to get access into a loading dock or delivery area. Complicate this with required project roadwork, concrete trucks pumping several stories into the air and tough community standards on when trucks can be in the street idling, and coordination issues become critical immediately.

Union labor buildings also require tough standards in making sure only union labor is delivering into the dock areas. Teamsters will often check store fixture and cabinetry deliveries to make sure they have union labels on them before letting them be off-loaded onto a dock.

A strong delivery access program must be put into place by the devel-

When you have retailers stacked over each other, work has to occur in tight coordination, continuously. This busy Manhattan shot shows concrete being pumped into a store under construction five stories up.

opment team. The criteria should then be given to the Tenant Coordination team, which is responsible for passing it on to the tenants and making sure their construction and operations teams understand how to get materials in and when to do it. When things get particularly busy in a loading area due to a mass opening of stores at one time, tenant coordination needs to plan on stationing a person in the loading dock to assist in getting store operations teams down onto the docks and materials offloaded and back up into the tenant spaces as soon as possible.

MIXED-USE COMPONENTS ALL UNDER CONSTRUCTION AT ONE TIME

Mixed-use projects have several components all fighting for deliveries and staging areas at one time. If you have multiple openings going on with retailers, it becomes even more critical for intense planning on how to get materials and supplies into the building. If possible, tenant coordination should insist that a section of the loading dock be cordoned off just for retail use at critical times. They should also be adamant that they need control of oversized elevators and freight and passenger elevators at critical construction and merchandise delivery times.

CONTROLLED TECHNOLOGY ACCESS

Controlled technology access is not unusual for office buildings or residential apartment complexes. Most building owners in those real estate arenas understand that by controlling access to the building, the technology delivery can become a source of additional income. This concept is new to retail, though, and tenants who have a large amount of stores with their own national accounts and providers will resist being required to use landlord-designated providers.

LOCALLY SAVVY TENANT CONTRACTORS

Landlords in mixed-use projects should require through the lease the right to approve the tenant contractor. Many tenants have relationships with national retail contractors. Unfortunately, those contractors might not always be the best choice for that particular project, even though they know the store design and construction issues best.

Landlords should require the tenants use savvy retail contractors who know the needs of the community and work in that municipality the most. Those contractors will know how to get deliveries in, move people and materials in and out, have the proper union relationships and know the local codes and restrictions. The landlord should also insist that the tenant contractors be obligated to get the signage installations done and coordinate all merchandise deliveries instead of letting the tenant operations teams try to do it after the fact. By using a local contractor, the tenant will ultimately save themselves and the landlord a lot of time and money as well as aggravation. If the tenant feels they must use their national contractor relationship, then specify that they can hire the national contractor to provide a superintendent as a consultant who is on site to direct construction. However, the delivery coordination and union relationships should be done through someone locally licensed and experienced.

Depending upon the community, the design criteria of the center and the capability of the development team, additional challenges such as union labor protests and strict community work prohibitions might need to be faced and resolved.

The main key to successfully completing a high-rise project is a strong communications program between the developer, the tenant and their design team and the contractor's superintendent. By keeping the lines of communication open and resolving conflicts daily, the developer can maintain control and create a successful working environment for all involved. The payoff? Timely store openings, despite tough circumstances.

14 | Regional Mall Challenges for Retail Coordination Teams

Regional mall coordination is not a cookie-cutter process, as some people would assume. Each property has its own unique personality determined by its location; building design; shared mechanical, electrical and plumbing systems; operating team and design and finishes. Centers that are already operating or that are under renovation also demand special attention from the tenant coordination team as they try to integrate store construction within an active environment controlled by operating strategies already in place.

The opportunities for Tenant Coordination teams to work on new regional centers are becoming rarer. More typical to a mall developer's in-house Tenant Coordination team's daily activities are working with tenants taking over old store locations or renovating stores they are already in possession of. As the shopping center industry matures, more mall Tenant Coordination teams will be involved in renovation of older centers versus construction of new regional malls in this country. These renovations, often extremely challenging as they involve keeping tenants open while reworking sections of the mall infrastructure, require just as much attention to the communication process as it does to the construction work that will occur.

Tenant coordinators who do have the opportunity to work on new regional centers or major renovations will enjoy the exhilaration of creating a new product as well as the challenges of opening up as many tenants as possible all on one opening-day thrust. Tenant coordinators working on renovating or building out individual spaces will experience the challenge and rewards of helping tenants and their teams through a myriad of construction challenges. Either way, the ultimate goal is the same—generate more income for the developer, the store owner and the contractor by getting the stores open as soon as possible.

Melding a store's branded image with a center's design criteria can be a challenge for both the tenant design team and the tenant coordinator. When the negotiations were concluded, the result was a stunning Solstice store.

Design Criteria

Regional mall design criteria demand strict attention to the actual infrastructure of the center as well as to the integration of the tenant's branded image into the mall theme and design. Mall tenants typically share not only common operating systems, but also back-of-house corridors and loading docks, which create construction coordination issues related to getting materials and supplies in and through them while leaving room for tenants also under construction or already operating.

Tenant coordination teams not only need to convey to the tenant construction and design teams the design requirements for architecture and engineering, but also to alert them to other unique coordination issues that might impact how they design and build their store. Some of these critical pieces of information include how many levels the center is and who or what is next to, above or below them; where the loading docks and freight elevators are; what kind of mechanical systems the center runs off of and a map showing where their conduit or pipe and duct runs will have to be run through to get to special exhaust shafts or utility connection points if they are not in the store or they have to run out to obtain more; any special requirements by the operations team if the center is already open, such as construction rules and regulations; and any unique structures, neutral piers and bulkheads they will have to tie into.

Design criteria that are supplemented by visual renderings, illustrated details and photographs are helpful to tenant design teams as they try to picture how their client's store is going to sit within the framework of your building. Tenant coordinators working with existing centers can include actual photographs of the center, adjoining tenants and how other stores have successfully linked into the mall structure with their storefront attachments and transitions of mall to tenant flooring.

TELL THE STORY

If you are working with a brand-new center or a renovation, then the design criteria should tell the developer's story of what the retail component of the project is going to look like. This story should help motivate the tenant design teams to create unique touches for their client's image that help meld the tenant's look into the landlord's vision. While this can be a tough sell when you are dealing with huge national chains and their own branded images and requirements, it can also be successfully accomplished through open communication and flexibility of both the tenant and landlord.

Design criteria for malls already open should include actual photographs of the wing or court where the tenant is going, along with photographs of field conditions related to that space and samples of how other tenants have successfully tied into the infrastructure. Also include examples of typical details for attachments not only for architectural components but also mechanical and structural components such as VAV boxes, taps into chilled water systems, use of specific types of electrical conduit, grease guards, fire alarm tie-ins, repairs to fire walls and flooring membranes for waterproofing. The more typical details tenant coordination gives the tenant's design team, the quicker the plan review process will go and the more assurance the management and operations teams will have that the tenant is adhering to the overall rules and regulations of the center. This will also result in quicker construction build-outs and less oversight by tenant coordination and operations of the tenant contractor during construction.

ARCHITECTURAL SPECIFICATIONS

How do you want to have the tenant's store connect into your bulkhead? Do you have a particular request for where the doors sit and how your tile bumps into theirs? What is the type and quality of the finishes you want? Do you have a special merchandising control zone? Are pop-out windows encouraged? Is there a unique signage requirement? What are your waterproofing requirements? Where will the tenant contractor get his mall tile?

Malls and galleria-type shopping centers require absolute attention to storefront details and merchandise presentations, more so than any other type of projects. Tenant coordinators need to be very precise in working with the tenant design teams on making sure it is clear how the store will fit into the mall framework by providing as much detail as possible. They also need to be strong in conveying what the landlord's expectations for interior presentation are. The more that is caught in the design and planning phase, the less that has to be worked out in the field during construction, which often results in conflict endangering the future landlord-tenant relationship as well as increased construction costs and loss of time in opening.

The more detailed and the better the visual aids, the easier it will be for the tenant's architectural team to understand your vision and requirements and the less time you will spend trying to assist them or their contractor at a later date. Take the time to put together practical working suggestions and components to the design criteria. The more detail-specific information you provide, the less time you will spend answering questions and reviewing drawings or dealing with irate construction and operations managers from both the tenant and the mall management teams.

MECHANICAL REQUIREMENTS

Most regional malls share sanitary and domestic water lines as well as fire protection, fire alarm and electrical systems. While stores in single-level centers might have stand-alone mechanical systems, other tenants in multilevel centers might share mechanical systems, which limit how much chilled water, steam, fresh air intake and exhaust are available. It is extremely important that the tenant's design team gets as much MEP information as possible and that they understand that if the tenant's demands outstrip what is available, getting more is not always an easy or cheap solution.

On projects where the coordination of the mechanical, electrical and plumbing systems and distribution is critical due to limited availability or strict controls, insist that the design team have their engineers contact you separately. Explain to them the project requirements and get them as much information as you can on what is being provided as per the lease and building design to their client, the tenant. Also get to them specific requirements on life safety, communications and technology and systems testing. Send them files for the entire retail component and guide them to where to look for their electrical and mechanical distribution connection points. If they have to run through back-of-house corridors, get them scaled drawings showing the runs and locations and alerting them if they have to pass through any existing stores or common areas.

The more tenants are stacked and the smaller the footprint of the building, the more challenges tenant coordinators will have in finding available connections and supply for power, fire alarm, air and exhaust for tenants. It becomes even tougher when tenants start coming in and asking for more than what was originally planned for or allotted to their space, or when other tenants have already completed their work and routes for conduit or pipe and duct to additional connections have been shut off.

It is essential that developers take into account during their project planning how they are going to get additional power and air to tenants and where they are going to run conduits and pipes. They need to plan for not only second-day management contingencies, but also for overruns during the initial construction. Developers also need to make sure that the leasing team is aware of how much power and utilities are actually available before each construction exhibit is written so that they do not give away what is simply not available.

CONSTRUCTION ISSUES

Regional malls are not all the same when it comes to construction issues. Each mall is going to have its own unique personality, just like any other type of retail product or project. Some things do tend to be consistent, though, especially in the construction process.

Smart retail contractors working in mall environments will want to know where the store is located in relation to loading docks and back-of-house corridors, whether it is an open and operating center or not, what designated contractors and fees there are and if they have to buy any parts or components to tie into mall systems or purchase flooring materials. They also need to know if it is a union environment, what other stores and common areas are located around them, if there is anything existing in the store that needs demolition and if they need a barricade and what type. All of this information will help them determine their construction costs and schedules. While a busy tenant coordinator is tempted to just tell them to go look, often it is not that simple and they rely upon you to help their client, who is your tenant.

Tenant coordinators working on existing centers should take the time to routinely inventory all spaces that are currently empty or whose leases are coming up for renewal so that they can answer not only design but also construction questions, not only for the tenant design and construction teams but also their own leasing agents, who might have questions.

Both new and existing centers should have construction handbooks available to give to tenants when they are starting the bid and construction process. This handbook should not only contain rules and regulations, but also a list of designated subcontractors, explanations of where to go to get mall requirement materials and typical details for tying in key components such as the mall and tenant flooring transitions. Even though this information might have been made available to the design team and you are hoping it will be picked up in the plans by the time the tenant contractors start to price and bid, this does not mean it will be conveyed to the contractor by the time he is estimating. Information available in the construction handbook also ensures tenant contractor accountability to the mall tenant coordination or operations team when it is time for construction to begin.

Just like urban and mixed-use centers, regional malls with multiple floors have stacking issues that require special attention. Restaurants can be a particular challenge. Typically, in regional malls restaurant operations tend to be grouped closer to front entrances or into food courts where the mall design makes connection to existing fire shafts and grease traps and freight elevators available. However, occasionally food operations tenants go into areas where the infrastructure is not available, and the Tenant Coordination team has to pay particular attention in assisting the tenant design team on figuring out how to get them connected to or create the infrastructure for their typical operational needs. In existing centers, this can be particularly challenging, as underslab penetrations into open tenants or finished common areas might need to be done.

Occasionally retail tenants will also need to work over the top or come through the middle of another operating tenant or into a common area for plumbing lines, elevator pits, additional structural supports or conduit for tie into mall systems. This all needs to be coordinated with extreme care by the tenant coordinator and operations teams. Most leases allow for landlords to get access into adjoining spaces so that they can do this, but only with the cooperation of the impacted tenant.

Other typical regional mall construction issues include building storefront barricades to contain noise and duct, negotiating back-of-house corridors and loading dock requirements, tying into existing mall systems without impacting the mall or its tenants and noise limits and construction hours. The more information conveyed in advance by the tenant coordinator to the tenant design and construction teams, the quicker and more successful the construction and store opening will be and the quicker everyone will be making money.

Coordination of Moving Materials

In a regional center with limited loading dock and freight elevator access, the coordination of moving in materials is a major issue that can cost the contractor and his client money and time. On new centers or in renovated malls with new wings, on-site tenant coordinators working during mass openings or with a lot of store and base building renovation going on around them need to create dock offloading plans and schedules. They can also provide maps to give to each contractor showing them where their offloading areas are and how to get through back-of-house corridors and elevators.

If a center is operating, the focus switches from trying to get them into the loading docks when multiple tenants are competing for off-loading time to one of coordination with other tenants who might be bringing in merchandise deliveries. In this case the general contractor and tenant coordinator need to work with the center operations team. If there are back-of-house corridors, often contractors will be allowed to offload and deliver during the day. However, if there is competition for these areas with large retailers or with restaurants that are bringing in food early, then the contractor might be required to come in during off hours or at night. Contractors working in existing centers should also plan on bringing in oversized items through main mall entry doors after hours and be coordinated through operations with security so that someone is available to actually let them in and watch the door so that unauthorized personnel do not try to enter after them.

Tenant coordinators and operations people also need to make sure that the tenant contractor who is bringing deliveries in through mall common areas understands that he is responsible to protect all finishes, and actually then watch or spot-check them to make sure they do.

During large openings of malls and wings, tenant coordinators also need to remember that not only construction but merchandise deliveries need to be taken into account and coordinated. The reality is that retail contractors usually understand the reality of working in a mall environment. That is their bread and butter, and they make sure they understand the rules and play right. They want to work in your center again. When it comes to getting things in, the ones who usually create the most problems are the mom-and-pop tenants who do not understand the rules and are not using a professional retail contractor, and the tenant merchandising teams who do not care what the rules are.

If unions are involved in your center, then a dock master might need to be employed to deal with getting things into the center. Since the developer would probably not have a direct relationship with the union, this person should be hired through someone who does. A word of warning here: it should be made clear to the unions that after the center is open, operations will handle the dock and union rules will no longer be observed.

Tenant coordinators need to become police officers at this time and make sure that the small tenants understand that they cannot just do things without considering the impact on others.

When dealing with national chains, tenant coordinators and mall operations teams also need to communicate strongly to the tenant merchandise and operations teams what the loading dock hours and delivery rules are and require that they coordinate with them when they want to schedule deliveries. Some centers are now using Web-based technology dock master programs to allow the tenants to look at available times and schedule deliveries. This is especially helpful for national firms, with hundreds of stores scheduling months in advance.

Tenant coordinators often have to get creative to assist their tenant contractors with getting things into the center or finding staging. Sometimes kitchen equipment might need to be lifted down through an open skylight, carpet might need to be unrolled and cut in a parking lot or a delivery made and carried through a corridor not closely located to the store under construction due to conflicts in other offloading areas. Successful on-site tenant coordinators and mall operations people have to participate with their tenant contractors to solve problems and help them get their construction done quickly with less impact on others.

Construction Coordination

Flexibility in assisting tenants with difficult construction coordination can pay off for developers and their on-site construction teams. By alerting tenants in advance when certain wings or corridors are getting closed off and arranging for them to get key oversized components in advance and stored where they won't impact the base building or tenant contractors, landlords can save all parties a lot of time and aggravation. Just as in urban centers, if a developer's construction team can do something to lessen impact or conflict between two tenants or in a critical common area or mechanical room, then it might even pay for the developer to do the work themselves and charge the tenant back

On-site tenant coordination or operations need to be extremely vigilant in walking through tenant spaces while under construction and making sure all connections to major building systems are correctly done and tested. They need to watch contractors to make sure no more than what was allotted to the tenant is used in utility allocations. Tenant coordinators also need to make sure all above-ceiling air passages for building smoke exhaust and air exchange are not blocked by tenant construction and that required plenum openings that need to be built by tenants are done so with the properly rated dampers and grills.

On-site tenant coordinators and operations teams also need to make sure the contractors are building structural components as per approved design and that they are not putting undue stress on building components or penetrating fire-rated rooms and corridors without proper approval and repair. If the center is subject to union labor, then the developer's construction oversight team needs to make sure that the tenant contractor's labor is compatible. Incompatible labor can shut down construction on an entire site, resulting in delays to the overall project.

Stores with wet areas need to abide by strict waterproofing standards. Testing to make sure that water from the pipes or faucet overruns in the wet areas do not leak over or through demised walls into other tenant areas, common areas or mechanical rooms below requires coordination. Successful coordination of testing of a waterproof membrane includes making sure there is access to all adjoining spaces, adequate personnel with equipment to clean up water in each space that might be impacted and instant communication between all parties involved. If the adjoining store is an operating tenant, sometimes the contractor will have to arrange to pay overtime to the other tenant to bring in a staff member to be there during the water test. Tenant Coordination needs to ensure that all is properly coordinated and observe the test and results.

Coordination in new centers or wings for mutual access is much easier. There the tenant coordinator needs to make sure the adjoining space superintendents have met each other and let them work something out between them. Many of these superintendents have worked together before and know each other and can handle it more efficiently between themselves. The tenant coordinator will still need to be involved to check the test results or make sure the connection inside the store is right, but it will not be as time-consuming.

Tenant coordinators and operations teams involved in regional mall tenant construction need to be constantly patrolling landlord rooms and space to make sure that the tenant contractors adequately protect those areas when working above or in them. They also need to be directly involved in any conversation concerning coordination that involves an open and operating tenant or impacts a finished common area or typically locked landlord room.

Unique Issues

Issues particularly unique to regional centers include special parking locations, limited building access for deliveries and getting debris out, service corridor use, utility coordination and storage of material.

SPECIAL PARKING LOCATIONS

One of the biggest ongoing fights a regional center tenant coordinator or operating team has is getting the tenant contractor's subcontractors to understand that parking spaces close to the doors of the center mean big dollars to the tenants. The subcontractor who wants access to his van for supplies and materials gets irate when told he has to move it to the far hinterlands of the parking area. During new construction this is not as much of a problem, but once a center is operational it is.

Mall management will threaten to tow the trucks. Tenant coordinators typically try to get the tenant contractor to police his own subcontractors. If a tenant contractor does not assist, tenant coordinators will call in the tow trucks themselves to make a point to the contractor or trade who will not comply. While this does work to a limited degree, tenant coordinators who try to negotiate special parking zones and arrange for offloading and open doors early in the morning for the trades to get supplies in and out will have more success and respect from contractors and property management, though it takes more effort.

LIMITED BUILDING ACCESS FOR DELIVERIES AND GETTING DEBRIS OUT

Actual coordination of how to get things in and out is critical in regional malls. Most regional malls have small loading dock zones that cannot be cluttered with debris containers or hold more than a couple of small delivery trucks at a time.

Debris containers need to be stored on-site somewhat close to the door opening or back-of-house corridor that the tenant contractor is using. If the mall is opening a lot of tenants at one time, tenant coordination might just choose one zone and place a couple of containers there and charge the tenant contractors for a debris removal program based on square feet. The tenant coordination team then becomes responsible for making sure the containers are emptied and replaced as needed. During an opening, this might require one person with a radio who is in direct contact with the trash removal or hauling company and who is constantly patrolling the parking lot area.

If just a few stores are under construction, then the contractors would bring in their own containers and keep them in a small section of the parking lot away from the stores. Occasionally a fight will occur when someone dumps in the other's container or if the community sees the open tops as a means of clearing out their garage without having to go to the dump. Mall security can assist the tenant coordinator and contractor by driving by occasionally and making sure no one is dumping illegally.

If a tenant contractor is doing demolition, often operations people will allow a special arrangement where they can bring in a container the evening before and demolish the store at night, making sure the container is pulled and out of the dock or closest fire lane or parking spaces early the next morning. If operations allow a tenant to use a fire lane, they must alert the fire department and make sure it is okay with them. A similar arrangement can be made for getting large deliveries of materials and supplies as well as merchandise in during the night through a loading dock during store renovations and buildouts.

Creative utilization of side entries, main mall corridors and fire lanes might be needed if the loading dock is too small to accommodate the truck. If the Tenant Coordination or operations team allows this, then arrangements need to be made with security to let the contractor and merchandise teams in and to stand watch or patrol. In addition, the contractor will need to protect the floor with plywood and possibly paper and make sure carts with balloon tires are used.

When it comes time to bring semi trucks full of merchandise in, keeping the contractor involved to make sure the doors are opened and the floors properly protected is recommended. A good practice for tenant coordination teams is to tell the tenant and their contractor that the contractor only is responsible for coordination of all deliveries with them and operations, including owner-supplied materials such as oversized graphic packages, exterior signs and merchandise. Since the contractor already knows how to get things in and knows the center personnel and regulations, they can make this happen more easily than getting others involved. They might not want to do this, but in order to service their client and with their client's persuasion, they will often agree.

SERVICE CORRIDOR USE

Another area of touchy concern with regional malls requiring coordination and constant policing is the use of service corridors. Since staging is limited in stores, contractors tend to allow their trades to do some staging of materials, carts and supplies in the back corridors. Once merchandise comes in, it also gets stacked back there awaiting store personnel to bring it in. However, these corridors are service areas to other stores and tempers will start to fly if other contractors and tenants cannot get through them.

In addition, the corridors are critical to safe exiting and cannot be blocked in case of an emergency. Operations and tenant coordination teams during openings, and whenever stores are under construction during second-day operations, need to be constantly monitoring and walking the passageways.

The best policy is to state in the rules and regulations that no materials or goods can be stored in the corridors and to ensure the policy is adhered to when walking back-of-house. If the policy is not stated and followed up on and a fire breaks out, the loss of life and property because people could not get out through the corridor or firemen into it could be disastrous.

UTILITY COORDINATION

Since mall systems tend to be based off of one meter box, particularly for domestic or chilled water, valves into the store tend to be metered through the use of submeters or meter checks. Tenant contractors need to find out in advance if special arrangements need to be made to get these meters in place before they hook up their systems to get water or power into the space. Tenant coordinators who provide this information in their construction handbooks in advance can save a lot of confusion for the contractors.

STORAGE OF MATERIAL AND MERCHANDISE

Regional malls generally have no protected exterior staging areas that can be used by the tenants and their suppliers and contractors. Occasionally landlords are required or volunteer to assist tenants by putting items in nonleased spaces or spaces where the other contractor has not checked in yet.

Landlords do not like to do this, since once a tenant is in, it is hard to get them out. Tenant's employees who come in will occasionally use the area for breaks or to open boxes and will leave their trash in the space, forcing the landlord to clean again before the actual user comes in. This practice, specifically for merchandise storage, should be discouraged in centers where there is no active sprinkler protection in the space. Many building and fire departments frown upon bringing merchandise in without active fire protection and are entitled to stop work on a project until it is corrected or levy fines.

If an opening center runs into staging or certificate-of-occupancy difficulties and semi trucks of fixtures and merchandise for multiple retailers are coming in, arrange for the semis to go into one section of the parking lot and be dropped off. Cordon the area off and put security there. If a staging problem occurs that requires storage of construction supplies, fixtures or finishes, those materials can go into empty spaces with less risk, since they are deemed construction. Tenant coordination should make it clear in all cases that they are not responsible for loss or theft of materials, that they are only trying to assist, and that materials must be removed promptly upon demand and the contractor is responsible for cleanup.

Depending upon the community, the design criteria of the center and the capability of the development team, additional challenges might need to be faced and resolved. Strong planning and communication in advance, based on the team's collective experience and the personality and demands of the particular mall, will better equip the coordination and construction teams to handle the unexpected emergencies that always occur.

15 Outdoor, Specialty and Community Center Challenges for Retail Coordination Teams

The bread and butter of the shopping center industry is not in the glamorous malls and gallerias or the challenging and exciting urban mixed-use centers. It is in the grocery chain–anchored centers.

Few shopping center developers who work primarily within this product line have Tenant Coordination departments or teams dedicated to projects unless they are opening a group of stores at once. In most cases it is the developer himself, his construction manager or a property manager who is handling the tenant coordination. However, many of the practices of tenant coordination apply to these products, and a successful implementation of a coordination program of some kind can add value to a property through consistency of design, minimalism of operational interference and earlier rent commencements. An owner and developer who implement and maintain a strong, policed design program also reap the benefit of increased value to

Grocery-anchored and neighborhood centers can benefit from a tenant coordinator's attention also. By making sure the landlord meets the obligations of the lease in a timely manner while also encouraging small shops to open quickly, Tenant Coordination adds value in terms of quicker rent commencement. They also help protect and enhance the value of a property through strict design reviews and construction oversight.

the center in terms of market value through increased rents, increased sales per square foot and higher-quality tenants.

The grocery chain–anchored centers are grouped with their more glamorous lifestyle counterparts because even though the product line and tenant mix are different, the unique requirements for tenant coordination and construction are similar.

Design Criteria

Today's lifestyle and power centers are being built by experienced developers who often take their standard design criteria and construction handbooks and write them to meet the demands of the project. However, owners of community and neighborhood centers can also produce these documents and utilize them as a standard throughout all their projects, with variations for the specific project highlighted or inserted.

Unlike malls and mixed-use centers, these types of centers typically do not demand as strict attention to the project's infrastructure, as the storefronts are usually installed in advance by the landlord and access to the utility connections is provided within the store. They also have their own back doors and usually do not share loading docks or elevators.

However, they do still require attention from a developer who wants to make sure that the stores conform to the overall vision of the project. Some of the information that needs to be shared includes the center's design theme, store location, location of utility connections and what is actually available for tenant use, unique signage requirements and any landlord control zone requirements. Additional information on the requirements of the municipality and design review codes is also helpful. For existing centers, a copy of the landlord's inventory of space and as-builds, if available, is also helpful.

Outdoor centers present their own set of challenges to landlords, such as making sure the landscaping complements the stores and does not fight with the tenant signage.

Design Criteria			
Types of Center	*Power Center, Big Boxes*	*Lifestyle and Specialty*	*Community and Neighborhood Centers*
Definition	Power centers are typically 200,000-plus square feet, with multiple big box tenants as well as grocery store or homestyle anchors. They have regional draw.	Lifestyle and specialty centers have entertainment components that are likely to be the anchors, along with specialty stores and restaurants	Community centers are larger grocery store–anchored centers around 100,000 square feet, while neighborhood centers are usually non-anchored collections of small service stores, typically about 50,000 square feet total, that serve the immediate needs of the neighborhood.
Design Criteria	Typically will concentrate on facade and front window merchandise presentations only. Demand conformity on exterior.	Complete design criteria packages specifying facade as well as interior presentations. Encourage unique touches in tune with the overall project design.	Typically will concentrate on facade and front window merchandise presentations only. Encourage conformity.
Signage	Landlord requires conformance to center design requirements, allowing for branding	Landlord encourages unique looks and applications within scope of project	Landlord requires size conformance and encourages use of professional design and installation
Engineering	Landlord provides drawings showing service availability and connection points	Landlord provides drawings showing service availability and connection points	Landlord provides drawings or written information stating what is available for use by tenant and locations

Design criteria that are supplemented by visual renderings, illustrated details and photographs are helpful to tenant design teams as they try to picture how their client's store is going to fit within the framework of the project. Tenant coordinators working with existing centers can also include actual photographs of the center, monument signs, adjoining tenants and any other details such as awnings and exterior furnishings if the tenant needs to provide their own.

TELL THE STORY

Developers working on larger properties are more likely to include information on the overall project vision with their design criteria to tenant design teams, especially if it is a unique lifestyle or specialty center encouraging unique touches from the tenants to help create a sense of place. This project vision, or "the story," should serve to encourage the tenant design team to think outside the box and create unique touches for their client's image that help meld the tenant's look into the landlord's vision.

Power center and neighborhood and community center owners should also "tell the story" in their criteria. While they are not encouraging the unique touches, it still helps the tenant design team immensely to understand what the project is about, who will shop there and what the developer expects.

Design criteria that include photographs or renderings of the center, the signage and landscape packages and unique design touches the developer is adding will help convey to the tenant design team what the developer is looking for from them. Tenant coordinators should also include some practical details such as how to tie into the center fire alarm systems, typical rooftop unit tie- or boltdowns, landlord controls on any exterior sign bands, requirements for installation of grease guards and traps and information on specific details the local municipality's plan reviewers will be looking for during the plan review permit process that will help expedite the permit.

The more information the landlord provides up front to the tenant, the quicker the plans can be produced and permitted and tenants opened for business.

ARCHITECTURAL SPECIFICATIONS

Theoretically, the architectural specifications for a lifestyle or entertainment center are going to be more demanding than for a neighborhood or community center. However, the quality of the tenant and their design and construction team tends to be better also, and they are more likely to understand the landlord's goals and work with them. The reality is, no matter what type of center you have, the independent operators are the most demanding. Tenant coordinators working on a lifestyle center might have a few independents or mom-and-pop operators who have to be educated and assisted in the design and construction process. Owners of neighborhood centers are typically dealing with the majority of their tenants in this manner and will ultimately be spending a lot more time working with them if they

Community center design and construction teams are faced with the same challenge of blending a tenant's branded looks into the context of the overall center design, as are their mall and lifestyle center counterparts.

decide to adhere to a comprehensive design criteria program to protect the value of their center.

In lifestyle and specialty centers, the design specifications will be more along the line of specifying ceiling types, signs, finishes and lighting within the merchandise presentation zones while still encouraging retail creativity. In neighborhood centers, the criteria will be stricter, requiring the use of one type of sign and installation, specifically stating what kind of flooring can be used and mandating that only professionally made signage can be posted. In either case, at no time should an assumption be made that the tenant design team knows the rules. The unique type of tenant desired for a lifestyle or specialty center is going to want to push the limits just as much as the independent in the neighborhood center, but for different reasons. Power centers will require less vigilance from a tenant coordinator's point of view, since the tenants tend to be national ones who value conformity as long as they can still present their branded image without too much interference.

Colorful storefronts and signage add to the entertainment feel. Awnings help to protect the storefront merchandise from harsh sunshine.

As in any other type of product, the more detail-specific information you provide in your design criteria, the less time you will spend answering questions and reviewing drawings or dealing with irate construction managers or store owners.

Landlords and tenants can add magic to what are standard retail boxes through the use of furnishings, landscaping, signage and well-lit storefront displays.

MECHANICAL REQUIREMENTS

Tenants in these types of centers do not share a lot of the same operating systems. Typically they obtain their electric, water and phone directly from central riser locations or landlord rooms. Occasionally they have their own transformers and risers dedicated just to them.

If multiple tenants share common access to automatic fire protection, sanitary, grease trap and domestic water lines, then the use of designated building contractors can make life much easier for landlords. If a landlord does plan to specify a designated contractor, then it needs to be stated in the design and construction criteria and even in the lease, if possible. Typically landlords will specify designated contractors for shared life safety systems such as fire alarm and sprinkler, or where there are critical warranties to protect on behalf of the landlord and all tenants such as roof and storefront.

Conveyance of accurate information to tenants about the location of utilities and what is being made available to them is critical. Occasionally a tenant design team will come back to a landlord and tell them that more power or water is needed than is available. This can result in large unexpected construction costs to the owners if the availability of services is promised to the tenant without someone from the landlord's team knowing in advance and researching availability before the lease is signed. Freestanding buildings and outparcels will often have drawings in the lease stating what their requirements are and where their building design dictates the utilities be brought to or in. Landlords who do not look at these attachments and research the impacts of promises made by signing agreements to do this, do so at great financial peril to themselves.

CONSTRUCTION ISSUES

Construction issues tend to be different in outdoor centers. Since they have their own entrances, especially back doors, and since the store-fronts tend to already be installed, once a tenant contractor checks in they usually do not have to fight for loading dock space or build barricades. They still require assistance and policing, but of a different sort.

Both new and existing centers should have construction handbooks available to give to the tenants when they are starting the bid-and-construction process. Handbooks for these types of centers will be more along the lines of "constructability" versus design or where to obtain landlord-required materials and supplies. Construction handbooks should contain information on when and if barricades are needed, requirements on public safety when working in common areas, information on coordinating tie-in to building systems that will require shutdown of other tenants and requirements on use of designated subcontractors. Including information on how to get automatic inspections called in, where the building department is located and how to get pre-power and meters set are also invaluable.

As a typical practice, construction handbooks should also protect the landlord with standard construction commandments including but not limited to:

- No storing of chemicals or flammables
- No gas-fired generators in nonventilated spaces
- Must use fire protection when welding
- Must adhere to OSHA standards and regulations
- Cannot use nonlicensed contractors and trades
- Must use designated contractors
- Must follow mall or center procedures when tying into life safety systems
- Must notify center management if tying into transformers or utility systems that will impact other tenants
- Cannot place non-fire-rated materials in concealed, nonsprinkled spaces
- Cannot make excessive noise during center operating hours

These handbooks become extremely useful to landlords who own several neighborhood or community centers and do not have on-staff operations teams to police tenant construction. If there is ultimately a problem with store construction and the landlord did not catch it, they can show proof that the tenant and their representative signed for the construction handbook and were responsible for adhering to the center's insurance and safety regulations.

Coordination of Moving Materials and People

Outdoor centers have fewer problems when it comes to coordinating getting materials and merchandise in. However, they still need attention due to the product type and the number of tenants moving in at one time.

If you have several tenants moving into a lifestyle center at one time, tenant coordination might need to be involved in scheduling truck and semi delivery times and creating holding areas for trucks. A lot of lifestyle centers have limited or small alleys, and use of a huge semi truck might be prohibitive because they simply cannot get into that area. That information needs to be conveyed to the tenant and their design and construction team as soon as possible because it can impact deliveries of fixtures and merchandise that are planned months in advance of an opening. If a fixture company knows this, they will build and package their cabinetry to fit into several smaller trucks. Likewise, the operations team will plan for several small deliveries and have people available to offload them, versus one huge delivery.

If a center is operational and the community bans semi-truck parking on-site, then the property management team might also need to make special arrangements with their tenants to find off-site parking for semis until the time comes, generally in the evening or early morning, when they can bring the truck in to offload at the back door or in a fire lane, with the fire department's approval.

Some lifestyle and power centers do have areas where tenants share offloading or fire corridors. If a center developer or owner has multiple tenants building out in an area or large shipments of merchandise coming in for a new store, then coordination between the operations teams, existing store and restaurant managers and property management will need to be made. These issues sometimes take a lot of time to work out and require huge amounts of tact, since open and operating tenants are not as flexible as tenants still under construction.

Occasionally contractors and operations teams have no choice but to bring things in through the front entrances or need to work outside their stores in the front. If this happens, then it is preferable it happen after hours, at night or early morning. Whenever it does happen the landlord needs to make sure the tenant cordons the area off with barricades and safety tape and that a public access area to get around or through is available. The tenant or their contractor might even have to put a flagman or safety-vested laborer outside the store to assist the public in getting around the fixture or merchandise offloading or construction work and to protect the employees doing the work.

Critical attention needs to be paid to the protection of center finishes, furniture, landscaping and amenities. Tenant coordinators, property managers and operations people have to ensure that the tenant contractor and store manager who are bringing deliveries in through common areas understand that they are responsible to protect all landlord's work and actually watch or spot-check them to make sure they do.

Construction Coordination

Developers and their teams who turn a blind eye to their tenants' construction issues and problems often get slapped in the head when tenants come back claiming that the landlord is holding them up from building out their stores. Occasionally this leads to litigation that could have been avoided through communication and common courtesy.

If a landlord sees potential issues impacting their tenant's construction or owes the tenant things through the lease, then it is the landlord's responsibility to sit down with the tenant in advance and try to create a plan that will allow the tenant to construct their store while offering the least amount of impact to other tenants under construction or open. If the coordination issues are extremely challenging, such as having to reroute major underground utilities or shut down transformers that impact other stores, then the land-

Freestanding buildings and outparcels have their own unique coordination issues, such as landscaping, paving and site work that the landlord might be responsible for but cannot complete until the tenant's work is done.

lord will need to have continued dialogue with not only the tenant doing the work, but other tenants that might be impacted. Occasionally the landlord should even take the burden of construction directly upon themselves and do work on behalf of the tenant, since the landlord's other tenants have the most to lose if work is not done in a timely or suitable manner. Developers need to keep in mind that tenants do not have obligations to one another and are not required to communicate with one another. That is the landlord's responsibility.

On-site Tenant Coordination, operations or property management teams need to be extremely vigilant in walking through tenant spaces while under construction, especially in dealing with independent tenants who do not have the most professional contractors. In outdoor centers where the systems are not as likely to be tied together, special attention still needs to be made to ensure that no undue structural stress is placed on the building and that fire walls are repaired. They also need to make sure that the tenant hooks into the right riser locations for electric, water and gas and does not try to steal additional services from other future tenant locations and that any work done in landlord rooms is complete and the rooms cleaned up and secured. Where there are shared systems such as sprinkler and fire alarm, the Developer's staff member needs to make sure designated contractors are used or that the tie-ins are carefully coordinated through the operations or management teams and other tenants alerted. They also need to make sure that no debris was flushed down into the sanitary lines, all permits are pulled and proper inspections made, damages to landlord areas are corrected and doors and thresholds are not damaged. Other things they might look out for are to make sure that debris is cleared off the roof and out of any docks and corridors, grease guards are used, if required, and condensate lines are properly hooked up and routed. Specifically, anything that might damage a landlord system, common area or shell or another tenant or cause a warranty issue needs to be looked at.

Tenant coordinators and operations teams involved in centers where constructions is going on between several stores and a base building contractor also need to make sure that all parties have met each other and are motivated to work well together. Often savvy retail tenant contractors can be asked or will volunteer to pool resources in a way that assists both the landlord and the tenants, such as utilizing one trash container company or hiring a crane operator to lift several stores' rooftop units up in one day.

Unique Issues

The unique set of problems specific to outdoor, specialty, lifestyle, neighborhood and community centers is more related to the tenant mix than constructability.

UNIQUE MIX OF TENANTS
Entertainment, lifestyle and specialty centers will have theaters and restaurants in their tenant mixes. These tenants require more assistance due to their size, life safety requirements and staging and deliveries.

Power centers have big box tenants that require strict adherence to their store prototype design and construction, especially if the landlord is doing a build-to-suit for them. It is extremely important that the developer and his Tenant Coordination team make sure that the architects and contractors doing the build-to-suit work understand that conformance to the lease is compulsory or will result in damages to their own client, the landlord.

Neighborhood and community centers have more mom-and-pops and independent operators, who require more handholding through the design, permitting and construction processes.

All of these centers require a lot of attention to their tenants.

Today's lifestyle and community centers feature a mix of big box tenants and smaller retailers. Lease requirements and obligations for the big boxes are stringent and require tight attention by the landlord to their design and construction team's progress.

UTILITY COORDINATION

Availability of utilities has to be watched as carefully in a power center as it does in a regional mall. The difference becomes the source of availability to get more utilities in and the impact on the site versus the impact on the existing building infrastructure.

If an outparcel tenant wants his sanitary connections to key in with his typical building design, a landlord might be forced to rework his entire underground sewer, which could have major impact and costs. If a freestanding tenant on a ground lease wants additional pairs of telephone cables, the landlord might have to go back to a separate telephone pull box to see if he can steal lines from another area, since the one closest to the tenant is already maxed. If a tenant needs more power than what is available through the current electrical room, the landlord might have to go back to the transformer and bring another new service in at another location. All of these coordination issues, that can be dealbreakers if a tenant cannot get what he wants, impacts the landlord and other tenants and need special engineering and permitting as well as construction coordination.

ON-SITE STORAGE

A lot of communities have it written into their design standards and ordinances that semi trucks cannot be parked on-site, or trailers left. If a tenant cannot fixture or open due to occupancy issues, the landlord might need to assist them in making separate arrangements to drop the trailers.

If a tenant needs construction storage, they might have to arrange to bring special containers or trailers in and leave them, which might require permission from the community. If a contractor wants to build a protected or fenced area for staging, he might need special permits. All of these issues might require at the very least landlord's permission from the municipality. At the most, the landlord might have to approach the building department themselves and ask for permission on behalf of the tenant.

OVERSIGHT OF CONSTRUCTION

Landlords with a lot of centers in their portfolio who do not have daily construction oversight particularly benefit from use of designated and preferred contractor lists. By specially designating who can work on your project in what capacity, you create many more pairs of eyes and ears to make sure that tenants are doing things the "right" way. A word of warning: if you use a designated contractor, you need to have "in file" a letter stating what their unit costs are so that you cannot be accused of price gouging or kickbacks. You also need to periodically shop preferred contractors to make sure the people you are referring are competitive and competent. At all times, there must be a hands-off position between a landlord and a preferred contractor. The tenants must understand that you are not in a relationship to benefit financially, and the developer must stay out of means and methods other than what is in the handbooks so that if there is a problem, you do not share in the liability.

Owners and developers of power centers, entertainment and lifestyle and community and neighborhood centers also share another similarity: limited staffs to handle the oversight of their projects coupled with tight public scrutiny from code enforcement and the community, who are particularly wary of landlords who do not have an active daily involvement in their project. If you are a developer who owns multiple centers but do not have active property management oversight on a daily basis on-site, use of a Tenant Coordination team to build a relationship with the community will help you and your leasing team immensely when it comes time to assist other tenants. Use of key designated contractors can also greatly enhance your relationship with the local authorities while downsizing your risk of having tenants damage key components to your infrastructure or common areas or create conflict with other tenants.

16 Working with Tenant Coordinators

Tenant coordination is a relatively new profession within the retail industry, and many tenant design and construction teams are not particularly sure how to work with them, especially since the role and responsibility as well as the skill set seems to vary between coordinators, depending upon the developer they work for and their own professional background.

This chapter is geared to tenant design and construction teams and explaining to them how to work with tenant coordinators. However, it can aid developers who would like to start a tenant coordination department or implement a tenant coordination program, guiding them through the implementation process.

What is the definition of a tenant coordinator? A professional consultant or staff member who bridges the gap between the landlord's development, construction and leasing team and the tenant's design, construction and operations team to get the tenant open. Tenant coordinators pick up when the lease is signed and transition the open tenant over to property management, who works with the tenant from that point forward.

Tenant coordinators are professional "generalists" with a broad spectrum of skills and knowledge about design, engineering, construction, legal, development and retail fields.

More specifically, the tenant coordinator is assigned the tenant, using the lease as a guideline, and instructed to assist the tenant through the obstacles of design, permitting and construction to ensure that they open in a timely manner, while hopefully maintaining a good relationship between all parties involved.

Tenant coordinators come from a variety of backgrounds and play different roles, depending on the developer they represent. Some different tenant coordinators a tenant might encounter could include:

- An in-house tenant coordinator who handles design review and construction oversight for a number of tenants on designated properties
- A third-party, professionally trained architect or engineer who writes criteria only
- A third-party on-site construction representative who oversees tenant construction and troubleshoots
- A tenant coordinator who specializes in lease administration and tracking but has no expertise in design or construction issues
- A leasing agent tasked with tenant coordination as part of their responsibility to the landlord and gets paid their commission only when the tenant is open
- A property manager handling a large portfolio who has some tenant coordination functions as part of his role
- A developer's construction manager who oversees construction for base building as well as landlord build-to-suit work
- A mall operations staff member who oversees operations and also watches over tenant construction

The background of a tenant coordinator will also vary, adding challenges to the tenant design team. A construction manager might be trained in project management and have some lease administration knowledge, but not understand retail mix or store identity and branding. Another tenant coordinator might be a trained architect but not be experienced in the field or understand operations and delivery issues. A field representative might know construction but be uncomfortable talking about the lease requirements or reviewing tenant plans.

Developers will hire according to the needs of their projects and the skills required by their management, construction and development teams. Tenant coordination can be extremely demanding. Occasionally talented team members work as tenant coordinators, seeing it as an opportunity to learn more about construction management, design or operations instead of recognizing that it is a rewarding and challenging profession in its own right. This is unfortunate for the retail industry in general, which benefits immensely from professional tenant coordination. Experienced tenant coordinators bring with them the benefits of improved relations with tenants, increased value from earlier rent commencements, better construction and site oversight, stronger relations with local municipalities and the immense benefit of hard-won experience gained from past projects.

Included below are suggestions and ideas for tenants and their design and construction teams, recommending ways on how they can tap into the value of the developer's tenant coordinator in order to assist them in their own work.

Architects and Their Consultants

One of the first things a tenant's architect should do is call and introduce him- or herself to the landlord's tenant coordinator. At that time, during casual conversation, they should endeavor to assess the particular experience the tenant coordinator has and what their role is in the project. Architects who find themselves working with tenant coordinators who do not have an architectural background should be prepared to use layman's terms. They might also realize the need to take a more active role in trying to understand the landlord's design criteria themselves instead of relying on the tenant coordinator

This store designer created a unique way of catching the customer's eye and adds to the overall interactive and high-tech look of the center. Mounted behind frosted storefront glass are laser lights that change color. Shown above, blue, and below, red.

who is coordinating the issuance of information to the tenant. If they find that they are dealing with someone with specialized architectural and design background, they might need to be more flexible themselves, realizing that the landlord probably has tough design criteria that they expect the tenant to live up to and advising his client accordingly.

> *"Tenant coordinators need to treat all tenants fairly and if concessions are made to one tenant, they must be considered for all. Fairness and conformity to the lease document are what makes the tenant coordinator's job a challenge."*
>
> JUDY MURTAUGH
> Director Site Information Management,
> Store Design and Construction
> Limited Brands

Architects and their consultants also need to realize that tenant coordinators often handle multiple projects at one time and do not carry the design criteria for one project in their heads. The average tenant coordinator working for a developer might have anywhere from 15 to 50 tenants they are currently dealing with. As such, they might experience some difficulty in contacting the tenant coordinator, who might have an extensive travel schedule or be in the field. When they do contact them, the tenant coordinator might have to research their questions and get back to the architect. With that in mind, one good practice is to compile a list of questions, fax or e-mail them to the tenant coordinator and make an appointment to review the design criteria or ask all the questions at one time. Tenant design teams that try to skirt around tenant coordinators and go to field operations teams or base building contractors will often find that they have to redo their plans, since while their information might be correct, it is not presented in the manner required by the lease.

Most tenant coordinators enjoy dealing with the tenant's design team and are happy to answer questions, give feedback and walk through comments they made on tenant plans. They do resent being spoken down to, since their skill sets might not be required to be the same as yours, and tact should be used. It is highly advisable that tenant architects make sure their mechanical engineers use tact if they call directly.

Tenant coordinators will lose patience if they get multiple calls from a tenant design team fishing for information. If your client has not passed on the design criteria and a copy of the lease or construction exhibits, try to get them before you call and review. If they simply withhold it for some reason or, more typically, lose it, since they too are working on a large number of projects, then call and request the criteria, explaining to the tenant coordinator what has happened. At that time the tenant coordinator will probably step up and give you even more information than just the criteria, appreciating the bind you are in.

Experienced tenant coordinators will hear alarm bells go off when the following things occur:

1. Hand-drawn plans are submitted, indicating that the tenant has hired an architect not committed to keeping up with current technology. That can be indicative of an architect committed to doing things only their way who will end up being difficult to deal with and will cost their client more time and money than necessary.

2. Argumentative engineers who do not read the criteria or drawings and then try to save face by getting the landlord to give them the additional exhaust, fresh air, power or whatever they need, instead of admitting to their clients that they made assumptions.

3. Design teams who sold their services cheap, refuse to send someone out to verify or look at as-build field conditions and expect the tenant coordinator to drop what they are doing and go look for them.

4. Architects who are offended by marked-up drawings with a request to resubmit instead of understanding that the tenant coordinator is just trying to offset problems as well as to protect his development and construction team.

Tenant Contractors

Over time experienced retail contractors get to know certain tenant coordinators and develop a rapport with them. Tenant coordinators will often appreciate that relationship and will not hesitate to call the principal of a firm if a particular superintendent does not perform as per expectation.

One of the most aggravating things a tenant contractor can do is not recognize that the coordinator is dealing with many tenants at a time and does not have the time to answer endless questions about a project or set of plans, particularly if those questions should be directed back to the store construction manager, as they are about construction issues.

When bidding, the tenant contractor should call with a list of questions in hand and be prepared to wait for a return call. Tenant contractors who call three days before bids are due and then tell the coordinator that they are holding them back from getting their work done do not get placed on referral lists when other tenants call looking for a good contractor.

The use of e-mail and fax machines to transmit questions in advance is a good practice—however, one-on-one phone conversations are still better because sometimes a coordinator will give you even more information if one question triggers another thought. This can give you the advantage in bidding.

Questions to ask include:

- Is the shell complete?
- Do I need to tie into landlord systems and, if so, where?
- Is the space empty or will there be demolition?
- Where will I get my construction utilities from?
- Where is the loading dock and do I have a back door?
- Are there operating tenants around me?
- Can I get a list of designated contractors?
- What are my fees?
- Is this a union job?

Some landlords have clauses in their leases that they have the right to approve who the tenant uses as a contractor. If that happens and you are requested for a brochure or an interview, be quick to comply or you might lose the work.

Once the work is awarded to you, tenant coordinators like the following to happen:

1. A certificate of insurance, properly filled out, is faxed to them, followed by a hard copy
2. A copy of your license and occupation license is sent to them
3. You schedule an appointment to bring the superintendent in to meet them
4. You bring with you all fees and deposits as well as signed paperwork

If your project is particularly challenging and requires landlord interface, such as completion of site work or provision of utility connections, scheduling a preconstruction conference with the tenant coordinator and their construction team is in order. Support yourself by having the tenant construction manager for your project present also, as well as the architect if needed.

Make sure your superintendent is well versed in working in retail environments and gives his cell phone or job site number and an emergency phone number to the tenant coordinator in case of a problem. If a tenant coordinator calls you with a problem about the superintendent, be aware that they usually will not go over the superintendent's head unless they are experiencing problems with them. Be prepared to address these issues accordingly.

Like any business, you will occasionally run into unscrupulous employees who ask for kickbacks or freebies. Tenant coordinators who do this are often not operating in the best interests of their company, and you are entitled to ignore requests that you feel are out of order. A lot of tenant coordinators are uncomfortable if you even offer a lunch. In the long run, tenant contractors who offer coordinators money, trips, or other large-ticket freebies will probably find themselves not working on another of that developer's products, just like the unemployed coordinator.

Tenant Construction Managers

Tenant construction managers might find this hard to believe, but most tenant coordinators feel empathy for them and appreciate the challenges their own particular jobs demand from them. That is why some highly qualified design and construction consultants prefer to work for developers over tenants. While tenant coordinators might be away from home for a period of time, they are usually not in a different city every day, weeks on end. Nor do they have to deal with the tenant's operations and merchandising teams, who appear to change things on a whim.

Tenant coordinators do see themselves on the same professional level as the tenant construction managers and architects and do expect to be treated with equal respect.

Tenant coordinators will sometimes go through an entire project without communicating with the tenant construction manager if the tenant's consultants and contractor are doing their job right. If not, the tenant coordinator will call the construction manager and let them know. Some tenant coordinators do like to speak with the tenant construction managers as a courtesy at the beginning of a project, particularly if they have not worked with that tenant before. The tenant coordinator and the tenant's construction manager can often avoid problems by discussing expectations in advance and creating a plan to expedite the review and construction process.

A tenant coordinator does not need to feel as if they are a part of your team. They have a responsibility to the landlord and do not like being put into the uncomfortable position of being asked to disclose project information detrimental to their developer or owner.

Tenant coordinators do not appreciate tenant construction managers who bypass them to fish for information from the tenant coordinator's general contractor. They especially do not appreciate it if the tenant construction manager gives direction to the contractor, thus resulting in additional expense to the developer. In respect to that, the tenant coordinator also has to be careful to not do the same thing and give direction to the tenant's design and construction team, resulting in increased costs to their client without the approval of the tenant construction manager.

Tenant construction managers, like their consultants, should also approach tenant coordinators when initializing a project to determine what their background and skill sets are. Tenant construction managers should understand that tenant coordinators have generalist experience from working with multiple tenants and their design and construction teams, whereas a tenant construction manager is required to work with only one product line, although with many contractors and locations. Tenant coordinators are required to keep as many balls in the air as possible for a wide variety of tenants on tenant projects in different stages of design and construction. Most tenant coordinators do appreciate hearing from tenant construction managers on a regular basis.

Tenant Operations

If a tenant coordinator is doing their job well, their interface with the tenant operations team is usually limited to an introduction and periodic visits to make sure everything is going well with the merchandising and opening. Unfortunately, problems do happen during construction and a tenant coordinator might end up working with the operations team, sometimes in an adversarial manner.

Operations teams working with tenant coordinators should understand that they usually have the same goals in mind, getting the store open. However, tenant coordinators do not like being put in the role of having to police tenant merchandising and operations teams who do not respect the tenant's own contractor, as well as the base building management, construction and management teams.

Until the store is fully approved to open by all governing authorities, the tenant coordinator is often prohibited from letting you take occupancy or open. If you force the issue and do so, your own contractor can be heavily penalized along with the center itself.

Some developers do not require their tenant coordinators to interface with the operations team for the tenant. In that situation, the coordinator will suggest you contact the property or mall management team directly.

A successful opening of a store or a project often results in mutual respect and appreciation that carries over into future projects. It is a small industry and incestuous in nature. Tenant design and construction teams that understand the role of the coordinator and endeavor to work in nonadversarial roles whenever possible will benefit through better communications, earlier store openings and a willingness to assist the tenant when flexibility or creativity is required to solve a problem.

17 | The Tenant Coordinator as a Key Member of the Project Development Team

The personality of a project is created by several components that are often in place before tenant coordination is even brought on board. The trick to successful coordination is taking the stack of cards dealt the team and making them work.

These cards can include:

- Location
- Type of product
- Team members and consultants
- Design criteria
- Requirements of the municipality
- Community concern and oversight
- Construction demands
- Opening time frame
- Nature of the retailers
- Ownership demands and funding

Tenant coordinators take these cards and work them into the overall game plan of getting tenants open. The unique knowledge and experience they bring to a team widens the perspective of the team so that each of these unique cards becomes part of the overall landscape of the project and each requirement is planned for accordingly.

Define the Tenant Coordinator's Place on the Construction and Management Team

Tenant coordinators and operations teams who are brought into the mix early have a larger scale of understanding of who the players are

and can often try to influence decisions that will make construction easier for their tenants or lower their future maintenance and operations costs. The construction teams for developers do not always think long-term in terms of facility management; they are more concerned about getting a project built on time and on budget. The goals of tenant coordinators and operational managers are often in conflict with the construction management mentality unless the developer realizes this and requests input during the planning stages.

Tenant coordinators bring a unique perspective to a development team focused on the end goal of getting tenants open for business.

Tenant coordinators who are brought into the game at a later date have the additional challenge not only of trying to understand the components of the project, but of also having to sometimes arm-wrestle their way into a seat at the table so that their concerns and requirements are listened to and addressed.

The nature of tenant coordination is to project future needs on the here and now. Development teams that take important tenant coordination milestones and use those as part of their scheduling will be more prepared for the reality of actually getting space turned over to tenants within the schedule of the lease obligations. The earlier a construction manager plans with the lease obligations in mind, the more efficiently he can predict if the team is going to need to revise their schedule or accelerate costs to meet lease obligations or go back to the leasing team or project financial controller to ask for extensions of time, renegotiate delivery dates, or ask for more financing.

Development teams that recognize that the Tenant Coordination team is an integral part of the knowledge base and success of the overall project will not have as many surprises when it comes time to turn space over to tenants and open up projects.

Samples of organizational charts of how tenant coordinators can fit into a project or development team

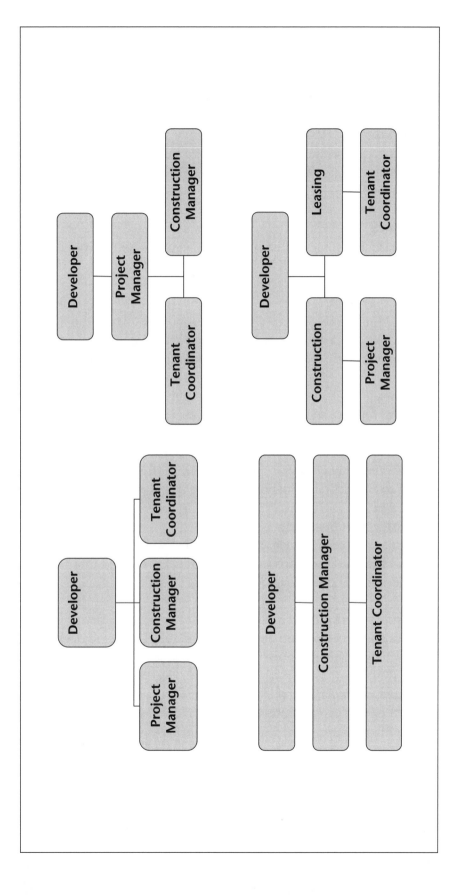

The Cards Development Teams Play With

Location:
Is the project located in the middle of a bustling city downtown or off a major cloverleaf or on the edge of a pier? How does that impact deliveries and staging?

Product:
Is it a stacked retail center in an urban area or a rural community center? What do we need to do to get people to the center and to the space?

Design Criteria:
Is it a three-page work exhibit or a four-color illustrated book? Is it available as a .pdf document on a Web page? Will the tenant plans require an extensive review that includes commenting on code-related issues, or will it consist of a spot check looking for utility locations and base building co-ordination? Will the municipality or community require a stamp showing landlord review and approval?

Local Oversight:
How does the community oversight impact the tenant and their design and construction? Work hours, visual displays, signage criteria?

Construction Demands:
Is it a union environment? Are there special mechanical requirements? What special inspections by the landlord are required that could impact their scheduling and costs?

Opening Time Frame:
Is this one large opening on a specified date or staggered openings after a shell completion or a one-on opening among already operating tenants?

Nature of the Retailers?
Are they independent operators who might need a lot of personal guidance? Big box tenants with specific prototype requirements? Chain store tenants with protected branding and national vendors to keep their operations consistent and simple?

Team Members:
What kind of control and who does each tenant have to interface with for plan review, inspections and communication? Is plan review internal or third-party? Does the tenant contractor have to work with the operations or on-site tenant coordination team? Does the tenant coordinator report to the developer, the construction manager or the leasing team? How much construction knowledge is expected of the tenant coordinator?

Ownership Demands:
Is it a hands-on owner that is interested and knowledgeable? Is it a small developer with limited resources and people? Does the owner intend to build and own long-term, or does he plan to sell and thus is not as interested in long-term operations?

Funding:
How does the construction funding work? What are the draw periods? How are the tenants' allowances scheduled and paid?

Receiving and Passing on Information in a Timely Manner

One of the biggest frustrations any tenant coordinator or coordination team can have is to not get the information they need to put together their opening plan or to create their design and construction documents and do their tenant plan reviews. Construction management teams that do not understand what the role of the tenant coordinator is and the type of information they need to perform their function impact the success of the center and its opening.

Tenant coordinators need to know as soon as possible the challenges and constraints of the projects that they are involved in so that they can react accordingly.

Tenant coordinators need to get the base building construction documents and develop a clear understanding of how the tenants will fit into the building framework. They need to know if there are special mechanical, electrical and plumbing requirements and testing and where the communications and electrical rooms are.

Tenant coordinators often have to negotiate with the local municipality to create special plan review processes or set up an expediting process. To do that, they need to know who the players are and be introduced to them. Sometimes tenant coordinators will end up having a better long-term relationship with the community than the other development team members due to the volume of interface they have with the municipality because of the number of tenants applying for permits. Construction teams that hold the tenant coordinator back from this interfacing can impact the success of the project.

Along with knowing the players, Tenant Coordination teams need a clear understanding of what the community requirements and construction restraints are in advance so that they can plan for any special needs and communicate to the tenants what they are. Tenant coordinators who are working in a vacuum from the rest of the design and construction teams cannot effectively assist their tenants in design and construction questions, resulting in confusion and poor landlord–tenant relations.

Tenant coordinators quickly prove their worth under tough challenges such as keeping retailers informed and open for business during renovations and expansions.

Designated contractors are another important source of the overall information a tenant coordinator needs. If there are roof or storefront warranties, the tenant coordinator needs to make sure the tenant is aware and that a procedure is in place to protect the building warranties. If a shell is still not finaled out yet and a tenant needs to make a change or tie into a base building system, Tenant Coordination has to know and coordinate through the base building contractor and their subcontractors so as not to impact final inspections or shell completion.

Tenant contractors working in sensitive electrical and mechanical rooms also need to be controlled to minimize damage as well as interruption of business to other tenants and operations. Tenant coordinators need to know who controls these systems and set procedures in place to supervise tenant contractors and their subcontractors when they are tying in. This is particularly critical when working with fire alarm systems and automatic sprinkler systems, where shutdowns and testing need to be coordinated with operations, monitoring companies, other tenants and fire departments.

Sharing Information with Tenants and Other Team Members

Tenant coordinators also have to make sure they are doing their part and letting the design and construction or management team know if there is information they need about tenants or lease obligations in order to make decisions or special arrangements. This information includes store delivery dates and requirements, impacts on staging and parking, over-sized equipment and millwork delivery dates, permitting issues and design and construction impacts the tenant has that will impact the project's base building contractor or operations team.

Tenant coordinators who attend project development team meetings can be invaluable as they share their experiences, which can be used for future planning. Since tenant coordinators tend to look out for delivery issues and be more experienced in the actual closeout of projects, the experience they provide can assist the project development team in long-range planning and construction issues. Tenant coordinators who are invited into the contractors' meetings can also provide insightful information geared toward getting tenant work coordinated and completed and tied into landlord systems, as well as sharing critical dates that need to be milestones in the project scheduling.

Large developers will often assign a lead tenant coordinator to a project and will have a reporting system already generated that the tenant coordinator uses to keep the development team current with required information. Third-party tenant coordination consultants will bring in their own reports and tailor them to the project or will utilize existing reports. Small developers and their tenant coordinators will often have to create reports, figuring out what will be needed as they proceed.

The more experienced the tenant coordinator is and the wider range of resources they have, the better they are able to assess at a glance what the project demands are or will be. Experienced tenant coordinators can create a reporting system to keep other team members informed of the lease obligations owed to the tenants, along with the status of key design, permitting and construction information.

Valuable Reports

There are certain tracking reports tenant coordinators ought to generate for their projects as standard procedure. These reports include key delivery dates, notices for delivery and dates of delivery, permitting,

> ### A Word of Advice
>
> Some developers want extensive reports. The more extensive and compli-cated they are, the harder it will be for the tenant coordinator to produce them during crunch times. Keep the reports simple and easy to fill out.

construction starts and certificates of occupancy and opening. These dates are needed not only for tracking the tenant's progress, but also for alerting the construction team for planning and for letting lease ad-ministration know if they need to be following up with delivery no-tices, defaults and rent commencements.

Other reports that can be invaluable, depending upon the project and its requirements, are:

- Tenant allowance and inducement forecasts for accounting
- "At-a-glance" status for leasing teams tracking progress
- Tenant lists with space addresses and permit numbers for internal use as well as for giving to local municipalities and fire departments
- Project directories for internal use with a list of tenants, architects, engineers and contractors
- Tenant lease abstracts with construction delivery and design re-quirements on one page for quick reference

An Appendix is attached in this book with sample reports and forms from various developers and projects.

Information Requirements				
Types of Center	*Mixed-Use and Residential*	*Malls and Regional Centers*	*Lifestyle, Specialty and Power Centers*	*Community and Neighborhood Centers*
Deliveries	Restricted hours and noise? Size of trucks? Front door deliveries? Narrow alleys?	Loading docks? UPS and FedEX front door deliveries during operations? Size of corridors and elevators? After-hours procedures?	Back-of-house procedures? Loading docks? Truck entries and paths?	Back-of-house procedures? Fire zones/lanes?
Staging and Parking	Where do they stage? Where can subcontractors park?	Is there empty space for fixture deliveries? Where are the trash containers?	If a big box opens, is there a requirement on the number of parking spaces available?	Where do the subcontractors park? Who polices parking in front of operating stores?
Design and Permitting	Are there requirements for window dressing and light levels? Is there a special community review along with the permitting?	Is there one expediter set up to handle permitting? Is there on-site review? Is there a stamp needed before plans can go to the municipality?	Are letters from the landlord required in order to allow the tenant to install their signs and pull permits?	Are letters from the landlord required in order to allow the tenant to install their signs and pull permits?
Construction and Inspections	Restricted work hours? Barricades? Required landlord inspections of tie-in to critical base building systems? Unions? Designated contractors?	Restricted work hours? Barricades? Required landlord inspections of tie-in to critical base building systems? Unions? Designated contractors?	Restricted work hours? Barricades? Required landlord inspections of tie-in to critical base building systems? Unions? Designated contractors?	Restricted work hours? Barricades? Required landlord inspections of tie-in to critical base building systems? Unions? Designated contractors?

18 | Tenant Coordination as a Career Choice

Professional recognition of the role talented and experienced tenant coordinators play is increasing in the retail construction and design industry. As more trained construction, design and operations professionals enter the field and stay in it as a unique and rewarding career choice, the diversity of skills required to perform the function are expanding and the needs for standardization of skills and training are increasing.

Professionals who can fill the demanding and rewarding role of a tenant coordinator are being increasingly sought after. Tenant coordinators are becoming recognized as powerful forces in their own right and expect equal footing on project teams with the project managers and construction managers.

Large development companies for malls have had tenant coordinators on board for a while and have set the standard to date for expected skill sets and experience. However, as more small developers see the increasing need for professional coordination of their projects, the skills of tenant coordinators will be more in demand and the variety of projects they are experienced in will increase immensely. Third-party consultants already bring to the table experience in multiple project types and demands and can quickly jump in to fill the gap of coordination on a complex project.

Tenant coordination as a unique career choice in a demanding and expanding industry is rewarding and challenging.

Creating a Tenant Coordination Department
by Martha Spatz

Tenant Coordination is an integral part of the retail real estate deal process. The TC department can usually be described as the last leg of a relay team. No matter how far behind any of the other departments get the deal, TC has to pick up the pace and get the deal, the store or restaurant, open on or before the required opening date. An effective tenant coordination program or department requires a group of individuals who like to work within time constraints and who can pick up the pace to a sprint when necessary.

Developing an effective tenant coordination program involves four basic stages, which together provide the groundwork for each TC team sprint:

1. Establishing a mission statement and goals
2. Creating a TC process for your organization
3. Structuring a TC Department
4. Finding and training a qualified core team

Stage One: Establishing a Mission Statement and Goals

Consider the steps involved in bringing a standard retail real estate deal from conception to store opening. A deal outline is the foundation for all aspects of the tenant coordination program and serves as the basis for developing the department's mission statement and goals. In business and management literature, "mission" and "goals" are sometimes used in various overlapping ways. Here, the deal outline might be compared to a course map for the "Real Estate Deal Race"; the mission statement, to the department's philosophy of running that race; and goals, to steps the department will undertake to win that race.

In addition to departmental mission and goals, each major project, such as a grand opening of a regional or lifestyle center, requires its own mission statement and goals. An on-site TC team will have a different mission than the corporate TC department. The TC department's mission and goals can serve as prototypes for each on-site TC team. Similarly, each stage in developing a TC program applies both to the TC department as a whole and to individual projects or teams within the department.

Without a mission and goals, department members will have no clear direction and may have difficulty explaining, to themselves as well as to others in the organization, what their department or team does; with these documents, employees will know—and be able to explain—where they are headed. A mission statement and goals also facilitate the remaining stages in developing a TC program.

Stage Two: Creating the Process and Developing Reporting Systems

Using the outline developed in Stage One, establish a preliminary flowchart including each step in the process. Record an estimated number of weeks required to complete each step. Once you have this preliminary flowchart, consider the various departments that impact your work flow. Add those departments' work to your preliminary chart, creating one master flowchart. Master flowchart in hand, meet with the other departments to agree on the flow and timing of all work.

The master flowchart can be modified for particular projects. The standard tenant coordination process involves these steps:

1. Review of deal and issuance of tenant package letter
2. Review of tenant's preliminary drawings
3. Review of tenant's working drawings

If there is a tenant coordinator on-site, then the steps below can be handled:

1. Conduct pre-construction meeting
2. Review tenant construction on a routine basis
3. Prepare final punch-list.

A stand-alone step that can be done either at the department level or at the team level:

1. Review request for construction allowance package

Some TC departments have more responsibility; some have less. Some have one person do all of the above steps for a deal; some have people assigned to specific tasks so that more than one person works on one deal. It is often most efficient to have one person handle a tenant's deal start to finish; the consistency of one person not only saves time, which equates with money, but prevents the tenant from playing one person against another.

Stage Three: Structuring the Department

STAFFING

There are five key roles that must be filled in a TC department:

1. A person with very good design sense
2. A person with very good technical knowledge
3. A very talented CAD person
4. A good leader
5. An administrative person who is extremely well organized and computer literate

Sometimes, due to the size constraints of the department, one person might need to fill more than one of these roles. On the other hand, all five roles must be filled in field offices that are created to handle one specific grand opening project, as well as in the corporate TC department staff. A tenant coordination staff must be balanced in design and technical strengths and function as a team sharing those strengths. This is true of both corporate and field-office staffs.

Before you start interviewing, clearly know the type of person that you wish to hire. Write a very specific job description. Review the job description in detail with the job applicant during the interview. Be certain that the applicant doesn't expect the job to be more—or less—than it really is. When interviewing for a tenant coordination position, applicants' expectations are at least as important as their previous experience. For example, a degreed architect who likes to design is likely to be frustrated in tenant coordination work, which involves review of designs, with occasional chances to suggest alternatives, but no opportunity to design projects from start to finish.

There is considerable discussion in the industry as to whether tenant coordinators should have architectural degrees, design backgrounds or construction backgrounds. Each company needs to find the proper mixture for their needs.

TEAM DEVELOPMENT

The TC department should be a team, with each person making up for the other person's shortcomings. Any individual working in the TC department should be:

- A good communicator, able to understand the message of others and convey their own
- Well organized
- Able to prioritize workloads
- Able to adapt to change
- Able to work with many different types of people
- Willing to set aside ego
- Able to work well under pressure
- Decisive yet flexible
- Focused on team, rather than individual, accomplishment

These final two characteristics are crucial and require some explanation. First, "decisive yet flexible": learning to recognize exactly when a deal is about to blow and knowing when to be flexible comes with experience. Good training and mentoring can help a tenant coordinator with this art; however, an open and flexible mind is key. Therefore, it is essential that every member of the TC team be flexible enough to yield when appropriate.

In addition, it is essential that each individual involved in tenant coordination work well as part of a team. The following interview topics help determine if a candidate will make a good team member:

- Describe a specific incident where you were a member of a team or group that accomplished a goal/task.
- What role did you play in accomplishing the goal/task?
- How did you work with others to accomplish the goal/task?
- With what kinds of people do you least like working?
- How do you deal with people with whom you don't like working?
- Describe an incident in which you were called upon to assist someone else in the completion of a task/goal.

Other aspects of finding and training TC team members are explored in Stage Four.

CONNECTIVITY

In addition to staffing, the computer network is an essential aspect of TC department structure. The TC department should either have its own computer network or be part of the company's network. At a minimum, each TC team member will need a computer that can be networked to the others in the department.

Depending on the location of the properties to be handled, some of the tenant coordinators might need laptops or at least a handheld

Blackberry. In current-day TC, the computer, scanner, PDF file, Auto-CAD, etc. have all become so integral to everyday work that a field office even needs an on-call computer tech person to keep their systems operating and their communications flowing. This is critical in a grand opening project, where losing one day of TC time could be life-threatening to the grand opening date.

Stage Four: Finding and Training Qualified People

FINDING GOOD CANDIDATES

Here are some ways to find a tenant coordinator:

- Contact all of your personal sources.
- Review the résumé file at your company. Sometimes there is a sleeper résumé in there that was never sent to you or human resources didn't think was suitable for the tenant coordination department.
- Ask the people who work for and with you for names of people who might be interested.
- Post the job on job-search Web sites such as careerbuilder or monster.com.
- Call your favorite college professor and ask if she/he knows anyone looking for a job.
- Run an ad.
- Promote from within your company or department.
- Contact architectural firms that you do business with and ask to review their résumé file.
- Contact the local AIA chapter and post your job description.
- Hire a headhunter.

Once you have received resumes, review them carefully to see if the person might be able to fulfill the job description that you have written. Remember to consider applicants' expectations as well as experience when interviewing and to seek candidates interested in teamwork.

After you have interviewed a number of candidates for your department and narrowed the selection to two or three, it is critical that you personally, not your human resources department, call their previous supervisors or professors. If you call only their character references, you will be getting only favorable recommendations. Previous supervisors or professors can supply you with information regarding quantity and quality of work, job responsibilities, cooperation, dependability, initiative, and relations with coworkers, but you have to ask the right questions. Try to speak to at least three references.

TRAINING TEAM MEMBERS

Training the person that you hire is one of the most important tasks in a successful tenant coordination program. As your organization runs the "Real Estate Deal Race," remember, your tenant coordinator will be the one taking the baton and running with it in your company's name. Do the training yourself or have the most competent person on your staff train the new person. If you do not do the training yourself, review the person's progress every two to four weeks: talk to the person doing the training and to the person who is being trained.

Training step one
Explain your TC department's mission statement and goals. This should not be a three-minute survey, but instead a thirty-minute discussion. Give examples of why these goals are important to your department and company.

Training step two
Explain the company's organizational chart, highlighting those with whom the tenant coordinator will interact. Personally introduce the coordinator to as many people as possible on their first day of work. It is critical that the new hire know which departments they will be working with on a daily basis.

Training step three
Outline, on a very basic level, how a retail real estate deal is put together and what purpose TC serves. Explain what you expect the coordinator to do at any point in tenant communications when it becomes clear that some part of the negotiations are not going well.

Training step four
Refer again to the job description for which they were hired and explain each task in detail; where appropriate, physically walk the trainee through the process for each task. Explain clearly what task they are expected to self-perform and what can be delegated and to whom.

Training step five
Explain in detail your TC department's process and flowchart. Discuss each step, including standard forms of communications that are associated with those steps.

Training step six

Discuss your department's philosophy on key items such as e-mail, telephone answering, voice mail, cell phones, returning calls, returning e-mails, written correspondence, etc.

Ongoing training

Try to bring the coordinator with you to as many meetings as possible during the first six weeks, just to observe. After the meeting, make sure you allow five or ten minutes for them to ask you questions about what went on.

During the first six months, try to attend all meetings in which the new coordinator is required to report. Listen to what the new employee is saying and doing, but don't take over the meeting.

The best way to nurture a new employee is to talk with them frequently. Try to get a sense if they are catching on to their new job and if the people that they have to work with are giving them the needed respect. If you do talk to the person face-to-face on a weekly basis, you will most likely be able to ascertain whether they are grasping what is important about the job. If you can't tell if they are grasping what is important, start the discussion this way:

- Ask them to tell you a story about their interaction with a tenant or tenant's architect or tenant's contractor.
- Ask them for an example of when they have had to be decisive and one when they have had to be flexible.
- Ask them if they can give you an example of the department's mission statement in action.
- Ask them for an example of how they have met one of the department goals.

Carefully selected, well-trained and nurtured TC team members coupled with a well-defined mission statement and goals, as well as a clearly stated master flowchart, are the key components in developing an effective tenant coordination program. Once these key components are in place, the TC department or team is ready to take up the final leg of the "Real Estate Deal Race," no matter how far behind they may be when they are passed the baton.

Glossary

Center Definitions

Community Center A community center typically offers a wider range of apparel and other soft goods than the neighborhood center. Among the more common anchors are supermarkets, super drugstores, and discount department stores. Community center tenants often include value-oriented big-box category-dominant retailers selling such items as apparel, home improvement/furnishings, toys, electronics or sporting goods. The center is usually configured in a straight line as a strip, or L, or U shape. Of the nine most common center types, community centers encompass the widest range of formats.

For example, certain centers that are anchored by a large discount department store often have a discount focus. Others with a high percentage of square footage allocated to off-price retailers can be termed off-price centers. These centers range between 100,000 and 350,000 square feet of gross leasable area encompassing 10 to 40 acres and the primary trade area is between 3 and 6 miles.

Galleria An arcade of shops typically anchored on both ends with high-end department stores. Gallerias tend to be associated with high-end tenant mixes.

Grocery-Anchored Centers Strips of shops, typically 100,000 to 150,000 square feet, with a large parking field where the main destination anchor is a grocery store. Tenants tend to be convenience- and service-oriented, such as pool companies, drugstores, cleaners and restaurants. Tenants tend to be independent franchisees.

Lifestyle Center   Most often located near affluent residential neighborhoods, this center type caters to the retail needs and "lifestyle" pursuits of consumers in its trading area. It has an open-air configuration and typically includes at least 50,000 square feet of retail space occupied by upscale national chain specialty stores. Other elements help make the lifestyle center serve as a multipurpose leisure-time destination, including restaurants, entertainment, and design ambience and amenities such as fountains and backyard furniture that are conducive to casual browsing. These centers may or may not be anchored by one or more conventional or fashion specialty department stores. These centers range between 150,000 and 500,000 square feet of gross leasable area encompassing 10 to 40 acres and the primary trade area is 8 to 12 miles.

Mixed-Use Center   A center that consists of well-integrated entertainment, office, hotel, residential, recreation, sports stadium, cultural venues, and/or other uses that mutually support a substantial retail component.

Neighborhood Center   This center is designed to provide convenience shopping for the day-to-day needs of consumers in the immediate neighborhood. These centers are often anchored by a supermarket and/or a drugstore anchor. These anchors are supported by stores offering drugs, sundries, snacks and personal services. A neighborhood center is usually configured as a straight-line strip with no enclosed walkway or mall area, although a canopy above the storefronts may provide shade and protection from inclement weather. These centers range between 30,000 and 150,000 square feet of gross leasable area encompassing between 3 and 15 acres, and the primary trade area is about 3 miles.

Outlet or Value-Oriented Centers   Centers that feature discount or off-price stores.

Power Center   A center dominated by several large anchors, including discount department stores, off-price stores, warehouse clubs, or "category killers," i.e., stores that offer a vast selection in related merchandise categories at very competitive retail prices. The center typically consists of several anchors, some of which may be freestanding (unconnected) and only a minimum amount of small specialty tenants. These centers range between 250,000 and 600,000 square feet in gross leasable area encompassing 10 to 50 acres, and the primary trade area is between 5 and 10 miles.

Regional Center   This center type provides general merchandise (a large percentage of which is apparel) and services in full depth and variety. Its main attractions are its anchors: traditional, mass merchant or discount department stores, or fashion specialty stores. A typical regional center is usually enclosed, with an inward orientation of the stores connected by a common walkway, and parking surrounds the outside perimeter.

Regional Malls Indoor centers anchored by two or three department stores, typically up to 1 million square feet.

Superregional Malls Indoor centers anchored by three or more department stores and anchors. They have a larger regional draw to customers and are typically over 1 million square feet.

Upscale Mall or Center A shopping destination with high-end retailers.

— A —

ADA Americans with Disabilities Act, which gives federal requirements for accessibility to buildings by people with physical handicaps.

Adaptive Re-use Adapting a building for retail use. Examples: old factories, school buildings, and warehouses are, sometimes turned into outlet retail projects.[1]

Additional Insured An additional person or entity, other than the primary policyholder (entity covered by the policy), who has certain rights and coverages under the policy.

Administration Fee The cost of actually administering the common area of a shopping center; a standard addition to the overall cost of common-area maintenance (CAM), typically set at 15 percent of tenant CAM contribution but may vary due to negotiation between landlord and tenant.

AIA Document Billing form typically used in the construction industry, produced by the American Institute of Architects.

Anchor Store A major store (usually a chain store) in a shopping center having substantial economic strength and occupying a large square footage. A major department store branch in a shopping center. The stores and other users that occupy the largest spaces in a center and serve as the primary traffic generators. Freestanding anchors are excluded.[1]

As-Built Plans   The final blueprints used by an architect when constructing a shopping center or tenant space. As-builts contain the most up-to-date information about a center.

As-builts are a final record set produced by contractor or architect to show what was actually built.

— B —

Back of the House or **Back Room**   Nonselling area of a store that includes stockrooms, restrooms, etc. Commonly referred to as BOH.[1]

Big Box   A single-use store, typically between 10,000 and 100,000 square feet or more, such as a large bookstore, office-supply store, pet store, electronics store, or toy store.[1]

Black Box   Minimum amount of work provided to a tenant by a landlord. Basically, it is a concrete slab, walls and roof.

Blackout Days   Refers to days when tenants are not required to accept delivery of store space from a landlord or to open. Usually a block of dates that are tied into their operationally busiest seasons. Most typically, blackout dates will occur from October through January, although blackouts during spring season selling periods for fashion are not uncommon.

Building Permit   The official permission granted by the local municipality or authority to begin construction on a building or sign. It is typically granted in written form, such as an oversized card that must be posted at the job site.

Build-to-Suit   When a landlord agrees to build out a store 100 percent to tenant specifications, including fixtures and finishes.

Business License   This is a written approval to open a business in a county or municipality; recognition of a business as a taxable entity. Some communities require both business and occupational licenses.

Business Plan   A detailed, carefully prepared road map for the operation of a business for the coming year or years; it sets a direction and destination (strategy) for the business and plots the course (tactics) to get there. Typically contains operations, marketing, leasing development, and a financial plan.

— C —

CAD   Computer-assisted drawings.

Can Signs   Signs that are built as one big box and have the letters or logo applied as an art element to the exterior finish, typically vinyl to acrylic. They are usually internally illuminated.

Cash-Wraps The front counter/checkout area of a store or retail merchandising unit (RMU) that houses the cash register and wrapping section.

CDP (Certified Development, Design and Construction Professional) A professional designation granted by ICSC to practicing shopping center professionals who achieve a passing score on a comprehensive examination. The designation stands for competency gained from knowledge and experience.

CenterBuild Annual conference for design and construction professionals within the shopping center industry.

Certificate of Completion A document that is issued by a local government or municipality to a developer stating that the building construction has complied with code standards and is considered complete as per the building plans by the local municipality. Completion does not mean occupancy can occur, and additional permits for interior work with inspections must be completed before occupancy will be granted. Also known as C of C.

Certificate of Insurance A document that is evidence that an insurance policy has been issued. A document that verifies the type and amounts of insurance carried by a policyholder.[1]

Certificate of Occupancy A document issued by a local government to a developer permitting the structure to be occupied by members of the public. Issuance of the certificate generally indicates that the building is in compliance with public health and building codes. Also known as CO or C of O.[1]

Channel Letters Referring to signage, these are individual letters constructed as cans that have their own internal illumination and are attached directly to a wall or building facade. The letters are usually strung together electrically inside the building facade and then tied back to an electrical power source.

Charge-Back The process for a landlord to recover expenses, e.g., CAM, real estate taxes, utilities, work done to tenant space, chilled water charges, through billing the tenant its share of the costs according to the lease agreement. Also known as bill-back.

Common Area The walkways and areas onto which the stores in a center face and which conduct the flow of customer traffic.

The portions of a shopping center that have been designated and improved for common use by or for the benefit of more than one occupant of the shopping center.

Common Area Maintenance (CAM)   The amount of money charged to tenants for their shares of maintaining a center's common area.

The charge that a tenant pays for shared services and facilities such as electricity, security, and maintenance of parking lots.

The area maintained in common by all tenants, such as parking lots and common passages. This area is often defined in the lease and may or may not include all physical areas or be paid for by all tenants.

Items charged to common area maintenance may include cleaning services, parking lot sweeping and maintenance, snow removal, security, and upkeep.

Construction Allowance   Money or financial incentives given to tenants for the cost of constructing their store space in a center. Construction allowance is also known as *tenant allowance* or *tenant inducement payments*. Generally determined at an allowance per square foot, based on what the tenant feels they need to build out their store, although sometimes determined by credit for work landlord did not do for tenant based on formulated unit pricing.[1]

Construction Criteria or Handbook   Information or criteria provided to tenants and their contractors, including specific rules and regulations of the mall for construction as well as information relating to where to find items required by the mall, such as matching floor tile, or who the designated contractors and mall contacts are.

Construction Days   Leases that allow for a tenant to have a certain number of days for buildout before their rent payments commence. Typically it is 60, 90 or 130 days. See **work period**.

Construction Draw   Financing tool for when a tenant or landlord makes an application for a partial payment against a total amount set aside by the landlord for the tenant under the lease or by the lender to the landlord as part of their construction financing.

Construction Drawings   Another term for architectural plans.

Construction Exhibit   The section of the lease that refers to or outlines tenant and landlord obligations in respect to what each is constructing or expecting from the other.

Construction Management   Construction management is a form of contracting. The construction manager acts as an agent for the developer or owner, taking no risk or financial responsibility for the outcome of the project, which is different from the responsibilities of a general contractor. The construction manager supervises, coordinates, and administers the work on behalf of the developer; however, all contracts are executed directly between the various trade contractors and the developer, with the construction manager signing as an agent of the owner. The construction manager might hire a general contractor or enter into multiple prime contracts with a variety of trade contractors. In either case, if there is a loss or overrun, the dispute is between the developer and the trade contractors, not between the developer and the construction manager.[1]

Construction Manager (CM)   An agent of the owner who supervises, coordinates, and administers construction work on a new project, renovation or redevelopment but takes no risk or financial responsibility for its outcome, unless hired as a construction manager at risk.

Consultants   Typically refers to the architects, engineers and planners involved in the design, permitting and construction of work. Typical use by an owner is "the consultants" as in relation to "the contractor."

Contractor's License   Most communities require general contractors to pass stringent exams and have personal recommendations and financial resources before giving them a contractor's license. Licenses ensure building owners of the professionalism and competency of contractors performing work. Unlicensed contractors, while often competent, do not have the same requirements and are not allowed to pull building permits.

Corporate Store   Occasionally franchisors will option to build a store within their formula but choose to run it themselves versus selling it as a franchise.

Co-Tenancy   A term that refers to a clause inserted into a tenant's lease stipulating that a reduced rent or no rent be paid until an agreed-upon percentage of the center is occupied.

CSM (Certified Shopping Center Manager)   A professional designation granted by ICSC to practicing shopping center professionals who achieve a passing score on a comprehensive examination. The designation stands for competency in shopping center management gained from knowledge and experience.

— **D** —

Date of Possession (DOP)   Date a space is deemed as substantially complete or complete and is turned over to the tenant or lessee to begin work. Date of possession is often referred to in a lease as *delivery date* also. The date of possession is the date the tenant can legally enter the space to start their own work and also the date that kicks off rent commencement and utility takeover by the lessee.

Default   The failure to perform on an obligation previously committed to. For example, failure to pay rent on a specific date may place a tenant in default of obligations under his lease.

Failure to comply with the terms of a lease.

Delivery Date   See *date of possession.*

Demising   Generally used to determine the separation of tenant spaces. Walls that separate tenant space.

Design Criteria   A number of different elements set out in a center's design criteria manual, including guidelines for store design; mechanical, electrical, plumbing, and structural requirements; and the different responsibilities of tenant and landlord.

Design Review   Review of plans submitted by the tenant architectural and engineering team to check to make sure they have incorporated landlord criteria and match base building requirements such as utility locations and availability.

Designated Contractors   Trades or contractors that tenants are required to use to protect the developer and tenant from violating warranties on the building or to protect the landlord and other tenants from damage to critical life safety or mechanical equipment and systems such as fire alarm, fire sprinkler, chilled water systems, roof, storefront or electrical distribution centers.

Development Team   Team of managers and consultants put together by a project owner to gain development and construction approvals for a project and to oversee design, construction, leasing and turnover to the operations team.

— E —

Estoppel Letter   The tenant or the landlord represents as to the current relationship of the tenant and landlord; that is, an estoppel letter will be set forth whether there are any defaults or whether rent has been paid in advance. This document would have each party agree that the lease is in full force and effect and that no covenent has been breached.[1]

Exclusives   A term referring to a store's being given the exclusive right to sell a particular category of merchandise within a shopping center. An existing tenant may have negotiated the right to be the only one in the center to offer particular goods or services, and therefore space may not be leased to another tenant offering the same goods or services in competition with the first tenant.[1]

— F —

Field Verification   Requirement that someone goes to the project site and actually inspects the premises for what is in place and where it is located. Also know as *site verification.*

Finish Board   Board that has samples of finishes tenant intends to use, such as carpet, tile and paint colors.

Fire-Rated   Stamped or approved or designed to withstand collapse or disintegration by fire usually for a unit standard of time such as 1, 2 or 4 hours.

Fire Wall   An interior or exterior wall that turns from the foundation of a building to the roof or above, constructed to stop the spread of fire.

Fixture Plan   Construction coordination plan or drawing showing layout of fixtures and display elements, including signage.

Fixtures   Racks and display furnishings for merchandise.

Franchisee   A business operator who has bought into a formulated business program for a type of store and has agreed as per the franchise agreement to run the business according to the formula prescribed.

Franchisor   The business operation that has created a formula for a store, including operations, advertising, image and training, and sells it as a package to an independent store operator.

Freestanding Building   Building that stands by itself within a planned development. The parking, site development and landscaping are typically provided and maintained by the developer or landlord up to a designated area such as five feet outside the building pad. The building usually has to blend in with the accepted overall center-approved design.

— G —

General Conditions   Indirect costs primarily covering the contractor's on-site staffing and management; for example, preconstruction services, field superintendent, contractor's project manager, field office, temporary utilities, and the like.[1]

General Contractor (GC)   A person who manages the construction process, holds the prime subcontracts, and guarantees completion for an agreed-on cost.[1]

Guaranteed Maximum Price (GMP)   An amount fixed in a contract, setting a limit on the reimbursement to the contractor for the cost of the work plus a fee; this hybrid of lump sum and time-and-material contracts has most of the advantages of the other types with few of the disadvantages.[1]

— H —

Halo Lighting   Referring to signage, halo-lit signs are mounted away from the face of a wall and the light escapes from the back of the sign or individually mounted letters to create a gentle wash of light around the letters or sign.

Hard Costs   The brick-and-mortar elements of a redevelopment project, such as the land, the building, and building improvements; excludes architectural fees, overhead, etc.

Heating, Ventilation, and Air-Conditioning (HVAC) Units   Fairly large machines that handle all the heating, cooling, and ventilation uses associated with a center.[1]

High End   Refers to tenants offering better-quality and/or exclusive merchandise at higher prices.[1]

— I —

Impact Fees   Fees charged by utility companies to tie into their services before they will commence monthly service. Impact fees can also be levied for roads and schools to offset the cost of new infrastructure to support development.

— J —

Junior Department Store   A store that, in both size and selection of merchandise, can be classified as being between a full-time department store and a variety store.[1]

— K —

Kickout Clause   An option that allows a landlord or tenant to terminate the lease before the end of the term. In the tenant's case, generally tied to the presence of another retailer.

— L —

Labor   Costs of manpower invested in a construction project.

Labor Harmony   A polite way of stating that if a project has unionized labor, then the tenant must make sure their contractor understands and hires the right subcontractors to ensure that there is no work disruption.

Landlord Control Zone   An area, typically at the entrance to the store, where the landlord specifies lighting, signage, display and merchandise requirements.

Lease   A contract transferring the right to the possession and enjoyment of property for a definite period of time.

The signed agreement between landlord and tenant that establishes responsibility, sets standards, and states what is recoverable from tenants for the maintenance process.

Lease Abstract   A short version of a lease, containing the most important facts about it in order to facilitate later reviews (for example, by new employees).[1]

Lease Commencement   Date lease goes into effect, usually execution date. It can be different from the rent commencement date.

Lease Exhibit   The section of the lease that refers to a particular item, such as location of premises on a siteplan, signage or construction responsibilities.

Lease Outline Drawing (LOD)   Material prepared for the tenant, showing the demised space and its relation to adjacent spaces and the center as a whole; electrical, plumbing, HVAC, and waste line entry points are identified, but existing partitions and fixtures are usually not shown.

Letter of Intent (LOI)   Generally a document submitted prior to a formal lease. It serves to delineate the intentions between the landlord and the tenant. Basic issues, including minimum rent, percentage rent, pass-through expenses and other major points of negotiation, are outlined. Generally subject to execution of a complete contract. The expression of a desire to enter into a contract without actually doing so. A letter that a tenant will send to a landlord indicating interest in signing a lease and what terms they will be looking for, including construction requirements.[1]

Lien   A charge, security, or encumbrance upon property for the payment of a debt.[1]

Life Safety   Refers to building systems that warn the public or help to assist the protection and evacuation of the public in an emergency, such as fire alarm and automatic fire sprinkler protection, emergency exit locations, signage and lighting and rated walls and stairwells. Typically life safety systems are inspected by electrical, mechanical, building and fire inspectors independently. See **NFPA.**

Light Boxes   Large internally illuminated sign boxes mounted on walls that are covered by translucent film with photographic illustrations, or that have a front door into which posters are slipped inside and front-lit.

Low-Voltage   Term used to refer to electrical equipment usually provided by tenants' vendors for cash registers, computers, telephone and security systems and signage. Typically run off of 110 volts and installed by low voltage–licensed vendors, requiring plug-in of final equipment and some cabling. Usually under separate contract from electrical equipment that is hard-wired directly back to an electrical panel by a licensed electrician. Some communities require permits for low-voltage work.

— M —

MEP   Mechanical, electrical and plumbing.

Merchandise   The goods or items that a retailer sells.

Merchandise Plan   A forecast, usually by months for a six-month season, of the major elements that enter into gross margin. It normally includes the planning of sales, stocks, purchases, markups, and markdowns.

Milestones   Critical dates within a project's timeline.

Mom-and-Pop Store   A store whose owners own only that single store. A common description of independent stores owned by entrepreneurs.[1]

— N —

Named Insured   The person or business entity designated on a policy as being insured.[1]

National Tenant   A retailer who operates a chain of stores on a nationwide basis.[1]

Negotiated Contract   A contract arranged on some type of fee basis plus costs with a cap, or guaranteed maximum cost. The fee covers the contractor's indirect (off-site) overhead and profit, while the costs cover all the other elements, such as labor, material, subcontracts, and job site supervision.[1]

Neutral Pier   The exterior separation controlled by the landlord between two tenant spaces, particularly in reference to regional malls.

NFPA   Building inspectors inspect as per the local building codes. Fire inspectors inspect as per the National Fire Protection Association and their collective codex of life safety code. Generally life safety issues will overrule building codes. See **Life Safety.**

Notice of Commencement or Notice to Owner   Some communities require that before work begins on a property, the legal ownership entity be notified and made aware.

— O —

Occupational License   Paperwork that registers official approval by the local municipality or authority showing that the tenant has registered with them and is approved to open their type of business within that municipality. Service tenants such as health care professionals, health clubs and restaurants often come under separate business regulations from retailers and need to undergo more stringent requirements to get an occupational license in hand.

OSHA   Occupational Safety and Health Administration.

Outparcels   Unused portions of a shopping center's site that constitute the perimeter areas, not including the center facility or parking lot, and that may be used or developed for similar or nonsimilar purposes.

Outsource   When a third-party consultant is utilized to perform functions needed by a developer or management team.

Owner's Representative   A person who represents the owner's interests on a project or works as an owner's agent on their behalf.

— P —

Pad   The exact parcel of land on which a department store's building stands.

Point of Sale Promotional materials displayed in a store near merchandise for sale, usually in close proximity to the cash register. When a center can include a company's logo or information on signage placed inside stores as part of a mall-wide program, this increases the value of the partnership program to the sponsor.

Project Management The organized, systematic approach toward planning, organizing, and managing the process of design and construction. A project manager operates as an agent on behalf of the owner.[1]

Project Manager The person who oversees the consultants and contractor to bring a project to successful completion.

Prototypical Drawings Plans and specifications build-to-suite tenants provide to the landlord to create their own construction drawings from.

— R —

Raceways Boxes that contain wire for tenant signage that sits on top of the building facade. Sign letters are mounted on it.

Redevelopment Usually a compehensive action that may include extensive leasing activity, renovation, expansion, and/or reconfiguration, but that typically substantially changes the leasing and marketing direction of an existing center.[1]

Regional Tenant A retailer who operates stores in a particular region of the country.[1]

Relocation Clause A lease clause that gives a landlord the ability to move the tenant to another location within the shopping center premises.[1]

Renovation Improvements or modifications of existing features of a shopping center, such as new ceiling, floor and wall surfaces, the addition of skylights or fountains, the redesign or addition of restrooms and other amenities, landscaping, furnishings, upgraded lighting, and resurfacing of parking spaces.[1] Renovation is usually undertaken as part of a redevelopment.

Rent Commencement This is the date the landlord can expect to start receiving rent. It can be different from the date the lease is executed and is usually tied into the day the store actually opens or the time the tenant has to complete their construction work.

Romex   Type of electrical conduit.

RTU   Rooftop systems

— S —

Shell   Basic building that houses tenants. *Shell* typically refers to roof, slab and exterior walls and storefront as well as any building systems that service the building as a whole, such as fire alarm and fire risers and roof drains.

Signage Criteria   Design criteria specifically written to give the guidelines of what will be acceptable to the landlord and community for the design of exterior signage.

Site   A specific tract of land proposed for center development, exhibiting qualities of size, shape, location plus accessibility, and zoning, and suited for the development of a center.[1]

Site Verification   Requirement that someone goes to the project site and actually inspects the premises for what is in place and where it is located. Also known as *field verification*.

Size Certification   Document from an architect, signed and sealed, stating that they have measured a space. Some leases have clauses requiring size certification; not all leases use the same means and methods in coming up with a size.

Soft Costs   Architectural fees, interest on loans, payroll, and indirect expenses in a redevelopment project.

Stacked Tenants   Tenants located over or underneath each other in a building.

Storefront Elevation Drawing   A plan that shows the tenant what the exterior front facade of the store looks like.

Substantially Complete   The condition of a store space that the landlord is ready to turn over to a tenant for them to begin work. The space might not always be complete, but it is considered substantially so if the tenant can work unhindered by the landlord and if it is considered watertight.

— T —

Technology Rooms   Operations rooms in a project where the building information systems are routed and maintained. More sophisticated projects will have building engineers stationed in them and will be monitoring air flow, chilled water and steam heat, security and telephone and Internet communication systems. Some malls will simply have phone rooms where telephone lines come into central distribution banks and then are distributed to tenant spaces.

Tenant Allowance (TA) A provision sometimes made by landlords to build a tenant space or provide rent concessions, even free rent, for a period of time to induce the tenant to lease.

Tenant Coordinators Staff members who oversee the transition of tenants from the point the lease is signed until a store is open. Generally charged with lease administration and design and construction responsibilities to make sure the stores are designed and built as per landlord's requirements and that the terms of the lease are met and fulfilled by both the tenant and the landlord.

Tenant Improvements Building improvements that enhance a tenant's space. May be paid for by either landlord or tenant and induce the tenant to lease. See **tenant allowance.**

Tenant Inducement See **construction allowance.**

Turn Key The landlord builds and finishes out a retail space; the tenant shows up with merchandise and is ready for business.[1]

Turnover (U.S.) The ratio of annual sales to inventory, or the fraction of a year that an average item remains in inventory. Low turnover is a sign of inefficiency, since inventory usually has a rate of return of zero. Also known as stock turns. (U.K.) Retail sales of a shopping center tenant, usually referred to as annual turnover sales.

Turnover Date Specific date when the space is considered complete as per the lease obligations and the lessee is notified in writing that the space has been deemed complete and is now being turned over into their possession. See also **date of possession.**

— U —

Utility Connection Points or **Points of Connection** Landlords are generally required to deliver to tenants the ability to hook up to utilities. Often the locations of these hookup points are actually defined in a lease or on a lease or construction prototype document within a lease.

— V —

Vanilla Box A space partially completed by the landlord based on negotiations between tenant and landlord. Although every landlord's definition is different, a vanilla box normally means HVAC (heating, ventilation, and air-conditioning), walls, floors, stockroom wall, basic electrical work, basic plumbing work, rear door, and storefront.

Vertical Transportation This refers to elevators and escalators; how to get people, freight and merchandise up and down within a project.

— W —

White Box A space partially completed by the landlord or licensor based on negotiations with the tenant, and usually including HVAC (heating, ventilation, and air-conditioning) systems, walls, floors, a stockroom wall and door, basic electrical and plumbing work, a rear door, and a storefront; also called a *vanilla box*.

Work Period The time that the landlord gives a tenant to construct the store, usually without paying rent; anywhere from 60 to 180 days or more, and spelled out in the tenant lease. See **construction days**.[1]

---

[1]ICSC's *Dictionary of Shopping Center Terms,* International Council of Shopping Centers, 2001.

Appendix:
Reports and Forms

Construction Estimating and Management

Space Assessment Form
Construction Request Form
Unit Pricing Worksheet
Contractor Selection Information Checklist
Lease Execution Notification Form

SPACE ASSESSMENT FORM

Suite Number _____ Prior Use _____

Length of time of prior tenant _____

Condition of space

Firewalls in place
Condition of storefront
Condition of back door and frame
Any evidence of asbestos
Any evidence of chemical storage
Fixtures or cabinets reusable
Extent of demolition to bring it back to white box
Extent of demolition to bring it to black box

Mechanical

Size of rooftop unit
Age of unit
Brand
Condition
Cost to service or repair if less than 5 years old

Electrical

Size of electrical service
Size of panel box
If 208/480, is a stepdown transformer in place and size
Estimate on age of box
Location in relation to meter

Plumbing

Size of water meter
Size of line coming into space
Backflow preventer in place
Number and size of bathrooms
Are the bathrooms handicapped-accessible?

Life Safety

Does the space have a separate fire alarm panel?
Is the space tied into landlord system? If so, how?
Are the exit signs in place and in good working order?
Are there any barriers to wheelchairs and strollers the landlord will need to fix?

Landlords dealing with asset managers for Real Estate Investment Trusts or pension funds often have to assess the condition of a space in advance of a lease expiring so that the costs of leasing or re-leasing the space can be assessed from a projected budget point of view. This is also a helpful form for property management firms with multiple centers who might be on-site only occasionally.

CONSTRUCTION REQUEST FORM

To: Construction Department

Fr: _____

Cc: Development Department

Provide:
- ☐ Preliminary ballpark construction cost estimate
- ☐ Firm construction estimate based on plans and specifications
- ☐ Space Information Package to Tenant

Requested by:_____ Date: _____ Phone: _____

Date Required by: _____

Project Location (Property/Space, lot number): _____

Tenant/Project Name: _____

Tenant/Project Contact and Phone Number: _____

Tenant Address: _____

Probable Lease Commencement Date: _____

Blackout Dates: _____

Construction to be managed by:
- ☐ Landlord
- ☐ Tenant
- ☐ Other

Probable construction start date:_____

Probable construction completion date: _____

Square Footage: _____

Special Requirements (Items not indicated on plans): _____

_____

_____

_____

Has project been estimated or bid before? Yes _____ No _____

If sending space information package, please return sheet with copy of transmittal.

This form can be used internally for estimating costs for leasing and construction purposes.

UNIT PRICING WORKSHEET

Work	Unit	Unit price	Number of Units	Estimate
Storefront				
Storefront—glass and metal	LF			
Storefront door—single	EA			
Storefront door—double	EA			
Back doors				
Exterior—new door, single	EA			
Exterior—new door, double	EA			
Exterior—relocation	EA			
Astragel	EA			
Relocation emergency lights	EA			
Canopy relocation	EA			
Add new canopy—single	EA			
Add new canopy—double	EA			
Additional exterior jar light	EA			
Sheetrock				
Demising walls	LF			
Partition walls	LF			
Wooden doors	EA			
Ceilings				
Hard ceiling	SF			
2 × 4 lay-in	SF			
Electrical				
New service, 200 amp.	EA			
Wall outlets	EA			
2 × 4 lay-in fixtures	EA			
Can lights	EA			
Emergency lights	EA			
HVAC				
RTU	TON			
Ductwork	TON			
Exhaust Fan	EA			
Sprinklers				
Add or relocate a head	EA			
Plumbing				
Toilet	EA			
Sink	EA			
Urinal	EA			
Stall Partitions	LF			
Lights/fans	EA			
Signs	EA			
Insta Heats	EA			
VCT	SF			
Mirrors	EA			
Grab Bars	EA			
Paper towel dispensers	EA			
Soap dispensers	EA			
Toilet paper holder	EA			
General Contractor				
General Conditions	%			
Overhead and Profit	%			
Cost of Permit	EA			
Estimate				

Tenant Coordination sometimes has to estimate what work will cost for budgeting purposes. This is a sample worksheet that can be used.

CONTRACTOR SELECTION INFORMATION CHECKLIST

Date: _____ Person completing form: _____

Company name: _____

Company address: _____

Company phone number: _____

Company fax number: _____

Contact person and position: _____

Type of contractor: General: _____ Trade: (specify type) _____

Years in business: _____ Licensed to do business in: _____

Annual dollar volume: $ _____ Value of backlog: $ _____

Number of full-time employees: _____

Value of projects: $_____ Average project value: $_____

Types of clients:

       Retail _____%   Commercial _____%   Institutional _____%

       Industrial _____%   Government _____%   Residential _____%

Labor affiliation: Open shop _____ Non-Union _____ Union _____

Safety record—the number of work hours lost due to accidents in the last 2 years: _____

Bonding capacity: $_____

Bonding Company: Name:_____

                    Address: _____

                    Contact: _____

Are you currently involved in or are there any pending or outstanding suits, claims or arbitration proceedings against the company or its owners?

_____

Have you been involved in any litigation within the last 5 years, and if so please explain:

_____

Please provide references from past clients, vendors and financial.

What is the name of your insurance company and its rating?

_____

Tenant coordinators who bid their own landlord's work or who qualify tenant contractors can use a form similar to this for background information.

Developer Name
LEASE EXECUTION NOTIFICATION FORM

To: Property Asset Manager
        Property Accountant
        Construction Department

Fr: Leasing Department

Date: 0/0/00

A lease has been fully executed with (fill in tenant name) for space number (fill in) at (fill in name of shopping center). You are authorized to proceed with the Landlord's improvements as defined in the attached.

_____
Vice President of Leasing

This form can be used internally as a sign-off to proceed on landlord improvements as per the lease.

General and Lease Correspondence

Introduction Letter
"Get in for Permit" Letter
Default No Plans
Update Letter
Pre-Delivery Notice
Delivery Notice

INTRODUCTION LETTER
Shopping Center or Developer Letterhead

Date

Name and Address of Tenant Contact, as per lease-required notifications

Re: Tenant Name and store number, if tenant has assigned one
       Space Number
       Name of the Center
       City, State

Dear Sir or Madam:

Congratulations! Welcome to (name of shopping center). We are proud to have you as one of our fine tenants.

Even though I have enjoyed working with you personally, now that you are officially open for business it is time for me to hand you over to our property management team.

Mr./Ms. (name) is the Property Manager. If you have any questions about operations, marketing or management issues, please contact him/her at 000-000-0000.

Property Accounting collects rent through our Phoenix office. You will be receiving a coupon book shortly. If you have any questions, please contact them at 000-000-0000.

Congratulations again.

Sincerely,

Name of Tenant Coordinator
Retail Tenant Coordination

Cc: Others as required for legal notice, the lease
       Property Manager
       Property Accounting
       Leasing
       Tenant File

The official handoff to property management after a store is open.

"GET IN FOR PERMIT" LETTER
Shopping Center or Developer Letterhead

Insert Date

Name and address of tenant as required by lease for notices
Address
Address
Address

Re: Name of Shopping Center and location

Dear Tenant Contact:

A lease outline drawing for the new *store name* at *shopping center name* has been sent to your office. Please have your architect or design manager contact me to arrange for electronic plans or hard copies for the shell to be sent to them so that they can commence their work.

We are planning a May '00 grand opening. We also allow you 90 days for construction. As such, we are planning on turning the space over to you on March 1. The building department has told us that they average 45 days for plan review. However, we would suggest at this time you give yourself 90 days for plan review and approval by the *Name of County* due to the number of stores that will be submitted all at the same time. Please submit your plans for permit review to the County no later than the first of January.

As the landlord, we also review plans. Working on a January submittal deadline to the County, I suggest you start your submittal process to us in October. You will need a letter stating that we have approved your plans as part of your permit application package.

If you have any questions, please call me at 000-000-0000.

Sincerely,

Tenant Coordinator
Retail Tenant Coordination

Cc: Others as per lease requirement
    Tenant File

Sometimes a little prod is needed to get a tenant to start thinking about getting their store scheduled to make any opening requirements you might have.

DEFAULT NO PLANS
Shopping Center Developer

Date:

Contact Name
Company Name
Address
City & State/Province
Postal Code
Attention:

Dear Sir/Madam:

Re: Name of Shopping Center
    Retail Unit Number _____
    Name of Store

Further to the terms and conditions stipulated in Section 0.00 of the Schedule "C" attached to and forming part of the Letter Agreement / Lease Agreement please, be advised that you have defaulted in submitting the Tenant's plans within the time periods provided in Section 0.00 of the Schedule "C."

As the drawing due date was _____, please advise the writer when your completed working drawings will be submitted for approval.

Yours truly,
Shopping Center Developer

Sender's Name
Title

c.c.

Some landlords require plan submittal within certain time frames after a lease is signed or the tenant can be put into default of their lease. This letter is a sample of a letter sent to alert a tenant that plans have not been received by that date. This simple clause can do much to get the attention of a tenant who might not be paying attention to your store due to the volume of other stores under construction. It is also useful when dealing with independent operators who might still be shopping for a design consultant.

UPDATE LETTER
Shopping Center or Developer Letterhead

Date

Name and Address of Tenant Contact you are working with
Address
Address
Address

Re: Tenant Name and store number, if tenant has assigned one
      Name of the Center

Dear *Contact Name*:

I would like to take this opportunity to update you and your design and construction team on a few things at *name of center and location*.

We are proceeding along quickly in shell construction and it is definitely worth a trip out to the center now to see the progress on your new store location. We plan to start delivering in-line shop space to our tenants shortly in order to make our 0/0/00 planned grand opening.

If you have not yet done so, we urge you to get your plans in to both myself and *Local Municipality* for review and approval. I currently show the following status:

Landlord plan review		Received and approved
Finish board approval		Received and approved
Landlord sign approval		Not received
Permit application process number		Not received
Selection of contractor made		Not received

Please note that there has been a change to the lease and design criteria that may impact your design and construction costs. The lease states that we are providing only metal studs for the demising wall. Due to *Name of Municipality* requirements relating to life safety, we are installing the demising wall sheetrock. This will result in a charge back to you for the associated cost. Please make sure your architect and contractor are aware of this and prices accordingly, as they might not have been called out as in place to the architect on any plans reviewed to date.

If you have any questions, please do not hesitate to contact me at 000-000-0000.

Sincerely,

Name of Tenant Coordinator
Retail Tenant Coordination

Cc: Others as required for legal notice, the lease
      Tenant File

Sometimes a second prod is needed to get a tenant to start thinking about adjusting their store schedules to make any opening requirements you might have.

PRE-DELIVERY NOTICE
Shopping Center or Developer Letterhead

Date

Legal Entity, Tenant, as per lease
Address
Address
Address

Re: Lease between Tenant Name and Landlord Name, Executed (Insert Date)
      Notice of Delivery, Section 0.00

Dear Sir or Madam:

In accordance with the provisions of the above referenced lease, please be advised that the landlord's construction in your leased space will be substantially completed as per _____ days from this notice, as per Exhibit X of the lease, and will be ready for commencement of tenant construction.

Tenant shall not commence construction until landlord has approved all construction documents, and all pre-construction requirements, as outlined in the lease, exhibits and attachment or referenced to in the lease, are satisfied by the tenant and tenant's contractor.

Sincerely,

Name
Retail Tenant Coordinator
Shopping Center or Developer

Cc: Tenant File
      Tenant Construction Manager
      Mall or Property Manager
      Any other cited in lease

Via Certified Mail or Signature Required Express

Sample of a pre-delivery notice or letter to a tenant stating that the landlord anticipates work being completed by a certain date. Tenants who request this letter often use it to trigger ordering fixtures and merchandise. There is usually some sort of fine attached also if the landlord cannot make the delivery as stated. This letter has to be issued with great care, since many times it is based considerably far out in the future, scheduled on construction dates that might not be able to be met due to a variety of reasons.

DELIVERY NOTICE
Shopping Center or Developer Letterhead

Date

Legal Entity, Tenant, as per lease
Address
Address
Address

Re: Lease between Tenant Name and Landlord Name, Executed (Insert Date)
Delivery Notice, Section 0.00

Dear Sir or Madam:

In accordance with the provisions of the above referenced lease, please be advised that the landlord's construction in your leased space is substantially completed as per Exhibit X of the lease and is ready for commencement of tenant construction.

Tenant shall not commence construction until landlord has approved all construction documents, and all pre-construction requirements, as outlined in the lease, exhibits and attachment or referenced to in the lease, are satisfied by the tenant and tenant's contractor. The Tenant Contractor is to check in with on-site tenant coordination (or mall management office) before commencing construction. Please call 000-000-0000 to make an appointment.

Sincerely,

Name
Retail Tenant Coordinator
Shopping Center or Developer

Cc: Tenant File
Tenant Construction Manager
Mall or Property Manager
Any other cited in lease

Via Certified Mail or Signature Required Express

Sample of a delivery letter to a tenant stating that work is completed as per the landlord's scope and that the space or store is ready for turnover to them for their scope of work. This is a lease document, and your legal department should be involved in formulating it.

Design Criteria and Approvals

Transmittal Design Criteria
Tenant Lease Outline Drawings
Design Criteria
Photo Information
Site Plan
Storefront Detail
Plan Approval
Plan Approval Transmittal
Authorization to Submit Building Plans for Permit
Sign Approval
Sign Approval, Letter
Authorization to Submit Sign Plans for Permit

TRANSMITTAL DESIGN CRITERIA

Tenant Coordination
Name of Developer
Address
Address Phone

Shopping Center

Transmittal

To:	Tenant Contact Name Address	**From:**	Tenant Coordinator
CC:		**Pages:**	1 plus Design Criteria, Plans
Phone:	000-000-0000	**Date:**	0/0/0000
Re:	Name of Store	**Via:**	US Mail

☑ **Attached** ☐ **For your approval** ☑ **For your use** ☐ **As requested** ☐ **For review/comments**
☐ **Approved as submitted** ☐ **Approved with comments** ☐ **Not approved, please resubmit**
☐ **Letter** ☑ **Lease Outline Drawings** ☑ **Plans** ☐ **Samples** ☑ **Design Criteria** ☑ **Specifications**
☐ **Record of E-mail Transmittal** ☐ **Submittal** ☐ **Other**

Attached are the following for your design team's use:

- ☐ Design Criteria
- ☐ Engineering Specifications
- ☐ Lease Outline Drawing
- ☐ CAD file, Base Building Plans
- ☐ Sign Criteria
- ☐ Copy of Construction Exhibit, the Lease
- ☐ Submittal Requirements

As per the lease, plans are due to Tenant Coordination for review as of 30 days of execution of the lease. We anticipate having plans by 0/00/0000.

Please call if you have any questions.

This is a sample form that can be used to transmit design criteria to a tenant or their architect when sending out hard copies to them.

TENANT LEASE OUTLINE DRAWINGS

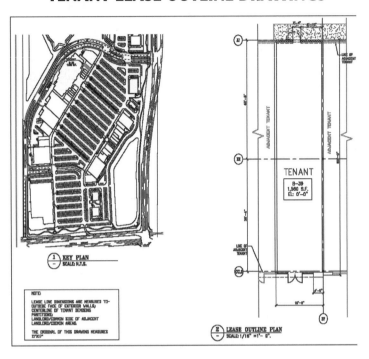

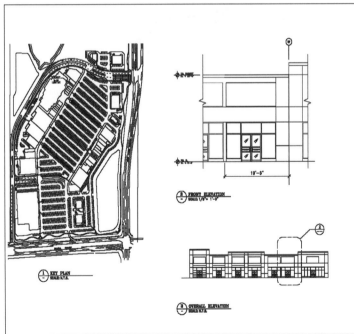

This is a sample of a lease outline drawing. This is an important document that is often attached to the lease and is used for design, construction and rent determination. It should include the name of the tenant, date and size.

DESIGN CRITERIA

The overall storefront impression should be inviting and captivating. All Retail Tenants are encouraged to integrate unique design features, common design elements and a well defined entry to their storefronts. The overall design should "entertain" the customer by introducing oversized props or graphics and special lighting effects.

A definite sense of the three-dimensional is encouraged and the storefront profile should be contoured, de-emphasizing the straight and flat path of the lease line. Storefronts that demonstrate the creative placement of pop-outs and geometry of display windows are also encouraged.

The following storefront conditions will not be permitted:
* *Fully enclosed opaque storefronts*
* *Wide open storefronts*
* *Full storefront bulkheads spanning straight across between demising caps*

DESIGN CONTROL ZONE: All elements in the front 6'-0" area are subject to stringent Landlord review. Quality flooring, ceiling materials, light fixtures and displays must be used within this highly visible area to the public. *No resilient flooring materials, t-bar or exposed ceilings, or fluorescent fixtures will be permitted within the control zone.*

Fluorescent light fixtures without lenses or diffusers will not be permitted anywhere within the public area of the store.

The Landlord poses the challenge to the Retail Tenant to create a successful and innovative transition between the mall tile and the Tenant flooring finish. All finishes and materials visible to the public should be of high quality and must be approved by the Landlord.

The overall integration of a well designed storefront entry, lighting, graphics, signage and creative merchandising and display is essential.

ALL STOREFRONT DESIGN ELEMENTS INCLUDING BULKHEADS, DOORS AND GRILLES, SHALL BE SUPPORTED FROM THE TENANTS PREMISES AND NOT SUSPENDED FROM THE LANDLORD'S OVERHEAD STRUCTURE.

Sample of storefront criteria from a design manual provided by Oxford Properties Group. Photos and professional presentation help tenant design consultants better visualize the requirements of the design criteria, resulting in quicker design times and fewer revisions and comments.

PHOTO INFORMATION
Shopping Center Name

Photos of Food Court Area

Here are some photos of the food court area. Please take a few minutes to open each file and see how we have incorporated natural material and colors from the local region to add regional flavor to the center. When designing your space, please utilize materials and graphics that tie in to our regional theme.

MVC-016S.JPG   MVC-009S.JPG   MVC-007S.JPG   MVC-008S.JPG   MVC-010S.JPG

MVC-011S.JPG   MVC-012S.JPG   MVC-013S.JPG   MVC-014S.JPG   MVC-015S.JPG

The use of the Internet and Web sites as tenant coordination tools to show tenant design teams the context of where their store will sit and the design theme in place is invaluable. Literally, a picture is worth a thousand words in this efficient context.

SITE PLAN

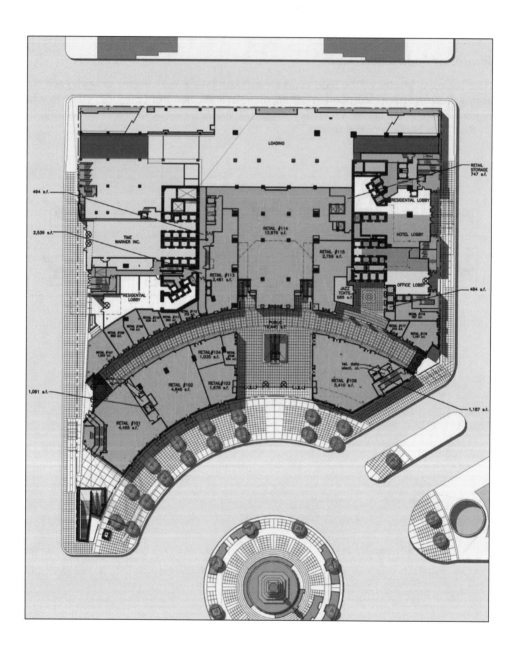

A site plan showing store locations is extremely helpful for tenants trying to understand where their store is in relation to entrances, features and themed courts. This is from the Time Warner building design criteria.

STOREFRONT DETAIL

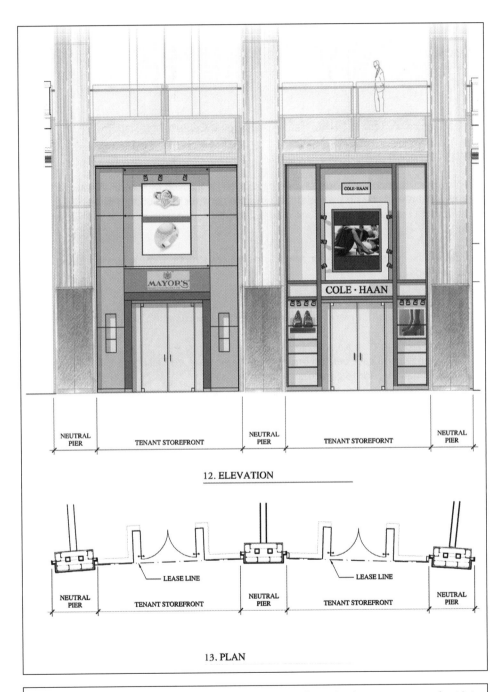

NEUTRAL PIER | TENANT STOREFRONT | NEUTRAL PIER | TENANT STOREFORNT | NEUTRAL PIER

12. ELEVATION

LEASE LINE

LEASE LINE

NEUTRAL PIER | TENANT STOREFRONT | NEUTRAL PIER | TENANT STOREFRONT | NEUTRAL PIER

13. PLAN

This is a sample of storefront criteria from a design manual, illustrating how a tenant storefront is to fit within the landlord's neutral piers in a galleria setting. Illustration from The Shops at Columbus Circle, Manhattan, New York.

PLAN APPROVAL
Shopping Center or Developer Name

Insert Date

Tenant Name
Address
Address
Address

Re: Plan Approval, Tenant Name, Name of Shopping Center, City, State

Dear Sir or Madam:

The plans for the above-mentioned store have been "approved as noted." A copy of the approved plans must be on the job site during the construction buildout phase. If additions or revisions to the approved plans are made, Tenant Coordination must be notified and copied.

In order to take possession of your space to begin construction, the following items must be completed:

1. A lease fully executed by both parties
2. Approved buildout plans, approved by Tenant Coordination and by the building department
3. Approved sign plan as per your lease
4. Insurance certificate per the provisions of your lease, to be submitted to Tenant Coordination prior to construction
5. List of subcontractors, emergency contact numbers, and any required licensing, bonding, or insurance certificate to be submitted to Tenant Coordination
6. Building permit, original to be posted at the jobsite with copy submitted to Tenant Coordination
7. Pre-construction meeting scheduled with Tenant Coordination to discuss rules and regulations during construction.

As always, if you have any questions, do not hesitate to call. I can be reached at 000-000-0000.

Sincerely,

Name of Tenant Coordinator
Tenant Coordination

Cc: Property Manager
    Tenant File

This is a sample of a letter that can be used to signify the landlord's approval of plans to a tenant.

PLAN APPROVAL TRANSMITTAL

Tenant Coordination
Name of Developer
Address
Address Phone

Shopping Center

Transmittal

To:	Architect Name	**From:** Tenant coordinator's name
	Address	
CC:		**Pages:** 1 plus plans
Phone: 000-000-0000		**Date:** 7/30/2005
Re:	Store name—comments on plans	**Via:** Federal Express

☑ **Attached** ☐ **For your approval** ☑ **For your use** ☐ **As requested** ☐ **For review/comments**

☐ **Approved as submitted** ☐ **Approved with comments** ☑ **Not approved, please resubmit**

☐ **Letter** ☐ **Lease Outline Drawings** ☑ **Plans** ☐ **Samples** ☐ **Construction Handbook**

☐ **Specifications** ☐ **Record of E-mail Transmittal** ☐ **Submittal** ☐ **Other**

Dear Architect:

Please resubmit only the pages requested. A copy of the plans with standard comments will be given to the GC upon check-in. Resubmittal and approval needs to occur before construction begins.

A1.1	Need waterproof membrane in wet areas where there are shared demising walls with other tenants
A2.0	Sign separate submittal
M1	Pipe condensate into gutters—see sketch for pipe with metal strapping on wooden block sitting on top of roof membrane on top of roof
	County will require tie-down or bolt in detail on RTU's engineered to meet 110 mph windload (FBC)
	Submit revision

This is a sample form that can be used to transmit comments to a tenant or their architect when sending back to them a copy of your comments on their plans. This is a useful form because it serves as a transmittal, which is a log of correspondence, and also as a means of conveying information.

AUTHORIZATION TO SUBMIT
BUILDING PLANS FOR PERMIT
Shopping Center or Developer Letterhead

Date

Municipality
Address
Address
Address

Re: Plan Submittal, Name of Tenant, Space and Official Address
      Interior Alteration Permit

Dear Sir or Madam:

The tenant contractor is submitting plans for construction for the interior alteration permit for the *Name of Tenant* space at the *Name of Shopping Center* on behalf of the tenant, *Name of Tenant*. The tenant has a signed lease with us and is submitting and building with our permission.

We will be requesting a copy of the process number from them and will be assisting them with items related to our work and the site.

Please feel free to contact me if you have any questions at 000-000-0000.

Sincerely,

Name
Retail Tenant Coordinator
Shopping Center or Developer

Cc: Tenant File

Some municipalities like the comfort of knowing that the plans they are reviewing have been reviewed by the landlord in advance. This also serves to protect them from reviewing plans with a tenant who has not been given legal rights to assume use of a space.

SIGN APPROVAL

Size is acceptable. Sign Approved.

1. No comments on color or branded image
2. Installation will need to be coordinated with on-site co
   date and access
3. All signage must be fully weatherproof and shall be co
   weather-resistant materials. All illuminated signs shall b
   compliance with all applicable building and electrical c
   Underwriter's Laboratory (UL) label. No exposed racew
   will be permitted. All cabinets, conductors, transformer
   to lighting controls must be concealed from public viev
   are an integral part of the design. All exterior Tenant si
   a time clock. All permits for signs and installation will b
   with a copy sent to the Landlord's Tenant Coordinator
   shall be fabricated in compliance with all applicable building and electrical codes.
   Signs meeting the Landlord's Sign Criteria, but not meeting local sign code requirements, shall be the responsibility of the Tenant.
4. Installers must provide proof of licensing and insurance. Trucks must be substantial
   with outriggers. Installers must protect asphalt with plywood. Methods of
   installation must be acceptable to on-site tenant coordination.
5. Sign and tenant responsible for pulling all permits, including electrical, and making
   sure all permits finaled. Open permits create unacceptable property violations.
   Please comply.

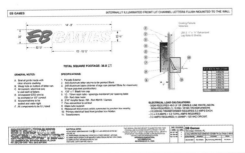

Sample of a sign approval based on .pdf forms e-mailed to the landlord.

SIGN APPROVAL, LETTER
Shopping Center or Developer Letterhead

Date

Sign Company
Address
Address
Address

Re: Sign Submittal, Name of Tenant, Space and official address for exterior centers

Dear Sir or Madam:

The submitted sign plan has been approved as noted. Please contact the center management office to schedule your installation. Note that a copy of the approved sign permit and sign contractor's insurance certificate must be sent to the Mall Manager prior to the sign installation.

In addition, please note that the following procedures must be followed at time of installation:

☐ Installation before 9:30 A.M. or after 9:00 P.M.
☐ Proper barricade of all common areas and roads to protect the public
☐ Installation vehicles must have plywood to protect asphalt under the outriggers
☐ Trucks cannot go onto sidewalks
☐ All signs must be finaled and proof of completion given to center management

Please feel free to contact me if you have any questions at 000-000-0000.

Sincerely,

Name
Retail Tenant Coordinator
Shopping Center or Developer

Cc: Tenant File

This letter is a sample of approval of a sign package for a tenant to install. Some communities re-quire letters of authorization from landlords also, showing that the landlord has agreed to let the tenant put a sign on their building.

AUTHORIZATION TO SUBMIT SIGN PLANS FOR PERMIT
Shopping Center or Developer Letterhead

Date

Municipality
Address
Address
Address

Re: Letter of Authorization, Sign Submittal, Name of Tenant, Space and Official Address

Dear Sir or Madam:

Name of sign installer is submitting plans for the construction and installation of exterior signage for the *Name of Tenant* space at the *Name of Shopping Center* on behalf of the tenant, *Name of Tenant*. They have our permission to install a sign at the *shopping center* on behalf of our tenant, *Name of Tenant*.

The tenant has a signed lease with us and is building with our permission.

The tenant is allocated 30 square feet as per their storefront size and we have verified that they are within that allotment and meet our design criteria.

Please feel free to contact me if you have any questions at 000-000-0000.

Sincerely,

Name
Retail Tenant Coordinator
Shopping Center or Developer

Cc: Tenant File

Technically speaking, a tenant is in possession of a space by leasehold estate. Many municipalities want proof that the sign they are about to review has been approved by the landlord and that the landlord will let the installer put it on their building. Some sign companies will give you a form to sign also.

Tracking Forms

Lease Abstract
Tenant Contact Data Form
Tenant Status Report
Tenant Status Conversation Log
Small Tenant Questionnaire
Big Box Build-to-Suit Report
Tenant Tracking Form
Tenant Fixturing Status
At a Glance Form
Architectural Plans Tracking
Tenant Tracking, Administration and Architectural
   (Form 1)
Tenant Tracking, Delivery, Permits and
   Construction (Form 2)
Tenant Contractor Check-In Paperwork
   Requirements

LEASE ABSTRACT

Tenant Name:	Smith's Town Store, LLC
Address:	Smith's Town Store
	2300 Regency Place Park, Suite 3500
	Atlanta, GA 30326
	Attention: Real Estate
Others for notices:	Joseph Brown, Esq.,
	Brown, Group and Jones, LLP,
	1500 Peachtree Center Avenue, N.E.,
	Atlanta, Georgia 30303
	And
	James Adler
	Construction Manager
	2300 Regency Place Park, Suite 3500
	Atlanta, GA 30326
Size:	3000 sf
Location:	J520
Date of Execution:	3/20/05
Lease Commencement:	The first to occur of 90 days from the day of delivery or date tenant opens.
Delivery Information:	Pre-delivery notice due 30 days prior, delivery notice day of delivery
Plan Submission:	Within 30 days from lease execution. Landlord has 10 days to respond and comment. Tenant has 15 days to address.
Landlord's Responsibility:	White box, see construction exhibit.
Utilities:	Upon delivery
Signage:	No pylon, mall directory allowed, coming soon banners allowed
Exclusivity:	None
TI	$120,000 evidence of work satisfactorily completed, reasonable evidence all work is paid for, all liens satisfied or waived, open 1 month, tenant not in default, estoppel, tenant in good standing
Chargebacks:	Landlord has right to charge back for signage directory, awnings and additional work as per requested by tenant with 15% administration fee
Approvals:	Tenant can install satellite, Landlord to approve location
Blackout:	Tenant not required to open between August 1 and September 15, November 1 to January 15
Closeout:	Landlord and tenant must walk space 10 days after letter sent out; LL has 15 days to complete outstanding items—tenant must give LL list within 30 days

---

Property management or lease administration might do a more information-filled abstract. Tenant Coordination's needs are more construction- and delivery-oriented, and a simple form with information related to landlord construction obligations can be sufficient.

TENANT CONTACT DATA FORM

TENANT CONTACT DATA SHEET					
SPACE NUMBER:				Center:	TPA
TENANT NAME:				RCD:	G.O.
SQUARE FOOTAGE:	New:	Ren:	Rel:	T.O.	90 (7/15/05)
LPG RECEIVED:			TLP/HB ISSUED:		
TENANT:					
			PHONE:		
			FAX:		
			e-mail		
ARCHITECT:					
			PHONE:		
			FAX:		
			e-mail		
CONTRACTOR:					
			PHONE:		
			FAX:		
			e-mail		
OTHER:					
			PHONE:		
			FAX:		
			e-mail		
SCHEDULE:					
Preliminary drawings:					
Final drawings:					
Construction start:					
Construction completion:					
COMMENTS: (Special construction/requirements/instructions)					
NOTES:					

DATE:	CONTACT:	COMMENTS:

A log for recording conversations with tenants is a good practice. This form serves that purpose as well as keeping handy information at your fingertips.

TENANT STATUS REPORT

Tenant Name:	Center:
Suite Number:	Wing:
Store Number:	Leasing Agent:

1	Letter of Intent		**Tenant Contact Info:**
2	Lease/Exhibit Review		
3	Request for Tenant Manual		
4	Tenant Manual Sent to Tenant		
5	Lease Execution Date		
6	Notice Letter Sent		
7	Possession Date		
8	Architect's Name Received		
9	Preliminary Plans Received		**Architect Contact Info:**
10	Preliminary Plans Approved		
11	Final Plans Due		
12	Final Plans Recevied		
13	Sample Board Received		
14	Final Plans Approved		
15	Sprinkler Engineering		
16	Sign Plans Received		
17	Sign Approval		
18	Building Permit Applied For		**Tenant Contractor:**
19	Building Permit Received		
20	Insurance Certificate Received		
21	Subcontractor List Received		
22	Contractor Schedule Received		
23	Construction Start Due		
24	Follow-Up		
25	Opening Date Due		
26	Construction Start Actual		
27	Opening Date Actual		**Special Lease Provisions:**
28	Invoice-Construction Chargebacks		
29	Punch List Letter		
30	Punch List Completed		
31	Closeout Letter		
32	Contractor Deposit Released		
33	Allowance/Date Processed		
34	Construction Allowance Amount		

This is a sample form that can be used as a tracking report on a tenant-by-tenant basis by a tenant coordinator or lease administrator.

TENANT STATUS CONVERSATION LOG

Tenant Name:	Center Name:
Space Number:	Leasing Agent:

Action Item	Date of Conversation	Projected Date	Actual Date
Lease Signed			
Tenant Design Criteria Sent			
Tenant Plans Submitted for Review			
Tenant Plans Approved			
Sign Plans Submitted for Review			
Sign Plans Approved			
Plans Submitted for Permit			
Plans Approved			
General Contractors Bids Due			
General Contractor Chosen			
Construction Start Date			
Electric Meter Set Date			
Fixturing Date			
Merchandise Date			
Certificate of Occupancy			
Opening Date			

Comments:

This is a sample form that could be modified to use as a conversation log. It would be particularly helpful to tenant coordinators in large departments dealing with a volume of tenants.

SMALL TENANT QUESTIONNAIRE

	Call Date	Call Date	Call Date	Answer Confirmed

Architect and Engineer
Who is your architect?
Are they state-certified?
When will I get plans from them?
Who is their engineer?
Are they state-certified and -licensed?
When are you submitting for a permit?
Who is expediting your permit?

Permitting Questions
When did you submit?
Have you received comments back yet?
When are you sending in corrections?
What issues are you running into?
When do you expect to have the permit?

Contractor Questions
Are you out for bid?
Who are you talking to?
When do you expect to award the contract?
Are they state-licensed?
Is their license current with the municipality?
When are they starting?

Fixturing Questions
Have you ordered your millwork?
In unionized states, does it have a UL label?
  (union label)
If internally lit, does it have a UL label?
  (approved UL lighting certification)
Where is it coming from?
Where are you storing?
When will it get here?

Kitchen Equipment Questions
Do you have an ansul system?
How will it be tied into landlord systems?
Have you submitted to the board of health for review?
Have you sized any grease trap requirements?
What is your occupancy and have you sized your
  water meter yet?
Do you have a walk-in cooler?
How are you installing it and will you need a sprinkler
  head in there?

Life Safety Issues
Do you have your own fire alarm control panel?
How are you planning to tie into landlord systems?

Management and Operations
Have you selected a store manager yet?
When do you plan to merchandise?
When do you plan to open?

This form is more detail-oriented for asking questions to see what status the tenant is at.

BIG BOX BUILD-TO-SUIT REPORT
LANDLORD'S WORK

Project: Amy's Big Box	
Location: B1	
Center: Ideal Shopping Center	

			Tenant Design Contact Info:
1	Lease exhibit sent to architect		
2	Plans from tenant sent to architect		
3	Plans sent to tenant for review		
4	Plans approved by tenant		
5	Required turnover date		
6	Plans sent to contractors for bid		
7	Bid date		
8	Award date		
9	Contractor chosen		Tenant Construction Manager:
10	Construction start date		
11	Plans sent in for permit		
12	Permit ready date		
13	Sign drawings received		
14	Sign submitted permit		
15	Sign permit approved		
16	Construction start date		
17	Estimate completion		
18	Notice of intended delivery sent		Landlord Architect:
19	Sign installed		
20	Punch list walkthrough with tenant		
21	Turnover for fixturing		
22	CO date		
23	Merchandising start date		
24	Opening date		
25	Completion punch list		
26	Close out construction		Landlord Contractor:
27	Warranty books received by GC		
28	Allowance to tenant received		
29	Turned over to property manager		

This report form is handy for when the landlord is responsible for building the store for a tenant.

TENANT TRACKING FORM

Tenant Tracking Document Date: 11/1/05

Initial Administration

Joe's Dept.	Lease Status	LOI Received	Lease Request Received	Lease Executed Date	TC Received Copy	LOD Sent	Shell Plans Sent	Design Criteria Sent
	signed	12/21/03	3/1/04	4/5/04	4/23/04	na	na	3/1/04

Plan Review

Prelim. Plans Received	Final Plans Received	Days to Review	Final Plans Date Approved		
			No	Yes with comments	Yes
6/24/04	7/24/04	20	na	7/30/04	na

Delivery Info

Blackout Dates	Pre-Delivery Notice Required	Date Sent	Delivery Date Required	Date Sent Actual	Date Tenant Accepted
0	no	na	3/1/05	3/1/05	

LL Obligations

Pad Box	Black Box	White Box	BTS	Punch List Status
yes	na	na	na	

Permits

Date Submitted	Shell Permit Number	Tenant Int Alt	Tenant Occupancy Number	Approval Date
12/13/2004	P04–01501	na	na	3/9/2004

GC Info

Days for Cons.	Date Started	Date C/O	Date Open
270	3/17/2005	10/9/2005	10/12/2005

Detailed tracking form, tenant by tenant.

TENANT FIXTURING STATUS

NEW/EXISTING TENANT FIXTURING STATUS FORM		
Tenant Legal Name:	Contact:	
Address:	Phone:	
	Fax:	
Tenant Trade Name:		
Unit Number:		
Possession Date:	Opening Date:	
Tenant Contractor:	Contact:	
Address:	Phone:	
	Fax:	
ITEMS		**DATE COMPLETED**
A. Tenant Package		
(i) Initial Contact Letter		
(ii) Design/Contractors/M&E/ Manuals, Base Building Drawings and/or Previous Tenant Drawings		
(iii) Building Permit Application		
(iv) Liability Insurance Form		
(v) Landlord's Standard		
(vi) Key Location Plan		
(vii) Landlord Prior to and During Construction Requirements		
B. Drawing Submission		
(i) Architectural		
Received from Tenant/Designer		
Forwarded to Tenant Coordination (Head Office) by Property		
Reviewed and Approved by Tenant Coordination		
Returned to Tenant by Property/Tenant Coordinator		
(ii) Mechanical		
Received from Tenant/Designer		
Forwarded to Base Building Consultant by Property/TC		
Reviewed and Approved by Consultant		
Returned to Tenant by Property/TC		
(iii) Electrical		
Received from Tenant/Designer		
Forwarded to Base Building Consultant by Property/TC		
Reviewed and Approved by Consultant		
Returned to Tenant by Property/TC		

An internal tracking form for a large tenant coordination department. There are three pages in this sample.

ITEMS	DATE COMPLETED
C. Prior to Construction	
(i) All Drawings Approved	
(ii) Lease Signed	
(iii) Building Permit and/or Application Posted	
(iv) Insurance Received	
(v) Site Meeting Between GM/OMS and Tenant Contractor	
Hand Over Approved Drawings (To Be Kept On-Site at All Times)	
Keys Given to Tenant Contractor	
Review Site Rules and Regulations and Health & Safety Policy	
After-Hours Access Permit & Security for Arrangements (If Required)	
Sprinkler Shutdown Scheduled (Postdated Check Received)	
Coordinate Hot Work Activities, tag for welding and burning permit	
D. On-site Preparation by Landlord	
(i) Barricade Installed	
(ii) Landlord's Work Completed in Tenant Premises (If Applicable)	
(iii) HVAC Turned "OFF" and Sealed or Construction Filters Installed	
(iv) Utility Meters Read (Gas, Water, Electricity, Other)	
E. During Construction	
(i) Regular Site Inspections	
(ii) Site Supervision and Coordination	
F. Prior to Tenant's Opening	
(i) Add Tenant to Directory, Signage, All Other Administrative Tenant Listings	
(ii) Tenant Emergency Contact Listing Received	
(iii) Send Flowers and/or Gifts	
(iv) Meet New Manager to Provide Welcome Package	
G. Final Inspections	
(i) By GM	
(ii) By Base Building Consultants on Mechanical and Electrical Installation	
(iii) By City Official Building Inspectors (Obtain Copy for File)	
(iv) Obtain Air Balancing Report	

ITEMS	DATE COMPLETED
H. Deficiencies	
(i) Issue Initial Deficiency Letter with Statutory Declaration to Tenant by GM/OMS	
(ii) Issue Follow-up Deficiency Letter (If Required)	
(iii) Deficiencies Completed by Tenant or Landlord	
(iv) Issue all or part of $3000.00 Construction Deposit	
I. Issuance of Tenant Inducement and Recoverables by Property	
(i) Drawing Review Fees	
Architectural ($350.00)	
Mechanical (Property-Specific)	
Electrical (Property-Specific)	
(ii) Barricades ($45.00 ft.)	
(iii) Sprinklers ($100.00/Drain Down for Retail, $200.00 for Office)	
(iv) Security (Property Specific)	
(v) Landlord's Work	
Construction Deficiencies	
Upgrades to Electrical/ Mechanical Services	
Roof Openings	
Core Drilling	
Landlord's Tile S/I Thermostat(s) Check Meter Calibration F.A./Evac Speakers Verification	
Others	
J. Forward Store Photos to Tenant Coordination at Head Office by Property	
K. Post Tenancy Checklist	
(i) Remove Required Chattels	
(ii) Clean Premises and Any Required Equipment	

AT A GLANCE FORM

Date: 0/0/00

A1: Joe's Department Store
Design:
1. Utility locations have been modified on landlord site plan to match tenant building
2. Elevations approved
3. Expect interior plans next week

Permit:

Turnover:
1. Required to turn over pad with utilities on 0/0/00

Construction:
1. Tenant is doing building
2. No contractor chosen yet

B1: Amy's Big Box—Red Flag!
Design:
1. Landlord plans approved by tenant 0/0/00
2. Tenant final fixture plan needed for coordination
3. Exterior sign drawings approved

Permit:
1.   Submitted 0/00/00

Turnover:
1. Pre-delivery notice to be sent prior—120 days as per lease
2. Need delivery by 0/0/00
3. Will need warranty books as turnover
4. Need sign panels in place 0/0/00

Construction:
1. GC has not started construction; weeks behind schedule for turnover
2. Shell and interior completion scheduled for 0/0/00
3. GC shell construction schedule dated 0/0/00 does not reflect milestones of electric and water meters needed for CO of building

B3: Small Shop Tenant
Design:
1. Tenant interior plans approved by landlord 0/0/00
2. Sign drawings reviewed, not approved

Permit:
1. Tenant submitted 0/0/00

Turnover:
1. Must make 0/0/00 turnover or will go into blackout and cannot deliver until 2/1/00

Construction:
1. Tenant contractor chosen

B5: Small Shop Tenant
Design:
Permit:
Turnover:
Construction:

This form can be used to inform other interested parties of status of work in an easy-to-read narrative form.

ARCHITECTURAL PLANS TRACKING

Landlord plans that need approval from tenants—Information as per lease 0/0/00

Tenant	Date Shell Plans sent to Tenant	Date Plans Received for LL Obligation	Landlord Obligation	Date LL Architect Released	Days to Work	Date Due Tenant	Date Sent to Tenant	Tenant Days to Review	Date Due back from Tenant	Date Received from Tenant	LL Days to Respond	Date Due Back to Tenant	Comments
Joes Dept. Store	7/15/04	9/5/04	BTS	9/10/05	60	11/5/05	11/2/05	20	11/23/05	11/20/05	30	12/10/05	Tenant comments
							12/10/05	20	1/2/05	1/3/05	30	1/23/06	Tenant comments, need resubmittal
							1/23/06	20	2/13/06	2/10/06			Plans approved as noted
Amy's Big Box	6/30/04	7/15/04	BTS	7/20/04	45	8/5/04	8/10/04	30	9/20/04	9/10/04	15	9/25/04	
							9/20/04	30	10/10/04	10/15/04	15	10/30/04	approved letter sent to tenant
							10/30/04	30	11/30/04	11/25/04	15		
Dan's Big Box	na	6/04*	BTS	6/15/04	60	8/4/04	8/4/04	20	8/24/04	8/23/04	0		
							9/7/04	20	9/27/04	9/17/04	0		
							9/27/04	20	10/22/04	10/1/04	na	na	approved letter sent to tenant
Smith's Big Box	7/15/04	exp. 8/15 to 8/30	BTS	8/24/04	30	9/28/04	9/10/04	30	10/20/04	9/23/04	30	10/22/04	
							10/15/04	30	11/19/04	10/26/04	30	11/25/04	revisions as per second comments
							11/19/04	30	12/19/04	12/2/04	30	1/1/05	set sent to build dept and GC for pricing
							1/24/05	30	2/24/05	1/26/05	30		working out details on door
							3/14/05	30	4/14/05	3/21/05	30		tenant approved 4/5/05
							3/28/05			4/5/05			

This form can be used to keep track of status of plans requiring tenant signoff on work the landlord is responsible for.

TENANT TRACKING, ADMINISTRATION AND ARCHITECTURAL (FORM 1)

Ideal Shopping Center
Tenant Tracking Document Date: 0/0/00

Tenant Name	Space	Size	LOI Received	Lease Request Received	Lease Executed Date	TC Received Copy	LOD Sent	Shell/LL Plans Sent	Design Criteria Sent	Prelim. Plans Received	Final Plans Received	Current Status	Final Plans Date Approved — No	Yes	Yes with comments	Yes
												Plan Review				
					Initial Administration											
Joe's Department	A1	88248	12/21/03	2/1/04	4/5/04	4/23/04 na	na	3/1/04	6/24/04	10/30/04	construction underway	1/0/00		11/30/04	na	
Amy's Big Box	B1	30185	5/1/03	7/1/03	4/24/04	4/25/04	5/1/03	7/9/04	5/1/03	5/19/04	9/2/04	open	5/25/04	na	10/1/04	
Small Shop Tenant	B3	8041	11/3/03	1/4/04	2/24/04	2/27/04	2/28/04	2/28/04	2/29/04	3/30/04	4/12/04		10/13/04	4/15/04	3/3/04	na
Small Shop Tenant	B5	5770	11/3/03	12/23/03	1/15/04	1/15/04	1/7/04	1/15/04	1/15/04	2/25/04	3/1/04					

Use this form for tracking plan review and permit status.

TENANT TRACKING, DELIVERY, PERMITS AND CONSTRUCTION (FORM 2)

Ideal Shopping Center
Tenant Tracking Document Date: 00/00

Tenant Name	Space	Size	Black Out Dates	Delivery Info					LL Obligations					Date Sub.	Permits			Days for Cons.	GC Info		
				Pre Delivery Notice Received	Date Sent	Delivery Date Received	Date Sent Actual	Date Tenant Acc.	Pad	Black Box	White Box	BTS	Punch List Status		Shell Permit Number	Tenant int. alt. permit	Approval Date		Date Started	Date C/O	Date Open
Joe's Dept. Store	A1	88248	0	no	na	3/1/05	3/1/05	3/1/05	yes	na	na	na	1/0/00	12/13/04	P04-015019	na	3/9/09	270	3/17/05	1/0/00	1/0/00
Amy's Big Box	B1	30185	Oct-Dec	120 days	1/6/05	5/1/05	5/9/05	5/9/05	na	na	na	yes	30 days	11/2/04	P04-004561	P04-011217	12/28/04	90	1/3/05	5/18/05	5/18/05
Small Shoe Tenant	B3	8041	2/15-6/15; 8/1-1/15	0	na	6/16/05	6/16/05	6/17/05	na	na	yes	na	5 days	3/16/05	P04-007536	P04-014118	5/17/05	60	6/20/05	1/0/00	1/0/00
Small Shoe Tenant	B5	5770	0	0	na	7/1/05	6/31/05	7/1/05	na	yes	na	na	na	3/20/05	P04-007537	P04-015113	4/30/05	45	7/2/05		

Use this form for tracking permits and construction.

TENANT CONTRACTOR CHECK-IN
PAPERWORK REQUIREMENTS

Tenant Name	Joe's Restaurant
Copy of Building Permit	Received 1/7/05
Copy of GC License	Received 1/11/05
Copy of Certificate of Insurance	Received 1/11/05
Deposit	$2500 check number 546
Additional Construction Fees	$800 check number 547
Signatures on check-in forms from construction handbook	Received 1/11/05

Tenant Name	Bloom's Department Store
Copy of Building Permit	Received 1/15/05
Copy of GC License	Received 1/15/05
Copy of Certificate of Insurance	Received 1/15/05
Deposit	$2500 check number 9687
Additional Construction Fees	$4000 check number 9688
Signatures on check-in forms from construction handbook	Received 1/15/05

Tenant Name	
Copy of Building Permit	
Copy of GC License	
Copy of Certificate of Insurance	
Deposit	
Additional Construction Fees	
Signatures on check-in forms from construction handbook	

Tenant Name	
Copy of Building Permit	
Copy of GC License	
Copy of Certificate of Insurance	
Deposit	
Additional Construction Fees	
Signatures on check-in forms from construction handbook	

If you have a lot of tenant contractors checking in at one time, it can be helpful to use this as a running form to keep up with what paperwork is outstanding, as it is not uncommon for pieces of your check-in documentation to come in at different times.

Construction Check-In Forms and Tracking Status

Tenant Construction Handbook, Cover
  and Contents
Contractor Check-In Requirements
Construction Sign-In and Drawing Receipt
Construction Check-In Paperwork Requirements
Designated Contractors
Utility Account Information
Insurance Requirements
Insurance Requirements When Dealing with
  Risk/Underwriter
Memorandum of Insurance
Liability Insurance Certificate
Hot Work Indemnification
Construction Fees Calculations
Construction Rules and Regulations Sign-In Form
Contractor Information Form
Lease Acceptance Form
Turnover Checklist Acceptance by Contractor
Contractor Start Date
Field Coordination Report
Fire Alarm Tie-In Request
Request to Use Freight Elevator
Oversized Delivery
Roof Penetrations
Sprinkler Shutdown
Sprinkler Shutdown When Dealing with Risk/
  Underwriter

TENANT CONSTRUCTION HANDBOOK,
COVER AND CONTENTS

Name of Shopping Center
Name of Municipality
Date

Sample of a construction handbook for a lifestyle or power shopping center.

HANDBOOK CONTENTS

1. Maps—Location of Center and Building and Utility Departments
2. Check-in Procedure
3. Contractor Responsibilities and Paperwork
4. Pre-opening Services—Tenant-Provided Services
5. Contractor's On-Site Work
6. Landlord's Responsibilities
7. Tenant's Responsibilities
8. MEP Requirements
9. Exterior Elevation Signage
10. Roof Penetrations
11. Use of Mall Areas with Service Corridors
12. Waterproofing
13. Work Practices and General Housekeeping
14. Strictly Prohibited Work and Practices
15. Corrective Work Done by Landlord
16. Designated Contractor—Information
17. Utility Contacts—Information
18. Pre-Power information
19. Insurance Guidelines
20. Roof Access Request Form
21. Automated Inspection Information
22. Revision Form
23. Legal Description
24. Internet Permit and Inspections Status
25. Occupational License Information
26. Contractor Fees Calculations
27. Construction Rules and Regulations Acceptance Form
28. Contact Info and Subcontractor List
29. Space Acceptance Form
30. Grease Guard Specs, use this or like product
31. Waterproofing Specs, use this or like process
32. Construction Deposit Request

This is a sample of the type of information that can be included in a construction handbook. Construction and design criteria can be posted on the Internet or made available through electronic plan reproduction firms for fast, inexpensive delivery.

CONTRACTOR CHECK-IN REQUIREMENTS

All Tenant Contractors are required to check in with on-site Tenant Coordination. All check-ins must be scheduled 24 hours in advance by contacting Name of Coordinator at 000-000-0000. Contractors may not start work until they have provided to the Field Tenant Coordinator the following:

Certificate of Insurance—The Contractor shall furnish proper evidence of required insurance coverage and workman's compensation. (See insurance requirements in lease and attached.) All policies shall provide 30-day written notice of nonrenewal or cancellation. Liability limits in tenant's lease govern. The following is to be listed as insured:

Shopping Center legal entity
Attn: Name of Coordinator
Business Address

The following are to be named as an additional insured:
Any additional insured

Building Permit—The Contractor shall furnish a copy of the Tenant's building permit.

Construction Deposit—The contractor shall provide a security deposit to cover any damage not addressed while on-site. There are no exceptions. Contractors doing more than one buildout are expected to provide said deposit per each location. The deposit will be in the form of a check made payable to *Ideal Shopping Center* for the amount of $2,500.00. This will not be kept in an interest-bearing account. The deposit will be returned upon application by the tenant contractor at the end of the construction.

Contractor Prepaid Fees—Payable at check-in, payable to *Shopping Center legal entity* except as noted. These fees will cover temporary trash, toilets, trash, power and water.

Landlord- and City-Approved Drawings—Contractor shall exhibit a set of landlord-approved drawings to use as a working set. This set of drawings is to remain on-site at all times along with the permit drawings. All drawings are to reflect all Building Department requirements. Please be aware that you will not get inspections without approved plans, stamped by the Building Department. These must be kept in a secure place on-site along with the permit card.

Contact and Subcontractor List—Contractor shall furnish the names and phone numbers of contractor's supervisory personnel, including a 24-hour emergency phone number. (See attached form.)

A **site-specific OSHA safety program** must be written for each location the contractor is working on within the center. The plan must include an emergency plan as well as standard items required by OSHA. One copy must be provided at the time of check-in and a separate copy kept on-site by the superintendent. The safety program must also include MSDS sheets and a copy of the hazard communication program. *Please note, storage of hazardous materials and chemicals and the use of gas-fueled generators are not allowed inside tenant spaces.*

Hard Hats and Proper Attire—Hard hats will be required by the base building general contractor, unless officially notified that it is no longer a hard hat job. Anyone not complying with proper OSHA dress and head and eye gear is subject to being asked to leave the site. Neither the General Contractor nor the Owner and Owner's Representatives will accept responsibility for any accident that results or occurs due to negligence of the tenant contractor or noncompliance with federal standards and regulations.

There is a **no drugs, no alcohol, and no weapons policy.** This will be strictly enforced by Tenant Coordination. Any personnel caught in violation will be asked to leave the job immediately.

Lease Premise Acceptance—Contractor signs Lease Premise Acceptance Form acknowledging any construction deviations and/or omissions. Tenant's taking possession of the premises shall be conclusive evidence of tenant's acceptance thereof in good order and satisfactory condition. (See attached form.)

Contractor signs **Construction Rules and Regulation Signature form** acknowledging receipt of a copy of these Construction Rules and the Tenant Handbook. (See attached form.)

Contractor furnishes **Construction Schedule** for tenant buildout. Tenant Coordination requests the schedules in Microsoft Project printout form.

Contractor reviews **Construction Completion checklist** and Tenant Criteria with Field Tenant Coordinator on-site.

This is a form that can be included in the construction handbook or sent out independently to a tenant's contractor so that they know what they will need to commence work on-site.

CONSTRUCTION SIGN-IN AND DRAWING RECEIPT

Property: _____

Retail Area No.: _____

Tenant Name: _____

Under the terms of the executed agreement to lease, the tenant is required to carry out its construction in strict conformity with the working drawings as reviewed by the Shopping Center Developer.

The undersigned hereby acknowledges receipt of one set of such working drawings indicating such review, and relative to the tenancy noted above. It is required by the agreement that these drawings be kept on-site and available for review by the landlord's representative during the tenant's construction period.

The undersigned acknowledges that the *name of shopping center's* Construction Site Rules and Regulations and the landlord's Health & Safety Policy (attached) has been reviewed and understood and that the tenant and all of its contractors, agents and employees are required to abide by these regulations in carrying out the tenant development work on the premises.

Each tenant is responsible for obtaining all necessary permits and approvals from all authorities having jurisdiction over the work to be carried out by the tenant or its contractors, prior to the commencement of the work on-site.

Contractor: _____

Address: _____

Phone: _____

Site Supervisor:_____ Phone: _____

Architectural Drawings:

Mechanical Drawings:

Structural Drawings:

Mall Rules/Regulations and Health & Safety Policies:

Signature: Date:

This is another sample check-in form that requires the tenant contractor to acknowledge the rules and regulations of the property.

CONSTRUCTION CHECK-IN
PAPERWORK REQUIREMENTS

Prior to construction commencement, the following items must be delivered to the landlord:

- ☐ Certificate of Insurance, including proper additional insured endorsement and insurance requirements per the attached "Construction Contractor Insurance" requirements
- ☐ Copy of building department permit and paid receipts
- ☐ Roof penetration drawing (if applicable)
- ☐ Names, addresses, telephone numbers, and emergency phone numbers of contractors performing work
- ☐ Copy of contractor's Construction Contract

Any damage to the landlord's work (i.e., sidewalks, storefronts, slabs, studs, drywall, ceiling, ductwork, electrical work, plumbing, plumbing fixtures, painting, etc.) caused by the contractor or any of the subcontractors will be repaired by the landlord's contractor at the contractor's expense. All contractors must work in harmonious accord.

The undersigned has received the keys to the storefront and service doors of the referenced space and is responsible for its contents upon acceptance of the space.

Signed   _____

Company   _____
                                         (General Contractor)

Sample tenant contractor check-in form.

DESIGNATED CONTRACTORS

Fire Protection—sprinkler—for all buildings

The overhead sprinkler system is monitored on behalf of the *Name of Municipality* Fire Department as well as center administration. Contractors must not tamper with the system. Any modification to the system must be done by the landlord's designated contractor. *If relocating more than two heads, a permit will be required. Allow yourself time for permitting.*

Name of Contractor, Company and Phone

Fire Protection—fire alarm—for all buildings

Only the landlord's designated contractor can tie or land the tenant into the fire alarm system. A permit will be required by *Name of the Municipality* for fire alarm hookup and testing as part of the construction process. The permit will need to be finaled as part of the Certificate of Occupancy. It is the tenant's responsibility to make sure that their devices are compatible with the landlord's systems.

If the tenant's internal policies require a separate fire alarm panel or system, then the tenant can hire our fire alarm contractor direct. If the tenant chooses to use someone else, then their fire alarm contractor will be responsible for pulling the permits and doing the work. However, they must subcontract our fire alarm contractor to do the smoke detector connections if we installed the rooftop units and to connect their system to ours. No outside company will be allowed to connect into our system.

General contractors for restaurants are required to arrange a pretest (using air) of the ansul system in coordination with the fire alarm contractor and tenant coordination prior to their final walkthrough with *Name of the Municipality* Fire Department.

Name of Contractor, Company and Phone

Roof Penetrations

If setting rooftop units, condensing units or large equipment requiring service, the landlord requires walk-pads. Rooftop units and equipment requiring condensate lines may be tied into existing lines or piped into the roof drains. Condensate lines must be set on blocks and walk pads also. Installation of any satellite dishes must be coordinated through Tenant Coordination. If sign contractors penetrate flashings, the tenant contractor will be responsible for hiring the designated roofer to come out and repair. A list of all penetrations must be given to tenant coordination at check-in. General contractor will contract directly with roofer.

Name of Contractor, Company and Phone

This is a sample of a designated contractor list for use in the field. If possible, it should be supported in the lease with a clause that says landlord-designated contractors must be used.

UTILITY ACCOUNT INFORMATION

Any account opened under the landlord's name will need to be moved to the tenant as soon as possible. Landlord reserves the right to charge administration fee on any accounts still under their name after a 4-week period following any requests to change the account name.

Electric
Name of Company
Phone: 000-000-0000

For tenants to make application for meter or turnover, please fill in a commercial business application. You will need proof of rental, a copy of the personal ID of the person making application, a tax ID number, a deposit and mailing information.

Water/Sewer/Reuse
Name of Company
Phone: 000-000-0000

The landlord is setting the water meters. When it is time to put in your own name, go to *Name of Municipality* and make application for power and water in your business name. They will handle the billing.

Telephone Orders for Service
Name of Company
Phone: 000-000-0000

They will need the business name, tax ID, physical address and billing address.

Gas
Name of Company
Phone: 000-000-0000

They will need the business name, tax ID, physical address and billing address. You also need to provide them with a schedule showing equipment and load summary.

Post Office

Fire Dept – knox box

A form that is easy to f[...] [...]o handle the setup of utility accounts [...]

INSURANCE REQUIREMENTS

The tenant, tenant's general contractor and subcontractors are responsible for obtaining the proper insurance. A primary policy or primary policy plus an umbrella policy can satisfy liability requirements. Please consult the lease for proper amounts.

Workman's Compensation
Workman's Compensation and Employer's Liability Insurance in an amount applicable by law.

Comprehensive General Liability
A blanket policy for an amount not less than $2,000,000.00, any one occurrence.

Comprehensive Automobile Liability
Include ownership, maintenance and operation of any automotive equipment in amounts indicated as follows:
Bodily Injury (Personal Injury or Death) in the amount of $2,000,000.00 for each occurrence
Property Damage in the amount of $2,000,000.00 for each occurrence

Additionally Insured
All insurance policies (except Workman's Compensation) shall include the following as insured and additionally insured. ***Demolition or construction may not commence until this information is properly indicated on the insurance certificate.***

The tenant contractor is required to keep all insurance in force and renewed 1 year from the time they start on the project, provided they are finished before that. As long as they are working on-site they will need to keep their insurance operational. In addition, they will need a certificate for each space worked on.

Ideal Shopping Center
Attn: Joe Smith
Address

The following are to be named as an additional insured:
General Contractor
Additional ownership entities

Tenant operations insurance is due to the property management team prior to store opening. Please consult the lease.

A form that is easy to fax or e-mail can be very helpful to a tenant's general contractor staff members who handle issuance of the certificate of insurance.

INSURANCE REQUIREMENTS WHEN DEALING
WITH RISK/UNDERWRITER
Shopping Center Developer

Date:

Contact Name
Company Name
Address
City & Province
Postal Code

Dear Salutation:

Re: Property's Name
Certification of Insurance Coverage
Tenant's Name

Pursuant to the conditions stipulated in the leasing documentation recently executed between us, your company is required to deposit certification of its insurance coverage with the landlord prior to the commencement of any construction within the leased premises.

Certification is required to be submitted on the attached Liability Insurance Certification form. Would you please have the form executed by a duly authorized signing officer of the insurance company that will be providing your coverage and return a copy to this office by no later than *enter date.*

Yours truly,
Developer's Name

Sender's Name
Title

c.c.

Enclosures ()

A sample of an insurance requirements form put together for tenant contractors in a required format. This sample consists of three pages.

MEMORANDUM OF INSURANCE

No.:
Date:

To:

This is to certify that Policy(ies) of Insurance as described herein has been arranged on behalf of the Insured named herein under the following policy(ies) and as more fully described in said policy(ies) and any endorsements attached thereto.

Insured: **Address of Insured:**

Coverage	Insurer	Policy No.	Effective	Expires	Limits of Liability
Comprehensive General Liability					$5,000,000 INCLUSIVE Bodily Injury and Property Damage, including Owners, & Contractors' Protective Liability, Products and Completed Operations, Blanket Contractual Liability, Employers' Liability, Tenant's Legal Liability, Non-Owned Automobile and Cross-Liability Clause.
Umbrella Liability					$ in Excess of Underlying Policy #
Automobile Liability					$5,000,000 INCLUSIVE Bodily Injury and Property Damage

It is understood that the entities listed below are added as additional insured to these premises with respect to liability arising out of the operations at the above-mentioned project.

Entities to be listed as Additional Insureds:

If the insurance provided under the said policy(ies) is altered, expired, cancelled or changed in a manner as to affect this Memorandum of Insurance, the Insuring Company hereby agrees to give thirty (30) days' written notice in advance, by registered mail, of such alteration, expiry, change or cancellation to:

Date: _____   _____
                                                Signature of Authorized Representative or
                                                Official of Insurance Company

Name and Address of Insurance Broker: _____

Contact Name & Phone Number: _____

LIABILITY INSURANCE CERTIFICATE

To be Completed only by the Insurer or his Authorized Representative

1. NAME OF INSURED:	2. ADDRESS OF INSURED:

3. OPERATIONS OF THE INSURED FOR WHICH CERTIFICATE IS ISSUED AT:

A. INSURING COMPANY   B. POLICY NUMBERS   C. LIMITS OF LIABILITY   D. EFFECTIVE DATE   E. EXPIRY DATE
Bodily Injury & Property Damage Inclusive
Excess Liability (If applicable) Inclusive

5. Provisions of Amendments or Endorsements of Listed Policy(ies)

A. Comprehensive General Liability is extended to include Personal Injury Liability, Contractual Liability, Non-Owned Automobile Liability, Owner's and Contractor's Protective Coverage, Products-Completed Operations, Contingent Employer's Liability, Severability of Interests and Cross Liability Clauses.

B. The Comprehensive General Liability policy is in the name of the Insured Tenant and as Additional Insured (only with respect to liability arising out of the operations of the Named Insured for which an agreement has been issued) OMERS Realty Management Corporation,

C. Any coverage so afforded shall not be invalidated as respects the interest of such Additional Insured by reason of breach or violation of any warranties, representations, declarations or conditions contained in the policies and shall apply only as primary and not excess to any other insurance available to such Additional Insured.

D. This is to certify that policies of insurance as described above have been issued by the undersigned to the Insured named above and are in force at this time. If cancelled or changed in any manner, for any reason, during the period of coverage as stated herein so as to affect this certificate, thirty (30) days prior written notice by registered mail will be given by the Insurer(s) to:

Oxford Properties Group

VERTIFICATION

This is to certify that the Insurance is in effect as stated in this Certificate and to confirm the authorization to issue this certificate for and on behalf of the insurer(s). This certificate is valid until the expiration date(s) shown in Item 3(e) unless notice is given in writing in accordance with Item 5(d).

BROKER'S NAME	ACCOUNT REPRESENTATIVE (Print Name)
ADDRESS	DATE
TELEPHONE NUMBER	SIGNATURE AND STAMP OF INSURER

Developer Name

HOT WORK INDEMNIFICATION
Hot Work Policy—Required Precautions Checklist

Available sprinklers, hose streams and extinguishers are in service and/or operable. Hot work equipment in good repair. Smoke/heat detectors bypassed where necessary.

Requirements within 35 ft (11 m) of work
☐ Flammable liquids, dust, lint and oily deposits removed.
☐ Explosive atmosphere in area eliminated.
☐ Floors swept clean.
☐ Combustible floors wet down, covered with damp sand or fire-resistive sheets.
☐ Remove other combustibles where possible. Otherwise protect with fire-resistive tarpaulins or metal shields.
☐ All wall and floor openings covered.
☐ Fire-resistive tarpaulins suspended beneath work.

Work on walls or ceilings
☐ Construction is noncombustible and without combustible covering or insulation.
☐ Combustibles on other side of walls moved away.

Work on enclosed equipment
☐ Enclosed equipment cleaned of all combustibles.
☐ Containers purged of flammable liquids/vapors.

Fire watch/hot work area monitoring
☐ Fire watch will be provided during and for 60 minutes after work, including any coffee or lunch breaks.
☐ Fire watch is supplied with suitable extinguishers, charged small hose.
☐ Fire watch is trained in use of this equipment and in sounding alarm.
☐ Fire watch may be required for adjoining areas, above and below.
☐ Monitor hot work area for 4 hours in total after job is completed.

Contractor's Hot Work Indemnification

The Contractor shall defend, indemnify and hold the Owner harmless from and against all liability, claims, demands, damages, losses and expenses (including reasonable attorney's fees) on account of property loss or damage of any kind, which arises out of or is in any way connected with the Contractor's performance or its work or the work of any of its agents, employees or subcontractors. This Defense & Indemnity shall include the right of the Owner to retain counsel of its choosing, and to be reimbursed for all reasonable attorneys' fees and costs.

The Contractor, its employees, agents and subcontractors agree to fully cooperate with the Owner, its employees, agents, subcontractors and insurers in the investigation and resolution of all claims and demands.

Signature (Contractor)

Company

Date

> *Some developers have extensive rules and regulations requiring when and how welding and soldering can be done. Hot work fire permits might be required. This form is a sample of a checklist—however, full hot work systems programs are available, and if your facility is interested in establishing a hot work permit system, further research is suggested.*

CONSTRUCTION FEES CALCULATIONS

Item	Square Foot Charge	X	Square Feet based on LL LOD only, not tenant plans	Total
Deposit				$2500.00
Trash	.25			
Electric	.10			
Toilets	.5			

Example for a 2,000-square-foot store

Item	Square Foot Charge	X	Square Feet based on LL LOD only, not tenant plans	Total
Deposit				$2500.00
(one time)				
Trash	.25	X	2000	500.00
(one time)				
Electric	.10	X	2000	200.00
(monthly)				
Toilets	.5	X	2000	100.00
(one time)				
				$3300.00

A handy form for tenant contractors as part of their check-in is a form that helps them determine what utility fees they might owe Tenant Coordination or operations upon check-in. A word of caution—generally if you collect security deposits, you must let the tenant contractor know if it will be in an interest-bearing account or not.

CONSTRUCTION RULES AND REGULATIONS
SIGN-IN FORM

To: Shopping Center Name
Re: Tenant Name
   Space Number

I hereby acknowledge that I am the duly authorized contractor for this tenant for the execution of constructing this tenant's new or remodeled premises, per the drawings approved by the landlord.

I acknowledge the receipt of, have thoroughly read and completely understand the landlord's rules and regulations for *Shopping Center Entity* dated* _____. I will fully abide by the same and will cause all my employees and subcontractors to abide by same. I will accept the consequences for failure to abide by same.

I acknowledge that I will review the landlord's required plans and if I see a discrepancy between my construction plans and the landlord's plans, I will notify the tenant.

Contractor: _____

Address: _____

Authorized Representative: _____

Title: _____

Signature: _____

Date: _____

This form can be used as part of the tenant's general contractor's sign-in package. Leave the date blank for the contractor to fill in as they check in, as you might have several handbooks printed over the course of a project and afterward; the dates should be updated, as information might change.

CONTRACTOR INFORMATION FORM

General Contractor: Name of Superintendent: _____
                                      Name of Project Manager: _____

General Contractor:	Name of Superintendent:	_____
	Name of Project Manager:	_____
	Home Office Address:	_____
	Telephone:	_____
	Fax:	_____
	Cell Phone:	_____
	PM's E-mail:	_____
	Superintendent's E-mail:	_____
	Site Fax Number:	_____
Electrical Contractor:	Name of Foreman:	_____
	Name of Project Manager:	_____
	Home Office Address:	_____
	Telephone:	_____
	Fax:	_____
	Cell Phone:	_____
Mechanical Contractor:	Name of Foreman:	_____
	Name of Project Manager:	_____
	Home Office Address:	_____
	Telephone:	_____
	Fax:	_____
	Cell Phone:	_____
Plumbing Contractor:	Name of Foreman:	_____
	Name of Project Manager:	_____
	Home Office Address:	_____
	Telephone:	_____
	Fax:	_____
	Cell Phone:	_____

We understand that we are responsible for making sure that we meet all job site safety requirements.

We understand that there is an enforced no drugs, no alcohol, no weapons policy. We will immediately remove any personnel who infringe on that rule voluntarily.

We understand that we are responsible for any damage done by ourselves or our sub-contractors on center interior and exterior finishes, including landscaping and sidewalks.

We understand that we are responsible to work with the base building contractor, landlord and landlord's representatives and other tenant contractors in a professional, respectful and polite manner at all times. We will respond to security requests in a prompt and respectful manner.

We understand that it is our responsibility to comply with all OSHA, federal, state and local laws, regulations and standards while working on this project. Should there be a conflict between a current law, regulation or standard and the contractual arrangement, the most stringent requirements shall be followed.

General Contractor's Superintendent, Signature Please: _____

*(One page will be required for each space worked on by the same contractor.
Replacement superintendents will be required to read and sign also.)*

This is a form that can also be used for check-in that serves many purposes. It makes the tenant contractor understand their responsibilities, and it also serves to assist in case you need to contact them or one of their subcontractors in case of an emergency. It is also a helpful tool for property management to have after a space is opened in case they have a problem in the space or would like to track down who did the work in the future.

LEASE ACCEPTANCE FORM

Tenant space and suite number: _____ _____

Date of walkthrough: _____

Those in attendance: _____

	Completion		Condition		Comments
	Installed	Not Installed	Acceptable	Not Acceptable	

Storefront
Glass
Doors
Locks
Threshold
Comments:

Exterior Back Doors
Door in
Frame condition
Hardware and locks
Comments:

Mechanical
RTU installed
Thermostat installed
Comments:

Electrical
Riser built
Disconnect installed
Conduit to space, pull string
Phone conduit installed, pull string
Fire alarm conduit installed, pull string
Comments:

Plumbing
Vent stack installed
Sanitary connection installed
Domestic water with shutoff valve
Size of water line, if different by lease
Gas line installed
Connection to grease trap marked
Comments:

Fire Protection
Sprinkler system installed
Comments:

Other items:
Space broom swept
Drywall finished, no nicks or holes
Drywall acceptable finish
Fire caulking in place
Comments:

Space accepted by: _____

Date of acceptance: _____

A sample of a lease acceptance form.

TURNOVER CHECKLIST
ACCEPTANCE BY CONTRACTOR

Date:_____ Property: *Ideal Shopping Center*

Store Name: _____

Space Number:_____

Contractor: _____

Phone Number: _____

The following items, unless otherwise noted, are provided by the landlord and constitute the completed landlord work. The contractor accepts these items "as is" and the space as being complete.

Completed	Work	Comments
	Demising partition	
	Floor slab	
	Storefront	
	Rear door	
	Ceiling	
	Toilet room, including roof vent	
	Toilet room partition, doors	
	Toilet room fixtures	
	HVAC electrical service	
	Electrical service	
	Power distribution (outlets)	
	Lighting	
	Emergency lighting, exit signs	
	Toilet exhaust	
	Rooftop unit(s)	
	HVAC distribution	
	Sprinkler system	

This is a sample of a lease acceptance form. This multipurpose form can also serve as a punch list of incomplete work for the landlord and their contractor; can be used to track condition of space at turnover for lease administration and legal purposes; and protects the tenant contractor from accusations of damage. If the space contains damage, such as to a door frame, it can be noted here for future reference.

CONTRACTOR START DATE
Shopping Center or Developer Letterhead

To: Lease Administration
         Property Manager
Fr: Tenant Coordinator
Re: Construction Start, *tenant name*
Date: 0/0/00

Please be aware that the contractor for *tenant name* has checked in and started construction on 0/00/00.

A simple format for a note to the file on what the actual start date of construction is for a tenant's contractor.

FIELD COORDINATION REPORT
CONSTRUCTION STATUS
DATE: 0/0/00

Store Name:
Need electrical permit
Need rough electrical inspection
Need final electrical inspection
Need final plumbing inspection
Need ductwork wrapping inspected
Need interconnect AC units
Need fire alarm tie-in
Need final mechanical inspection
Need flooring done
Need installation sales counters
Need telephone and computer equipment
Need low-voltage permit
Need final low voltage
Need electrical on sign
Need final on sign
Need fire inspection
Need final building
CO in hand

Store Name:
Need electrical permit
Need rough electrical inspection
Need final electrical inspection
Need final plumbing inspection
Need ductwork wrapping inspected
Need interconnect AC units
Need fire alarm tie-in
Need final mechanical inspection
Need flooring done
Need installation sales counters
Need telephone and computer equipment
Need low-voltage permit
Need final low voltage
Need electrical on sign
Need final on sign
Need fire inspection
Need final building
CO in hand

Store Name:
Need electrical on sign
Need final on sign
Need fire inspection for TCO
Need bldg. department approval TCO
Need TCO for stocking, training
Need final electrical
Need fire inspection
Landlord needs sign-off in landscaping
Landlord needs parking lot around building
striped and signed
Landlord needs sign-off by engineering
Need final building
CO in hand

Store Name:
Need electrical on sign
Need final on sign
Need fire inspection for TCO
Need bldg. department approval TCO
Need TCO for stocking, training
Need final electrical
Need fire inspection
Landlord needs sign-off in landscaping
Landlord needs parking lot around building
striped and signs
Landlord needs sign-off by engineering
Need final building
CO in hand

Store Name:
Open 0/00/00

This report is used as a status report to owners on issues and inspections for each tenant as they move toward opening. As the issues are resolved, they are dropped from the list. The idea is to get all issues to simply "dates opened." The closer to opening, the more the report is updated—at opening it is updated daily and handed to all parties involved.

FIRE ALARM TIE-IN REQUEST

Tenant Coordination
Name of Developer
Address
Phone

Name of Shopping Center

Fire Alarm Tie-in

To:	Mall Management	**From:**	Tenant Contractor
Phone:	000-000-0000	**Date:**	0/0/0000
Re:	Suite Number	**Via:**	☐ Fax Transmittal
			☐ E-mail
			☐ Hand Delivery

Date Work Requested:

Estimate of time needed to complete work:

Name and phone number of electrician coordinating work:

Please be aware—24 hours' notice is required. Please make sure you have received a confirmation back that your request is being honored. There is a $100 tie-in fee. All tenant fire alarm devices must be compatible with the landlord's system (insert Brand and Model).

Some properties do not require designated fire protection contractors. If it is an operating center, then a formal request asking for permission to tie into the landlord's fire alarm panel should be instituted. Operations should always be aware of when key systems are down and who is working on them.

REQUEST TO USE FREIGHT ELEVATOR

Tenant Coordination
Name of Developer
Address
Phone

Name of Shopping Center

Freight Elevator and/or Loading Dock Request

To:	Mall Management	From:	Tenant Contractor
Phone:	000-000-0000	**Date:**	0/0/0000
Re:	Suite Number	**Via:**	☐ Fax Transmittal
			☐ E-mail
			☐ Hand Delivery

Date Work Requested:

Items or materials being brought in:

Name of delivery service, shipping company or subcontractor that will be posted on truck:

Estimate of time needed to complete work:

Name and phone number of superintendent coordinating work:

Please be aware—48 hours' notice is required. Please make sure you have received a confirmation back that your request is being honored. All oversized deliveries come in during nonoperating hours only. Mall interior floors must be protected by the tenant contractor. The mall does not provide equipment or labor for offloading.

Special coordination for use of freight elevators or loading dock areas might be required. This form requests time in the dock areas or use of an elevator.

OVERSIZED DELIVERY

Tenant Coordination
Name of Developer
Address
Phone

Name of Shopping Center

Oversized Delivery

To:	Mall Management	**From:**	Tenant Contractor
Phone:	000-000-0000	**Date:**	0/0/0000
Re:	Suite Number	**Via:**	☐ Fax Transmittal
			☐ E-mail
			☐ Hand Delivery

Date Work Requested:

Items or materials being brought in:

Name of delivery service, shipping company or subcontractor that will be posted on truck:

Estimate of time needed to complete work:

Name and phone number of superintendent coordinating work:

Please be aware—24 hours' notice is required. Please make sure you have received a confirmation back that your request is being honored. There is a $15 an hour fee for security to be posted at the door. All oversized deliveries come in during nonoperating hours only. Floors must be protected by the tenant contractor. The mall does not provide equipment or labor for offloading.

Occasionally the only way an oversized delivery can get into a store under construction is through a set of sliding oversized mall doors used to get cars and maintenance equipment in. These doors are typically opened only when security is standing by during nonoperational hours. This form requests permission to bring in an oversized delivery.

ROOF PENETRATIONS

Tenant Coordination
Name of Developer
Address
Phone

Roof Penetrations

To:	Mall Management	**From:**	Tenant Contractor	
Phone:	000-000-0000	**Date:**	0/0/0000	
Re:	Suite Number	**Via:**	☐ Fax Transmittal	
			☐ E-mail	
			☐ Hand Delivery	

Date Work Requested:

List of and number of penetrations:

Name and phone number of superintendent coordinating work:

Please be aware—48 hours' notice is required. Please make sure you have received a confirmation back that your request is being honored. Attach an 8½-by-11 floor plan showing locations and sizes of penetrations. No penetrations will be made without the tenant contractor being present.

Most shopping centers zealously protect their roof warranties by limiting who is allowed to work on the roof, get access to it or make the actual penetrations. This form can be used to control who is working on the roof. The best control is to allow only one roofer to make any penetrations in order to protect the landlord's warranties. Any other trades wanting to get on the roof would have to request through a roof access request.

SPRINKLER SHUTDOWN

Tenant Coordination
Name of Developer
Address
Phone

Name of Shopping Center

Sprinkler Shutdown

To:	Mall Management	**From:**	Tenant Contractor
Phone:	000-000-0000	**Date:**	0/0/0000
Re:	Suite Number	**Via:**	☐ Fax Transmittal
			☐ E-mail
			☐ Hand Delivery

Date Work Requested:

Estimate of time needed to complete work:

Name and phone number of sprinkler contractor performing work:

Please be aware—48 hours' notice is required. Please make sure you have received a confirmation back that your request is being honored. There is a $100 shutdown fee per request.

Some properties do not require designated fire protection contractors. If it is an operating center, then a formal request asking for the shutdown of the system should be instituted. Operations should always be aware of when key systems are down and who is working on them.

SPRINKLER SHUTDOWN WHEN DEALING WITH RISK/UNDERWRITER

Sprinkler Shutdown Procedures

Date: 0/00/00

AON REED STENHOUSE
SPRINKLER SYSTEM SHUTDOWN
REPORTING PROCEDURES

The following is the procedure which **must** be followed when the sprinkler system(s) are proposed to be shut down:

1. Detach or launch the coversheet (Sprinklr.doc) attached below.
2. Print the sheet, and complete the form, providing the requested information. Please note that there is no need to provide an index number to Aon; the property name and location are sufficient.
3. Notify the Aon Reed Stenhouse office, **in Toronto**, of the shutdown by faxing the completed cover sheet to 000-000-0000. Please note that this is a 24-hour service.
4. When the sprinkler system(s) are operational again you must complete the box "Actual Date/Time Opened" and fax the sheet back to Aon Reed Stenhouse to confirm that the impairment is over.

Aon Reed Stenhouse will provide Sprinkler Impairment Kits to all properties for use whenever your sprinkler system is not operational. If you require extra kits or refills, please contact Joe Smith at Aon, or the Risk & Insurance Department. See Section 1.6 for contact numbers.

Please note that it is imperative that these procedures are adhered to, as failure to notify the insurer when a sprinkler system is shut down could result in denial of the claim if an incident should occur.

Continued

Often tenant coordinators have to protect the ownership of their centers by making sure the properties' risk provider's own standards are met and enforced. This is a sample of a sprinkler system shutdown request that actually has to go through the insurer. The use of impairment means the system is temporarily nonfunctional or impaired. There are two pages in this sample.

Fax Transmittal Sheet

Please deliver the following to:

Name	
Company	
Fax #	Cc
From	Phone: Fax:
Date	No. of pages (including cover sheet) 1

SPRINKLER IMPAIRMENT REPORT FORM

Property Name		City State or Province	
Sprinkler Valve Location/Number		Area Protected	
Reason for Impairment			
Date/Time to Be Closed	Actual Date/Time Closed	Date/Time to Be Opened	Actual Date/Time Opened
# of Turns to Close	# of Turns to Open	Fire Dept. Contacted	Fire Watch Instituted
Authorized By:		Date:	

Closeout Documents

Opening Date
Request Deposit Return
Construction Closeout Checklist
Tenant Deficiency Checklist
Turnover to Property Management
Tenant Possession Checklist
Request Tenant Allowance

OPENING DATE
Shopping Center or Developer Letterhead

To: Lease Administration
        Property Management
Fr: Tenant Coordinator
Re: Opening Date, *tenant name*
Date: 0/0/00

Tenant name opened for business today, 0/00/00.

A simple format for a note to the file on what the actual opening date of a tenant is. This is an important memo to have in the file in case there is ever a question about the actual opening date.

REQUEST DEPOSIT RETURN

Construction Deposit Request Form

Store: _____

Space Number: _____

General Contractor's Name: _____

Individual in charge: _____

Address: _____

Telephone number: _____

The following have been received and completed as noted. Please release our construction deposit for the above-mentioned store.

- ☐ As-built plans submitted
- ☐ Updated subcontractors' names and contact information submitted
- ☐ Updated emergency contact information for general contractor
- ☐ Copy of all rooftop equipment warranties and manuals
- ☐ Proof of payment, landlord's designated contractors
- ☐ Completion of punch list items from Tenant Coordination
- ☐ Copy of Certificate of Occupancy
- ☐ Copy of electrical signoff and building signoff, exterior signage
- ☐ All back charges have been paid and utility costs are paid
- ☐ Any claims for damages to exterior or interior work belonging to landlord or other tenants and contractors are deducted or the landlord has received a settlement from the tenant contractor's insurer. Deduction for damage from the damage deposit in no way relieves the general contractor from damages above the amount of the damage deposit.

Submitted by Contractor's Representative: _____

Agreed to by Tenant Coordination: _____

Date: _____

This is a checklist for a contractor to know what the requirements will be for when he or she wishes to get a return on their security deposit.

CONSTRUCTION CLOSEOUT CHECKLIST

Center:
Tenant:
Contractor:
Space Number:
Square Feet:

The tenant and/or their contractor are required to provide the following information upon opening of the tenant space:

- ☐ Copies of all applicable permits for tenant's work
- ☐ Copy of final certificate of occupancy from the local authorities
- ☐ Letters from all designated mall contractors showing work done on tenant's behalf has been paid for, other than what is backcharged.
- ☐ Final subcontractors list
- ☐ As-built or redlined set of plans
- ☐ The tenant's space has been inspected for compliance with the approved plan and sign drawing submittals and is complete.

Construction start date:_____   Opening date: _____

Back Charges:

Test for tie-in to chilled water	$
Test for tie-in to steamed water	$
Temporary electric	$
Temporary toilets	$
Temporary trash	$
Sprinkler modifications	$
Fire alarm wiring, devices and hookup	$
Mall tile	$
Repair to any damage, if any—notification attached	$
Additional work done by landlord on tenant's behalf—separate agreement attached	$

Construction allowance as per lease	$
Less back charges	$
Allowance due tenant	$

This form can be used by mall tenant coordinators as part of their closeout documentation with a tenant and its contractor and their real estate or accounting department to settle out release of any tenant allowances for construction.

TENANT DEFICIENCY CHECKLIST

Tenant Name: _____

Unit Number: _____

Opening Date: _____

Inspection Date: _____

FINAL INSPECTION ITEMS	Y/N	COMMENTS
A) Mall Tiles		
a) Extended to closure line or as per approved drawings		
b) Broken chipped or poorly installed tiles must be replaced		
c) Grouting and smooth edges or thresholds completed		
d) Floor receptacle locking bolts installed flush with floor finishes		
B) Bulkhead Interface		
a) Where tenant's soffit meets the landlord's soffit in a vertical plane, paint finish should be continued to an architecturally logical location		
b) Paint finish on landlord's soffit to be carried into a line of tenant's bulkhead unless a reveal is installed at the lease line to separate finishes		
c) Tenant's work as it interfaces landlord's bulkhead should not be visible		
C) Demising Caps/ Form Glass columns		
a) Clean and unmarred		
b) Furred-out demising wall or as per approved drawings		
D) Recessed Door Tracks		
a) Door tracks to be fully recessed and supported by threaded rods		
E) Door Pockets		
a) Closure panels complete with spring-loaded touch latches or flush locks		
b) Floor finish carried into pocket 1'-0"		
c) Door pocket closure panels in closed position when store is open		
d) All door pocket edges professionally finished		

FINAL INSPECTION ITEMS	Y/N	COMMENTS
F) Folding Grills/ Roll Down Grills		
a) Sliding grill is to be properly supported from structure above		
b) Sliding grill must be equipped with top and bottom locking pins		
c) Sliding grill to be equipped with tempered glass or perforated panel inserts		
d) Roll-down grills are permitted only where there is a second means of egress or as approved by city official having jurisdiction		
G) Signage		
a) In accordance with landlord-approved drawings		
b) Illuminated signs to be completely lit		
c) Neon to be completely lit, no humming		
d) Signage should not crowd bulkhead		
e) Fastening or mounting hardware should be painted a color that disguises it		
f) No exposed conduits		
H) Tile Bases		
a) Mall tile base as per landlord-approved drawings		
b) Durable, approved materials may be substituted for aesthetic purposes		
I) Lighting		
a) Fluorescent not permitted within 8'-0" of storefront unless concealed by tenant bulkhead		
b) Fluorescent fixtures must have lenses unless special consideration is given for a design concept		
J) Storefront		
a) Minimum height opening requirement of 8'-0" a.f.f. (including to u/s of tenant signage)		
b) Slatwall must be set back 2'-0" minimum from storefront if silicone butt joints are used in show window glazing, full and continuous silicone beading must be installed between glass panels		
K) General		
a) Pegboard is not acceptable in retail area		
b) Electrical hardware not visible to the public		
c) Air balance report submitted		

This form serves as a guideline to the tenant contractor on what the tenant coordinator is looking for upon completion. It also serves as an efficient record of the completion of the store for the file and to release any security deposits.

TURNOVER TO PROPERTY MANAGEMENT
Shopping Center or Developer Letterhead

Date

Store Manager
Address
Address
Address

Re: Lease Between Tenant Name and Landlord Name

Dear Sir or Madam:

Congratulations! I know that you are as pleased as we are to be open and doing business.

I have noted the following date, (insert date), as the day that the store opened for business.

At this time I would like to introduce you to our property management team. The property manager is (insert name). He (she) can be reached by calling or visiting the property management office located at (fill in address) or by calling 000-000-0000. If you have any questions or concerns, I know that they will be pleased to assist you.

Again, congratulations on a successful store opening.

Sincerely,

Name
Retail Tenant Coordinator
Shopping Center or Developer

Cc: Tenant File
    Tenant Construction Manager
    Mall or Property Manager
    Any other cited in lease

Via Certified Mail

This is a sample of a letter indicating turnover from tenant coordination to property management. This letter can also be used to indicate opening date, estoppel arrangements, convey certifications, or whatever the landlord wishes to convey to the tenant.

TENANT POSSESSION CHECKLIST

1) This section to be completed by Property Administration

Tenant:	Date Tenant Open for Business:
Current Address:	
Developer Address:	
Management Contact:	Telephone No.:
Office Contact:	Telephone No.:
Offer to Lease submitted:	Approved:
Assigned Storage No.:	Locations:
Term of Lease:	
Fixturing Commencement:	
Lease Commencement:	

Area:	Surveyed: Yes ☐ No ☐	Net:	Gross:
	Estimated: Yes ☐ No ☐		Gross:
Insurance Letter Sent:		Date Received:	

2) This section to be completed by Tenant Coordination Operations Manager

"Design Criteria Manual" sent (date):	
"Construction Guide Manual" sent (date):	
JDE Setup (date):	Tenant Address No.: Lease ID No.:
Janitorial Service Advised:	Storage Room Cleaned:
Landlord's Work Construction Scheduled:	Recycling Boxes:
Tenant Work Scheduled:	
Flowers Ordered:	For Delivery on:
Building Tour with GM/OM:	Tour Date:
Issue "Welcome Kit" Sent:	Called Office Contact:
Tenant Appreciation Photo Ordered:	Date Delivered:

3) This section to be completed by Operations Manager & Security Supervisor

Security Cards:	No. Requested:	No. Issued:	Date Issued:
Premises Keys:	No. Issued:	Key No.:	Date Issued:
Storage Keys:	No. Issued:	Key No.:	Date Issued:
Chief Engineer Advised:		Parking:	
Mail Box No.:		No. of Mail Box keys issued:	
Signage: Directional	Date Ordered:	Date Installed:	
Pylon	Date Ordered:	Date Installed:	
Comments:			
Elevator/ Loading Dock Booked		Date:	Time:
Additional Information:		Move-In Date:	
No. of Employees:		No. of Handicapped Employees:	
After-Hours Contact Letter Sent:		Letter Returned from tenant:	

COMMENTS:

> *Sample of an interdepartmental form designed to keep several people involved in opening a tenant informed of status.*

REQUEST TENANT ALLOWANCE
Shopping Center or Developer Letterhead

Date

Name and Address of Tenant Contact, as per lease required notifications

Re: Tenant Name, reference to executed lease, Tenant Allowance

Dear Sir or Madam:

Congratulations! Now that your store is open for business at (name of center), it is time to request release of your tenant allowance or construction funds from us.

A successful release of tenant allowance will occur upon the presentation of the following documents as per your lease requirements:

- ☐ Copy of full release of liens from your general contractor and all subcontractors and suppliers, as listed from Notices to Owners received (or list from a Contractor's Affidavit)
- ☐ Copy of the Certificate of Occupancy
- ☐ Letter of certification of completion from your architect that the work is satisfactory
- ☐ Copy of final as-builds, in CAD form on a CD/DVD disk
- ☐ Satisfaction of fees to landlord's designated contractors
- ☐ Payment of any back charges or work done on tenant's behalf by landlord
- ☐ Rent payments and opening fees paid

If you have any questions, please contact our accounting department at 000-000-0000 and ask for Joe Smith.

Congratulations again.

Sincerely,

Name of Tenant Coordinator
Retail Tenant Coordination

Cc: Others as required for legal notice, the lease
  Property Manager
  Property Accounting
  Leasing
  Tenant File

If you are carrying tenant allowances in your funding, sometimes it pays for you to contact the tenants and let them know what you will be requiring, as per the lease, in advance. This will put them on notice of what to provide and will assist your accounting or property management associates if they are handling the release of the funds.

Maintenance and Follow-Up

Biannual Checklist

BIANNUAL CHECKLIST

TENANT PREMISES BIANNUAL INSPECTION FORM

TENANT: _____ DATE: _____

FIRE PREVENTION		Grade	** IF APPLICABLE		Grade
1	Ceiling Tile in Place		10	Aisles Unobstructed	
2	Sprinkler Clearance as Per Code		11	Review Store Evacuation Policies	
3	Exit Lights Visible and Well Lit		12	Grease Trap Conditions	
4	Emergency Lights Working		13	Exhaust Hood & Duct—Last Date Serviced	
5	Unobstructed Exits		14	Is B.C. Extinguisher (Kitchens)	
6	No Extension Cords in Use as Permanent Wiring		15	Inspect Ceiling Space for Unauthorized Storage	
7	Portable Extinguisher(s) #_____		16	Condition of Smoke Head	
8	Extinguishers Last Checked (Date)		17	Fixed Extinguisher System Company & Last Date Serviced	
9	Electrical Panel & Transformer (Clear of Storage)				

SAFETY		Grade	**IF APPLICABLE		Grade
18	Storefront Glass & Mirrors		23	Lighting Within the Store Area	
19	Storefront Signage/Lease Line		24	Condition of Storage Area	
20	Tiles and/or Carpet Condition		25	Evacuation Map Posted	
21	Electrical Panel Clearance		26	Exterminator Co. & Last Date	
22	Integrity or Premises Perimeter				

SECURITY		Grade			Grade
27	Lock Integrity on All Doors/Gates		30	Tenant Rules & Regulations Manual	
28	Posted Rules & Regulations Sticker		31	Tenant Security Manual	
29	Posted Staff Parking Sticker		32	Alarm Monitoring Status Company	

INSPECTOR'S CHECKLIST (NOT GRADED)					
33	Any Tenant/Staff Concerns		37	Review Lost & Found Procedures	
34	Emergency Contact List Update		38	Check for Any Mall Equipment	
35	Security Numbers on Every Phone		39	Information on S.L.S. Seminars	
36	First Aid and Emergency Info		**Tenant Requests**		
				Grade Totals	

COMMENTS

RECOMMENDATIONS

GRADES: 2-Excellent, 1-Satisfactory, 0-Unsatisfactory

INSPECTED BY:_____ MANAGER: _____

SIGNATURE: _____ SIGNATURE:_____

REINSPECTION DATE:_____

A form that can be used for Operations and Tenant Coordination teams that inspect stores for compliance with mall rules and regulations, safety and operations.

Index